The Kelvedon Edition

C. H. SPURGEON'S SERMONS
ON REVIVAL

The Kelvedon Edition

C. H. SPURGEON'S
SERMONS
ON REVIVAL

Selected and Edited by
Charles T. Cook

MARSHALL, MORGAN & SCOTT

London

Marshall, Morgan & Scott, a member of the Pentos group, 1 Bath Street, LONDON EC1V 9LB.
© Marshall, Morgan & Scott 1958. This edition 1977.
ISBN 0 551 05575 8. Printed in Great Britain by Hollen Street Press Ltd at Slough. 775013L20

CONTENTS

I

A MESSAGE FROM GOD TO HIS CHURCH

"O Lord, I have heard thy speech, and was afraid: O Lord, revive thy work in the midst of the years, in the midst of the years make known; in wrath remember mercy."—Habakkuk 3: 2.

"O LORD, I have heard thy speech!" This is the language of reverent obedience, and is a fit preface to a fervent prayer. If we are not willing to hear God's voice, we cannot expect him to hear our voice. It is an admirable preparation for prayer, first to hearken diligently to what God the Lord shall speak, and then to be obedient to his commands. He who would hear God speak needs not to wait long, for God speaks to men continually by *the Scriptures*, which are given to us by inspiration. Alas that we should be so deaf to its teachings! This wonderful volume, so full of wisdom, is so little read that few of us could dare to gaze upon its pages and say, "O Lord, in this Book I have heard thy speech." At other times, the Lord speaks by *providence*; both national providences and personal providences have a meaning; providences that are afflicting, and providences which are comforting, all have a voice; but, alas! I fear that oftentimes to us providence is dumb because we are deaf. I am afraid few of you can say of it, "O Lord, in providence I have heard thy speech." The God of heaven speaks to men by his *Holy Spirit*. He does this, at times, in those common operations of the Spirit upon the ungodly which they resist, as did also their fathers. The Spirit strives with men; he calls, and they refuse; he stretches out his hands, and they regard him not. Though we have ears to hear, we frequently quench the Spirit; we grieve him, we neglect his monitions, and, if we do not despise his teachings, yet too often we forget them, and listen to the follies of earth, instead of regarding the wisdom of the skies. I am afraid that in looking into our own hearts and studying them in connection with the operations of the Holy Spirit, not one of us could dare to say, without exception, "O Lord, I have heard thy speech."

In the text before us we meet with a prophet whose ear had been spiritually opened, and who therefore heard the still, small voice of Jehovah, where others perceived neither sound nor utterance. There are times even with us when, being under the influence of the Holy Spirit, we hold near communion with our God; then are our hearts like wax to his seal, receiving the impress of the Divine Mind. Are you not conscious of having been in such a state? It must be so, in a measure, with all the Lord's servants; but especially must it be often so with those of us who are called to bear his messages to the people. I have most solemnly sought to hear the speech of Jehovah in my own soul before I came into this pulpit, and I pray that his divine power may enable me to convey that speech to you. I may be to some of you as an interpreter, and you who are spiritual men, you will discern and judge whether I have heard the speech of God or not. If you shall find it to be God's voice to you, I hope you will be led to the farther carrying out of the language of the text in that much-needed prayer, "O Lord, revive thy work."

There are three things in the text; *an alarming voice, an appropriate prayer,* and *a potent argument*—"in wrath remember mercy."

Hear, with solemn awe, THE ALARMING VOICE. The speech of God demands your humblest attention. We need not enter into particulars of the heavy tidings which came to the ear of Habakkuk when he set him upon the tower, and watched to see what the Lord would say unto him. Our business is to tell you, in all solemnity, what the voice of God has been saying to us. In my lonely meditations I heard a voice, as of one that spake in the name of the Lord. I bowed my head to receive the message, and the voice said, "Cry," and when I said, "What shall I cry?" the answer came to me as to Isaiah of old, "All flesh is grass, and all the goodliness thereof is as the flower of the field: the grass withereth, the flower fadeth: because the spirit of the Lord bloweth upon it; surely the people is grass." Then I thought I saw before me a great meadow wide and far reaching, and it was like to a rainbow for its many colours, for the flowers of summer were in their beauty. In the midst thereof I marked a mower of dark and cruel aspect, who with a scythe most sharp and glittering, was clearing mighty stretches of the field at each sweep, and laying the fair flowers in withering heaps. He advanced with huge strides of leagues at once, leaving desolation behind him, and I understood that the mower's name was Death. As I looked I was afraid for my house, and my children, for my kinsfolk and acquaintance, and for myself also; for the mower drew nearer and nearer, and as he came onward a voice was heard as of a trumpet, "Prepare to meet thy God." Moreover, as I mused on I heard a rumbling in the bowels of the earth, as though the destroyer were traversing the dark pathways which the miner has digged, and doing his fearful work among the stones of darkness which lie at the roots of the mountains. I wondered with sore amazement, and behold there came up from the mouth of the pit a thundering cloud of vapour, of smoke and fire, and dust, and rushing whirlwind, which told to wailing women that they were widows and their children fatherless; and the angel of death again cried in mine ears, "All flesh is grass, and all the goodliness thereof is as the flower of the field: the grass withereth, the flower fadeth: because the spirit of the Lord bloweth upon it: surely the people is grass." I have come here sore afraid, and much bowed down because of the mortality of man, and the certainty of death. We shall soon be gone, every one of us to his grave. Ye whom I now see before me are the meadows, and death is in your midst. Ye are the flowers, and I hear the terrible blast, which, alas! must wither even you. As the autumn leaves are gone, so are our fathers; and as the floods hasten to the ocean, even so are we hastening away to hear the judgment of the Great King.

As I thought upon this matter, and desired to hear God's speech therein, I saw a precipice, whose frowning steep overhung a sea of fire. Leading up to its brink I saw a road exceeding broad, a road which was crowded from side to side with a thronging multitude, who pressed and trod one upon another in their raging zeal to reach the summit of the crag. They went gaily on, merrily laughing, singing to sprightly music, many of them dancing, some of them pushing aside their fellows that they might reach sooner than was imperative upon them the end of what they knew so little. As I looked at that end which none of them could see, I saw a cataract of souls, falling in ceaseless, headlong stream into depths unutterably profound.

As the crowd came on rank by rank to the edge of this precipice, they fell, they leaped over, or were dashed from the treacherous crag, and descended amid cries and shrieks surpassing all imagination into a lake of fire, wherein they were submerged with an everlasting baptism, overwhelmed with destruction from the presence of the Lord. This is the broad road of which we had heard so often, wherein multitudes delight to walk. "Wide is the gate and broad is the way that leadeth to destruction, and many are they that go in thereat." Even if we could conceive that all who attend the places of worship were in the narrow way that leadeth unto life eternal, if we could be charitable enough to believe that, yet look at the multitude of outsiders! Look at this city, with far more than a million for whom the sound of the church-going bell is meaningless: who know not God, neither regard him, to whom the name of Christ is but a word to curse with or to ridicule: they are going, men of the same country as yourselves, men of the same race and tribe, speaking our own language, they are going downward to destruction! Scarcely were the first death a thing to be mourned over, if it were not for the second. It might be superfluous to shed so much as a single tear for all the men that died, if we knew that they rested in the arms of Jesus, and were for ever blessed; but this is the sting of death, its bitterness, its wormwood and its gall, that sinners are condemned by justice, and driven by vengeance from the presence of mercy into the place where hope can never follow them. Christian men and women, hear ye this voice of God and be afraid.

Over and above all this, there came upon me a horror of great darkness as I perceived something even more terrible than this. You will say to me, "How more terrible?" In certain aspects so it seemed to me. Hear it and judge. What if it be true that within the last twelve months the Church of the living God has scarcely made the slightest approach to an advance? What if this be true as respects a far longer period? Let the first sad fact rise before us with its proof. For the last twelve months no apparent increase has been made to the number of professed disciples of the Lord Jesus. Do you ask me for the proofs? I can prove it alas! too surely. Our own body, the Baptist denomination, is upon the whole, and all things considered, in as sound and healthy a state as any Christian community now existing; I am persuaded that in some respects it is more sound and more healthy; but do you know what will have been the increase during the twelve months of the entire denomination in England, Scotland, and Ireland, so far as we can ascertain it? Well, with the exception of London and the county of Glamorgan, in Wales, there will be no increase worthy of the name. In many parts of Wales, where we are strongest, there will be a positive decrease; and I think, in fifteen counties of England, we shall have lost numbers instead of making any advance, and when the whole are put together, the good with the bad, and this London of ours, wherein God has greatly blessed us of late, is counted with the rest, our entire increase for all the churches with all their ministers will not make up four thousand souls. It is true that our statistics are not very accurate, but if they were more accurate I believe the result would be more unfavourable. This is the more fearful to me to contemplate, because the increase of the denomination, which by God's grace we might naturally look for merely from the increase of population, should have been very much more than this. I believe it would be accurate and truthful, and could be borne out by statistics, that if at this day there were taken a census of the number of persons who commune at the Lord's table, it would be found to be smaller instead of larger than the number at the corresponding period of last year. As for abroad, what have our missions done? If there were but one soul we ought to rejoice, but the result of missions has been of late so terribly little as to call for great searchings of heart. Is it not a fact that there are missionaries of ten years' standing who never had a convert? Is it not also a sad fact that the number of members in all our native churches is probably less now than it was twelve months ago? Where are the nations that have called him "Blessed"? Not one, not one! There has been no visible advance. The armies of the living God have rather suffered a repulse than gained a victory, and instead of the morning coming and the light arising, and the sun advancing to a noonday height, it seems as though at the best he stood still, if the light did not even retrograde. Surely there is a voice from God here, and as I hear it I am afraid.

Meanwhile, what kind of an age has this been in which we have lived? Is it so impassive and thoughtless that progress is impossible? Are we living in one of those dark ages in which the mind is rocked to sleep and the soul is stupefied? Ye that love the Saviour, will you open your ears to catch the meaning of these things? Men dying, the Church slumbering, and error covering the land—doth not God say something in all this? Do you not hear out of this thick darkness the voice saying, "O my people, I have somewhat against you"? Did I not hear the Lord saying, "They shall perish, but their blood will I require at the watchman's hands?" I saw the Church of God folding her hands, given to slumber, saying, "I am rich, and increased in goods, and have need of nothing"; and all the while she was suffering multitudes to perish for lack of knowledge. Do you think the Church could have had it said that she remained a year without increase if there were not blame somewhere? You may remind me of divine sovereignty, if you will, but I remember that divine sovereignty always acts with wisdom and with love, and that the Lord has not said to us, "Labour in vain." If we had laboured, and if all the Christian Church had laboured as they should have laboured, I believe the promise would have been proved, "Your labour is not in vain in the Lord."

When one is thus bowed down with the voice of God, the most natural prompting of the regenerate soul is to pray; so we turn to the second part of the text which has in it AN APPROPRIATE PRAYER. It seems to me to be perfectly dreadful that there should be this constant dying, this constant ruin, this constant spread of error, and no progress in the Church. We must deal faithfully with ourselves and not be flattered. We would honestly enquire, How much of this lies at my door? How much of this burden of God ought I to bear today? Certainly enough to lead us to such prayer as that before us.

Habakkuk, being bowed down, first turns himself to God. His first word is, "O Lord." To the Most High we must carry both our own and our church's troubles. Habakkuk turns not to another prophet to ask of him, "My brother, what shall we do"; but he turns to the Master, "O Lord, what wilt *thou* do?" It will be well for us to confer with one another as to the causes of defeat and the means for securing success, but all conference with flesh and blood is idle unless it be preceded by solemn conferences with God. For God's church, God is needed; for

God's work, God's own arm must be made bare. Is it not delightful to notice how heavy trials drive us to God when we might not have gone to him else? The little child, when walking abroad runs before his father, but if he meets some strange man of whom he is afraid, he runs back and takes his father's hand directly; so should it be with us. If God had prospered all our churches, and everything had gone on as we had desired, we might perhaps have grown self-confident, and have said, "O Lord, thou hast given us power in ourselves"; but now, that we see the contrary, let us run back to closer fellowship and nearer communion with our God than ever, and taking hold upon the arm of his strength, let us stir him up by our continued and fervent prayers.

Notice next, that the prayer of Habakkuk is about God's Church. He knew that there were dark days coming over Palestine, but he does not pray about that land in particular. "O Lord," saith he, "revive thy work." The great thing to a Christian is, not the fate of earthly empires, but the state of the heavenly kingdom. As to what is to become of this principality or that empire, what have you and I to do with these things? We are the servants of a spiritual King, whose kingdom is not of this world. Let the potsherds strive with the potsherds of the earth, and break each other as they will; our business is with King Jesus and his throne. It is delightful to see the prophet rising beyond the narrow range of the Jew, getting out of nationalities, and praying, "O Lord, revive thy work." That is the one ship we care for in the storm, that one vessel in which Jesus Christ is riding at the helm, the Captain of salvation, and the Lord High Admiral of the seas. Let the nations mix in dire confusion as they will, God ruleth over all, and bringeth out his church in triumph from all the strife of earth. The one anxiety of our souls should be, the blood-stained banner of the Cross; will *it* wave high? Will King Jesus get to himself the crown, for we have neither will nor wish beyond. So, Christian men, if you have heard God's voice in the great judgments that are abroad, let those judgments lead you to pray, "Lord, remember thy Church—*thy* Church—thy Church in England, thy Church in America, thy Church in France, thy Church in Germany, thy Church anywhere, thy Church everywhere. O God, look upon thine elect ones; let the separate ones, scattered through all nations, receive of thy benediction ; as for all else, in providence, we leave it to thy will, for thou knowest what is best."

Observe next that the prophet uses a word which is singularly discriminative : "O Lord, revive *thy* work." He does not say, "Lord, prosper *my* work." How often do I go to God in concern about the work that is going on in this Tabernacle! I am thankful for all the blessing we have seen, and I grow increasingly anxious lest the Lord should withdraw his hand ; but when one looks abroad upon the world, and upon all the Lord's people in different denominations, one cannot pray, "Lord, prosper *my* work" ; at least, one *can* pray that, and then cover that over with another—"O Lord, revive *thy* work." For what about my work? Well, as far as it is mine it is very faulty. And what about the work of the Baptists? Well, there is doubtless much that is wrong about it. And what about the work of the Methodists, and the work of the Congregationalists, and so on? May God prosper them according as they walk in his truth ! but the way to come to the core of our prayer is to cry, "O Lord, revive *thy* work ; whatever is of thee, whatever is thy truth, whatever is thy Spirit's work in the hearts of men, whatever is genuine conversion and vital godliness—Lord, revive it. Lord, revive *thy* work, and if thy work happen to lie more in one branch of the Church than in another, Lord, give that the most reviving."

Note that the particular blessing he asks for is a *revival* of God's work, by which we mean in our time that there should be a revival of the old Gospel preaching. We must have it back. It comes to this—our ministers must return to the same Gospel which John Bunyan and George Whitefield preached. We cannot get on with philosophical gospels : we must bring together all these new geological gospels and neological gospels, and semi-Pelagian gospels, and do with them as the people of Ephesus did with the books—we must burn them, and let Paul preach again to us. We can do without modern learning, but we cannot do without the ancient Gospel. We can do without oratory and eloquence, but we cannot do without Christ crucified. Lord, revive thy work by giving us the old-fashioned Gospel back again in our pulpits. It is to be lamented that there are so many who are considered not to be bad preachers who scarcely ever mention Christ's name, and are very loose concerning atonement by his precious blood. You will hear people say they have gone to such and such a chapel, and whatever the sermon might have been about it certainly was not about the Gospel. Oh may that cease to be the case! May our pulpits ring with the name of Jesus; may Christ be lifted up, and his precious blood be the daily theme of the ministry!

This, however, would not bring back a revival unless there came with it a revival of the Gospel spirit. If you read the story of the Reformation, or the late story of the new Reformation under Whitefield and Wesley, you are struck with the singular spirit that went with the preachers. The world said they were mad; the caricaturists drew them as being fanatical beyond all endurance; but there it was, their zeal was their power. Of course the world scoffed at that of which it was afraid. The world fears enthusiasm, the sacred enthusiasm which love to Christ kindles, the enthusiasm which is kindled by the thought of the ruin of men and by the desire to pluck the firebrands from the flame, the enthusiasm which believes in the Holy Ghost, which believes that God is still present with his Church to do wonders.

You perceive that the prophet desires this boon at once. He does not say, "*at the end* of the years," but "*in the midst* of the years"; his prayer is for a present and immediate revival of genuine religion. Let it be ours, not from the teeth outward but from the heart outward to pray for revival; let us long for it with heart and soul and strength, and God will give it to us.

Once more note that the prayer of Habakkuk is a very intelligent one, for he indicates the means by which he expects to have it fulfilled; in the midst of the years *make known*. It is by making known the Gospel that men are saved, not by mere thumping of the pulpit and stamping of the foot, but by telling out something which the understanding may grasp and the memory may retain. To publish the doctrine of a reconciled God, to tell men that the Lord has laid help upon Jesus by punishing him instead of us; to proclaim that there is life in a look at the Crucified One, to tell them that the Holy Ghost creates men new creatures in Christ Jesus, to give a full and comprehensive view of the doctrines of grace; this is one of the surest ways, under God, of promoting a revival of religion.

And now we close with A POTENT ARGUMENT. He uses the argument of mercy—"in wrath remember mercy." If God were to say to the churches in England, "I will have nothing to do with you; you have been so idle, so worldly, so purse-proud, so prayerless, so quarrelsome, so inconsistent, that I will never bless you again," the churches of God in England might remain as astounding monuments of the justice of God towards the people who forsake his ways. We cannot therefore appeal to merit, it must be mercy. O God, have mercy upon thy poor church, and visit her, and revive her. She has but a little strength; she has desired to keep thy word; oh, refresh her; restore to her thy power, and give her yet to be great in this land.

Mercy is also wanted for the land itself. This is a wicked nation, this England; its wickedness belongs not to one class only, but to all classes. Sin runs down our streets; we have a fringe of elegant morality, but behind it we have a mass of rottenness. There is not only the immorality of the streets at night, but look at the dishonesty of business men in high places. Cheating and thieving upon the grandest scale are winked at. Little thieves are punished, and great thieves are untouched. This is a wicked city, this city of London, and the land is full of drunkenness, and the land is full of fornication, and the land is full of theft, and the land is full of all manner of Popish idolatry. I am not the proper prophet to take up this burden, and to utter a wailing; my temperament is not that of Jeremiah, and therefore am I not well called to such a mission; but I may at least, with Habakkuk, having heard the Lord's speech concerning it, be afraid, and exhort you to pray for this land, and be asking that God would revive his work, in order that this drunkenness may be given up, that this dishonesty may be purged out, that this great social evil may be cut out from the body politic, as a deadly cancer is cut out by the surgeon's knife. O God, for mercy's sake, cast not off this island of the seas; "revive thy work in the midst of the years, in the midst of the years make known; in wrath remember mercy."

While I have been addressing Christians, my object has been to bless the ungodly too, and I do trust that some here who are not converted will enquire, "What then is God's voice to me?" May you be led to seek salvation, and remember you shall find it, for whosoever trusts Christ shall be saved.

II

SOLEMN PLEADINGS FOR REVIVAL

"Keep silence before me, O islands; and let the people renew their strength: let them come near; then let them speak: let us come near together to judgment."—Isa. 41: 1.

THE text is a challenge to the heathen to enter into a debate with the living God. The Lord bids them argue at their best, and let the controversy be calmly carried out to its issues, so as to be decided once for all. He bids them be quiet, reflect, and consider, in order that with renewed strength they may come into the discussion and defend their gods if they can. He urges them not to bring flippant arguments, but such as have cost them thought, and have weight in them, if such arguments can be. He bids them be quiet till they are prepared to speak, and then, when they can produce their strong reasons and set their cause in the best possible light, he challenges them to enter the lists and see if they can maintain for a moment that their gods are gods, or anything better than deceit and falsehood.

I am not about to speak of that controversy at this time, but to use the text with quite another view. We also who worship the Lord God Most High have a controversy with him. We have not seen his Church and his cause prospering in the world for many a day as we could desire; as yet heathenism is not put to the rout by Christianity, neither does the truth everywhere trample down error; nations are not born in a day; the kingdoms of the world have not become the kingdoms of our Lord and of his Christ. We desire to reason with God about this, and he himself instructs us how to prepare for this sacred debate. He bids us be silent; he bids us consider, and then draw near to him with holy boldness and plead with him, produce our cause and bring forth our strong reasons. We have read of wonderful revivals; history records the prodigies of the Reformation, and the marvellous way in which the Gospel was spread during the first two centuries; we pine to see the like again, or to know the reason why it is not so, and with holy boldness it is our desire to come before the Lord and plead with him, as a man pleadeth with his friend. May God help us so to do in the power of the Holy Ghost.

First, then, LET US BE SILENT. "Keep silence before me, O islands." Before the controversy opens let us be silent with *solemn awe*, for we have to speak with the Lord God Almighty! Let us not open our mouths to impugn his wisdom, nor allow our hearts to question his love. What if things do not look as bright as we could wish? The Lord reigneth. And what if he seems to delay? Is he not the Lord God with whom a thousand years are as one day, and who is not slack concerning his promise as some men count slackness? We are going to make bold to speak with him, but still he is the eternal God, and we are dust and ashes. Whatever we may say with holy boldness, we would not utter a word in rash familiarity. He is our Father, but he is our Father in heaven. He is our Friend, but at the same time he is our Judge. We know that whatsoever he doeth is best. We would not say unto our Maker, "What makest thou?" nor to our Creator, "What hast thou done?" Shall the potter give account to the clay for the works of his hands? "It is the Lord, let him do what seemeth him good." When we look at what he doeth it may seem to our dim apprehension to be exceeding strange, and we may fail to read its meaning; but we need not wish to read it. It is the glory of God to conceal a thing, and if he chooses to conceal it, let it be concealed. Truly, God is good to Israel, and his mercy endureth for ever. If this world's history is to drag on through another score of mournful centuries, it will only reveal so much the more matter for praise when the great hallelujahs of the ultimate victory shall peal forth.

Our silence of awe should deepen into that of *shame*; for, though it is certainly true that the cause of God has not prospered, whose fault is this? If there has been straitening it has not been in God. God saith, "Is there not a cause? Can two walk together, except they be agreed? If ye walk contrary to me I also will walk contrary to you." Truly, when I see how God has blessed us, I am not so much astonished that he has

not given more, as I am amazed that he has given so much.
Does he bless such unworthy instruments, such laggards, such
slothful workers? Does he do anything by tools so unfit?
Does he place any treasure in vessels so impure? This is to
be ascribed to his grace. But if he doth not use us to the
highest point, let us take shame and confusion of face to ourselves, and before the throne of his glory let us sit down in
silence. What, indeed, can we say? We have no charges to
bring against him, no accusations against the Most High,
but we must silently confess that we ourselves are vile. Unto
us belongeth shame and confusion of face.

Go further than this, and keep the silence of *consideration*.
This is a noisy age, and the Church of Christ herself is too noisy.
We have very little silent worship, I fear. I do not so much
regret the absence of silence from the public assembly as from
our private devotions, where it has a sacred hallowing influence, unspeakably valuable. Let us be silent, now, for a
minute, and consider what is it that we desire of the Lord.
The conversion of thousands, the overthrow of error, the
spread of the Redeemer's kingdom. Think in your minds what
the blessings are which your soul pants after. Get a correct
idea of them, and then enquire whether you are prepared to
receive them? Suppose they were to be now bestowed, are
you ready? If thousands of converts were to be born unto this
one church, are you prepared to teach them, instruct them,
and comfort them? Are you doing it now, you Christian
people? Are you acting in such a way that God knows you to
be fit to have the charge of those converts that you are asking
for? You pray for grace—are you using the grace you have?
You want to see more power—how about the power you have?
Are you employing it? If a mighty wave of revival sweeps over
London, are your hearts ready? Are your hands ready? Are
your purses ready? Are you altogether ready to be carried
along on the crest of that blessed wave?

Consider. If you reflect, you will see that God is able to
give his Church the largest blessing, and to give it at any
time. Keep silence and consider, and you will see that he
can give the blessing by you or by me; he can make any one
of us, weak as we are, mighty through God to the pulling down
of strongholds, can make our feeble hands, though we have

but a few loaves and fishes, capable of feeding myriads with
the bread of life. Consider this, and ask yourselves in the
quiet of your spirits, what can we do to get the blessing. Are
we doing that? What is there in our temper, in our private
prayer, in our acts for God which would be likely to bring
down the blessing? Do we act as if we were sincere? Have we
really a desire for these things, which we say we desire? Could
we give up worldly engagements to attend to the work of God?
Could we spare time to look after the Lord's vineyard? Are
we willing to do the Lord's work; and are we in the state of
heart in which we can do it efficiently and acceptably? Keep
silence and consider. I would suggest to every Christian that
he should sit a while before God when he reaches his home,
and worship with the silence of awe, with the silence of shame,
and then with the silence of careful thought concerning these
things.

Then we shall pass on to the silence of *attention*. "Keep
silence before me, O islands": keep silence that God may
speak to you; that God's Word may be heard in your soul; not
parts of it only, but all of it; that God's Spirit may be heard
with his gentle monitions warning you, with his blessed
enlightenments revealing to you yourself and your Lord, with
his divine promptings urging you to greater consecration and
superior holiness, and with his divine assistances leading you
onward in the path of a higher life than you have yet attained.
Oh, it is well to sit still before the Lord, deaf to every voice
but the divine. We cannot expect him to hear us if we will not
hear him. "I will hear," says the prophet, "what God the
Lord will speak." Do you always do so? If you have heard
the Lord speak to you, you will own that there is no voice
like his. Be silent till you hear the Lord's word slaying all
your pride and self-will and self-seeking, and proclaiming his
sole glory in every part of your manhood.

If you have learned attention, be silent with *submission*.
For this you will need the gracious aid of the Holy Ghost.
It is not easy to attain to full submission of soul to whatsoever
the Lord wills. We are often like hard brass which will not
take the impression from the seal, but if we were what we should
be we should be as melted wax which at once takes the stamp
that is put upon it. Oh, to have a heart that is quite silent

as to any wish or will, or opinion, or judgment of our own, so that God's mind shall be our mind, God's will shall be our will. The Church would soon be healed of her sorrows, and delivered from her divisions, if she would for a while be silent. Oh, that the Church would sit at Jesus' feet, lay aside her prejudices, and take the Word in its simplicity and integrity, and accept what God the Lord, and he only, doth declare to be the truth.

In that silence LET US RENEW OUR STRENGTH. Noise wears us; silence feeds us. To run upon the Master's errands is always well, but to sit at the Master's feet is quite as necessary; for, like the angels which excel in strength, our power to do his commandments arises out of our hearkening to the voice of his word. If even for a human controversy quiet thought is a fit preparation, how much more is it needful in solemn pleadings with the Eternal One? Now let the deep springs be unsealed; let the solemnities of eternity exercise their power while all is still within us.

But how happens it that such silence renews our strength? It does so, first, by *giving space for the strengthening word to come into the soul, and the energy of the Holy Spirit to be really felt.* Words, words, words; we have so many words, and they are but chaff, but where is THE WORD that in the beginning was God and was with God? That Word is the living and incorruptible seed, "What is the chaff to the wheat? saith the Lord." We want less of the words of man, and more of him who is the very Word of God. Be quiet, be quiet, and let Jesus speak. Let his wounds speak to you; let his death speak to you; let his Resurrection speak to you; let his Ascension and his subsequent glory speak to you; and let the trumpet of his Second Advent ring in your ears. You cannot hear the music of these glorious things because of the rattle of the wheels of care and the vain jangle of disputatious self-wisdom. Be silent, that you may hear the voice of Jesus, for when he speaks you will renew your strength. The eternal Spirit is with his people, but we often miss his power because we give more ear to other voices than to his, and quite as often our own voice is an injury to us, for it is heard when we have received no message from the Lord, and therefore gives an uncertain sound. If we will wait upon the blessed Spirit, his mysterious influence will sway us most divinely, and we shall be filled with all the fulness of God. Even as we have seen the frost yield suddenly to the influence of the warm south wind, so shall our lethargy melt before his sovereign energy. Be silent then, that the Spirit may thus work upon you. Let other spirits be gone—let the spirit of the world, and the spirit of the flesh, and the spirit of self be banished, and let the Spirit of the Ever Blessed be heard speaking in your soul. Thus shall you renew your strength.

We must be silent to renew our strength, next, by *using silence for consideration as to who it is that we are dealing with.* We are going to speak with God about the weakness of his Church and the slowness of its progress. Be silent, that you may remember who he is with whom you are expostulating. It is God the Omnipotent, who can make his Church mighty if he will, and that at once. We are coming to plead now with one whose arm is not shortened, and whose ear is not heavy. Renew your strength as you think of him. If you have doubted the ultimate success of Christianity, renew your strength as you remember who it is that has sworn by himself that surely all flesh shall see the salvation of God. You are coming to plead with Jesus Christ. Be silent, and remember those wounds of his with which he has redeemed mankind! Can these fail of their reward? Shall Jesus be robbed of the power he has so dearly earned? The earth is the Lord's, and he will unswathe her of the mists which dimmed her lustre at the fall, and he will make this planet shine as brightly as when she first was rolled from between the palms of the omnipotent Creator. There shall be a new heaven and a new earth, wherein dwelleth righteousness. Think of that, and renew your strength. Hath not the Lord said concerning his beloved Son, that he shall divide the spoil with the strong, and the pleasure of the Lord shall prosper in his hands? Shall it not be so?

Think, too, that you are about to appeal to the Holy Spirit; and there again you have the same divine attributes. What cannot the Spirit of God do? He sent the tongues of fire at Pentecost, and Parthians, Medes, and Elamites, and men of every nation heard the Gospel at once. He turned three thousand hearts by one sermon to know the crucified Saviour to be the Messiah. He sent the apostles like flames of fire through the whole earth, till every nation felt their power. He can do the like again. He can bring the Church out of darkness into noonday. Let us renew our strength as we think of this. The work we are going to plead about is not ours one-half so much as it is God's: it is not in our hands, but in hands that cannot fail.

In silence, too, let us renew our strength by *remembering his promises*. We want to see the world converted to God, and he has said that "The knowledge of the Lord shall cover the earth as the waters cover the sea." "The glory of the Lord shall be revealed, and all flesh shall see it together, for the mouth of the Lord hath spoken it." "They that dwell in the wilderness shall bow before him; and his enemies shall lick the dust." "The idols he shall utterly abolish." There are a thousand promises. Let us think of that, and however difficult the enterprise may be, and however dark our present prospects, we shall not dare to doubt when Jehovah has spoken and pledged his word.

Our strength will be renewed, next, if in silence *we yield up to God all our own wisdom and strength*. I never am so full as when I am empty; I have never been so strong as in the extremity of weakness. The source of our worst weakness is our home-born strength, and the source of our worst folly is our personal wisdom. Lord, help us to be still till we have abjured ourselves, till we have said, "Lord, our ways of working cannot be compared with thy ways of working; teach us how to work: Lord, our judgments are weak compared with thy perfect judgment; we are fools, be thou our teacher and guide in all things. Crush out of us our fancied strength, and make us like worms, for it is the worm Jacob that thou wilt make into the new sharp threshing instrument, which shall thresh the mountain. After this sort shall you renew your strength.

Keep silence, then, and renew your strength most gloriously by *casting yourselves upon the strength of God*. More than ever before let your inmost souls be filled with trust in the arm that never fails, the hand that never loses its cunning, the eye that is never closed, the heart that never wavers. Jehovah works everywhere, and all things are his servants. He works in the light, and we see his glory; but he equally works in the darkness, where we cannot perceive him. His wisdom is too profound to be at all times understood of mortal men. Let us be patient, and wait his time. With no more doubt of our Father's power than the child at its mother's breast has of its mother's love; with no more doubt than an angel before the throne can have of Jehovah's majesty, let us commit ourselves, each one after his own fashion, to suffering and to labour for the grand cause of God, feeling well assured that neither labour nor suffering can be in vain in the Lord.

Our text proceeds to add, "Then let them draw near." Beloved, you that know the Lord, I would urge upon you to DRAW NEAR. You are silent, you have renewed your strength, now enjoy access with boldness. The condition in which to intercede for others is not that of distance from God, but that of great nearness to him. Even thus did Abraham draw nigh when he pleaded for Sodom and Gomorrah. May God the Holy Spirit draw us near even now; perhaps the following five considerations may help us in so doing.

Let us remember *how near we really are.* We have been washed from every sin in the precious blood of Jesus; we are covered from head to foot at this moment with the spotless righteousness of Immanuel, God with us; we are accepted in the Beloved; yea, we are at this moment one with Christ, and members of his body. How could we be nearer? How near is Christ to God? So near are we! Come near, then, in your personal pleadings, for you are near in your covenant Representative. The Lord Jesus has taken manhood into union with the divine nature, and now between God and man there exists a special and unparalleled relationship, the like of which the universe cannot present. Come near, then, O ye sons of God, come near, for you are near. Stand where your sonship places you, where your Representative stands on your behalf.

The next consideration which may help you to draw near is that *you are coming to a Father.* That was a blessed word of our Lord's, "The Father himself loveth you." God forbid I should say a word to make you think less of the splendour and majesty of God; but I pray you remember that, however great and terrible he is, he is our Father. I delight in those words of our poet:

> *The God that rules on high,*
> *And thunders when he please,*
> *That rides upon the stormy sky,*
> *And manages the seas :*
> *This awful God is ours,*
> *Our Father and our love.*

As surely as my earthly father is near akin to me, and I may come to him with loving familiarity, so may I approach the Lord, who hath begotten me again unto a lively hope by the Resurrection of Jesus Christ from the dead, and I may say to him, "Abba," "Father," and he will not disregard the cry. Hath he not given us the spirit of adoption? How can he despise that which he gives? Come, then, and speak in your Father's ear. O child of God, you are not talking to a stranger, you are not about to hold a debate with an enemy, you are not seeking to wring a blessing from an unwilling hand. It is to your Father that you speak. Come near to him, I pray you, and plead this day.

Remember next, that *the desire which is in our heart for God's glory and the extension of his Church, is a desire written there by the Holy Spirit.* Now, if the Holy Spirit himself indites the prayer, and he knows the mind of God, if he makes intercession in our hearts according to the will of God, we need have no hesitation to express our desires, because our desires are simply the shadow of the eternal purpose; and that which always was in the mind of God to give, the Spirit of God has inclined us to ask. True prayer is the intimation of God to man that he intends to bless him. It is the herald of mercy. Plead, then, O child of God, for the Spirit of God is pleading in you. Come and speak out that which he speaks within. When the Spirit prompts, what cause can there be for hesitation?

Remember next, that *what we ask,* if we are now about to plead with God concerning his kingdom, *is according to his own mind.* We are at one with God in this matter. If it were not for God's glory for sinners to be converted we would not pray for it. We desire to see thousands of sinners turn to Christ, but it is with this view, that the infinite mercy, wisdom, power, and love of God may be manifested towards them, and so God may be praised. Verily, much as our heart is set upon the prosperity of the Church of God, if it were conceivable that such prosperity would not glorify God we would not ask for it. We desire to see, not our notions, but God's truth prevail. I do not want you to believe as I believe except so far as that belief is according to the mind of God. I pray every believer here to search his heart and see whether his desire be a pure one, having God's glory as its Alpha and Omega. It is God's truth, God's kingdom, God's glory that we want to see promoted. If this be the case may we not come very boldly? We have not only the king's ear but his heart also, and we may open our mouths wide. When we have a question as to the Lord's will, we are bound to go no further than "nevertheless, not as I will"; but when there is no ground for hesitancy, with what sacred ardour may we press our suit!

Moreover, there is this further consideration; *the Lord loves to be pleaded with.* He might have given all the covenant blessings without prayer; wherefore does he compel us to use entreaties, unless it be that he loves to hear the voices of his children? God has given to the Church untold mercies in answer to intercession, for he delights to bless his people at the mercy seat. To this day we live by prayer. The Church of God has never gained a victory but in answer to prayer. Her whole history is to the praise of the glory of a prayer-hearing God. Come, then, if we have sped so well before, and if God invites us now, yea, if he delights in our petitions, let us not be slack, but enlarge our requests before him. Oh for grace that we may now this day and henceforward draw very near to God.

I now come to the fourth and last point which is, "LET US SPEAK." Be silent, renew your strength, draw near, and then speak. Let us first speak in the spirit of *adoring gratitude.* How sweet to think that there should be a Saviour at all; to think that there should be a heavenly kingdom set up, as it is set up; that it should have made such advances as it has made, and should still grow mightily! That Jesus Christ should be seen of angels is put down as a wonder, but it is mentioned next to it that he was "believed on in the world." He has been believed on by millions, and, however gloomy the prospects of the Church may appear, the kingdom of Christ is not an insignificant kingdom, even now. Those who deride her laugh too soon. She is in her twilight as Voltaire said, but it is the twilight of her morning, and not of her evening. Brighter times are coming; but even now, up to this moment, the history of the Church cannot be told without adoring gratitude to God. She has been foolish, and has lost her strength, but, like Samson's, it will return. Deceived and deluded in the days of Constantine, she suffered baptised heathen to proclaim an adulterous connection between the Church and the State, and from that day her glory has departed, and her power has fled.

When will she repent? When the visible Church gets back to her chastity to Christ, she will say, "We have nothing to do with parliaments and kings, except to convert them; ours is a spiritual kingdom, and statecraft is foreign to her. We ask not your endowments; we care not for your persecutions; let us alone; all we ask is a clear stage and no favour." The bride of Christ comes not into the world to toy with the politics of princes, hers is a higher work. She leans upon the Lord alone, and yields allegiance to none else. He keeps a chosen company, who follows the Lamb whithersoever he goeth; on whose banner is written, "One Lord, one faith, one baptism"; and whose watchword is, "One is our Master, even Christ, and all we are brethren." As to the world, we will seek its conversion, but we will never enter into alliance with it, much less bow down our necks before its kings and princes. May God grant us grace as we draw near to him, to speak out in adoration of him.

Next, let us speak in *humble expostulation*. I would earnestly urge upon my brethren in Christ to expostulate thus with the Lord. "O Lord, thy truth does not prosper in the land, yet thou hast said, 'My word shall not return unto me void.' Lord, thou art every day blasphemed, and yet thou hast said that thy glory shall be seen of all flesh. Lord, they set up the idols; even in this land, where thy martyrs burned, they are setting up the graven images again. Lord, tear them down, for thy name's sake; for thine honour's sake, we beseech thee, do it. Dost thou not hear the enemy triumph? They say the Gospel is worn out. They tell us that we are the relics of an antiquated race; that modern progress has swept the old faith away. Wilt thou have it so, good Lord? Shall the Gospel be accounted a worn-out almanack, and shall they set up their new gospels in its stead? Souls are being lost, O God of mercy! Hell is being filled, O God of infinite compassion! Jesus sees but few brought to himself and washed in his precious blood. Time is flying, and every year increases the number of the lost! How long, O God, how long? Wherefore tarriest thou?" In this manner order your case before the Lord, and he will hearken unto you.

When you have spoken by way of expostulation, then turn to *pleading*. Plead with all your skill in argument. "There is thy promise, O Jehovah; wilt thou not keep it? Thou hast said unto thy Son, Ask of me, and I will give thee the heathen for thine inheritance, and the uttermost parts of the earth for thy possession! We do ask in Jesus' name. Do it for thy promise, sake! Lord, thou hast done great thing sand unspeakable in times gone by: we have heard with our ears, and our fathers have told us the wondrous things which thou didst in their days and in the old time before them: thou art the same Lord, therefore glorify thyself again. By all the past, we beseech thee, reveal thyself at this present." Plead with the Lord and lay stress upon his glory. Tell him that it glorifies his mercy to save sinners, and glorifies his wisdom and his power, yea, every attribute of his divine nature. Then plead the merit of his Son. Oh brethren, plead the blood, plead the wounds, plead the bloody sweat in Gethsemane, plead the Cross, plead the Death and Resurrection, and come not away from the mercy-seat till with this mighty plea you have won the victory.

I wish I could preach like John Knox, but I wish ten times more that I could pray like him,—a man who would not take "no" for an answer, but won Scotland for Christ, and she remains Christ's still through John Knox's prayer. It is not possible for prelacy to flourish where Knox has prayed. Oh for prayer such as that again. This is what England, yea, the world, wants—men who can plead with God, men who can draw near and then speak.

Again, after we have been silent, after we have renewed our strength, and after we have drawn near to God, let us speak to-day in the way of *dedication*. Now, here I cannot suggest to any man what he in particular may speak. I charge you before the living God lie not unto him, but if you can say this, I pray you say it—"I give to God this day my whole being, absolutely and for ever, my body, my soul, my spirit. I have asked that his kingdom may come: I pledge myself in his sight to extend that kingdom by every power I possess or may be able to gain, by every opportunity he may put in my way, and by every means which I am able to use." I do not think Jesus ought to have less than that from us, but I know he gets far less. Perhaps the Lord may move some of you young men to say, "Lord, I want to see thy kingdom spread, and therefore I will give myself up to preach the Gospel." Perhaps some of you good women here may say, "I will undertake a work of usefulness of some kind or other for Jesus; I am resolved I will." And you who have this world's goods, I hope you will say, "I know that this good work always needs money: I have it: it shall be freely given. When I see that the Gospel does not spread, I will not have the reflection on my mind that it is retarded by deficiency of pecuniary means, while I have gold stored up." I will not suggest to any of you more than this—whatever the Lord moves you to do, do it; but I do think when we come to plead with the Lord after this fashion we ought to be able to say, "Lord, do spread thy kingdom; it is not my fault if it does not spread. I do for thee all I can. I boast not of it, for all I do I ought to do, and I wish I could do a thousand times as much; but still, Lord, during this year of grace I hope to do much for thee which I may have forgotten hitherto."

Last of all, let us speak still in the way of *confidence*. However we may complain of the spread of error, the deaths of good men, and the fewness of able ministers to take their places; however we may think the times to be dark and dreary, let us never speak as if God were dead. I walked some time ago with one of the most earnest Christians I know of, a very devout man, and he told me he was afraid one day the streets of London would run with blood. He was afraid of an educated democracy which, being uneducated in religion in School Board schools, would become clever Atheists, and cast off all reverence for God and law; and he gave me an awful picture of what was going to happen. But I touched him on the arm and said, "There is one thing you have forgotten, dear friend. God is not dead yet. What you are dreading will never occur in this land, I am sure. We have an open Bible, we have still some who preach the Gospel with all their hearts, and there is still a salt and leaven in the city of London that God will bless to keep down the rottenness and corruption. In spite of all his foes, the Lord reigneth." What, my friends, the Devil conquer our God? Never. Rome triumphant over Zion? Never. Rome has been very cunning; the Devil has done his best in Roman Catholicism; there is no more wisdom left in the Devil than he has put into that concern, and if that is confounded he has lost all. That is his *ultimatum*, the course of hellish craft can go on further. Therefore even now let every heart shout, "Hallelujah, Hallelujah," and yet again let us say, "Hallelujah, the Lord reigneth, and all must be well."

III

ENQUIRE OF THE LORD

"Thus saith the Lord God; I will yet for this be enquired of by the house of Israel, to do it for them; I will increase them with men like a flock. As the holy flock, as the flock of Jerusalem in her solemn feasts; so shall the waste cities be filled with flocks of men: and they shall know that I am the Lord."—Ezekiel 36: 37, 38.

MULTIPLICATION is a very ancient form of blessing. The benediction pronounced upon man was of this sort, for we first read in the first chapter of Genesis, "And God blessed them, and God said unto them, Be fruitful and multiply and replenish the earth." That same blessing was pronounced again when God accepted his servant Noah, and entered into covenant with him. We read in Genesis 9: 1 that "God blessed Noah and his sons and said unto them, Be fruitful and multiply and replenish the earth." This also constituted a main part of the blessing promised to faithful Abraham. In Genesis 22: 17, and many other places, we read to this effect, "In blessing I will bless thee, and in multiplying I will multiply thy seed as the stars of heaven, and as the sand which is upon the sea shore, and thy seed shall possess the gate of his enemies." This was the blessing of God's chosen people, a blessing which all the malice of Pharaoh could not turn aside, for the more the Israelites were oppressed the more they multiplied. David in the hundred and seventh Psalm uses the expression, "he blesseth them also, so that they are multiplied greatly": so that clearly increase of numbers in families and nations was anciently regarded as a token of divine favour.

In a spiritual sense, this is the blessing of the Church of God. When the Church is visited by the power of the Holy Spirit she is increased on every side. When a Church in the midst of a vast population remains stationary in numbers, or even becomes smaller, no man can see in such a condition the marks of God's blessing. Certainly it would be a novel sort of benediction; for the first blessing, the blessing of Pentecost, resulted in three thousand being added to the Church in one day, and we find afterwards that "The Lord added to the Church daily such as should be saved." We read in the Acts of the Apostles that the churches "walking in the fear of the Lord and in the comfort of the Holy Ghost, were multiplied." Ever since those early days, when the Lord has been with his people they have increased in numbers, their children have sprung up as among the grass, and as willows by the water courses. When they have been "minished and brought low" it has been because they have departed from the truth or lost their first love. The clearness of Gospel testimony has been dimmed, spirituality has been at a low ebb, the Holy Ghost has been despised, and he has suspended his operations, and then the Church has dwindled down till she has had little more than a name to live: but when the Lord has sent forth his power with the preaching of the Gospel, converts have been as the drops of the dew and as the sands upon the sea-shore, innumerable.

It is plain that one of the blessings which we as a Church should seek with all our hearts is that of continual increase. The entire Church of God should look for the daily multiplication of the spiritual seed. We have the promise of it in the text, but there is appended to it this condition, "I will yet for this be enquired of by the house of Israel to do it for them: I will increase them with men like a flock."

Every true Christian desires to see the Church increase; at any rate, I should pity the man who thinks himself a Christian and yet has no such wish. "Let the whole earth be filled with his glory" is the natural aspiration of every child of God, and if any man has persuaded himself into the idea that he is a child of God, and yet does not desire to see the glory of the Lord made manifest by the conversion of multitudes, I pity the condition of his heart and of his understanding. I trust we all feel the missionary spirit; we all long to see the kingdom of the Lord come, and to see the converts in Zion multiplied. But God has appended to the granting of our desire that we should pray for it: we must plead and enquire, or else the increase will be withheld.

Why has the Lord thus made prayer the necessary prelude to

blessing? He has done so in great mercy to our souls. The Lord knows how beneficial it is to us to be much in prayer, and therefore he makes it easy for us to draw near to him. He affords us a multitude of reasons for approaching the mercy-seat and gives us errands which may be used as arguments for frequent petitioning. When one knocks at a man's door it is a good thing to have some business to do, for then one knocks boldly. If the porter opens and enquires, "Why camest thou hither?" we can reply, "Good sir, I came on an important errand," and so we are bold to remain at the door. Now, as the Lord loves to commune with his people, he takes care to give them errands upon which they must come to him. We need never be afraid that we shall be interrogated at the gate of mercy, and this stern question put, "What doest thou here?" for we have always some reason for praying, indeed, every promise is turned into a reason for prayer, because the promise is not to be granted to us till we have pleaded it at the mercy-seat.

Moreover, if I may so say, God has in mercy compelled us to prayer by making the pleading necessary to the blessing. We must pray; we are unblessed unless we pray; and therefore our necessities drive us to the mercy-seat. Though we may be so low in grace and so unspiritual that we may feel little positive enjoyment for the moment in prayer, yet pray we must: a sacred compulsion lies upon us arising from our vast necessities. We thank God, then, that he gives us reasons for coming, yea, lays a stress upon us so that we are compelled to draw nigh unto him. First of all, WHY SHOULD WE AROUSE OURSELVES TO THIS ENQUIRY AT THE HANDS OF THE LORD? I do not thus put this question because I think that many of you need instruction as to the necessity for prayer, it is good to stir up your pure minds by way of remembrance upon this point. The first reason I shall give is this, because *it is a great privilege to be allowed to enquire at the hands of the Lord*. You will see this very vividly if you turn to the twentieth chapter of this prophecy, and read the third verse, "Son of man, speak unto the elders of Israel, and say unto them, Thus saith the Lord God; Are ye come to enquire of me? As I live, saith the Lord God, I will not be enquired of by you." Look again at the thirty-first verse of the same chapter, "For when ye offer your gifts, when ye make your sons to pass through the fire, ye pollute yourselves with all your idols, even unto this day: and shall I be enquired of by you, O house of Israel? As I live, saith the Lord God, I will not be enquired of by you." What a solemn curse to be denied an audience with God! How terrible a punishment it is when God shuts the gates of prayer, and declares, "I will not be enquired of by you: when you spread forth your hands I will hide my face from you; yea, when ye make many prayers I will not hear." A people may get into such a condition of sin, such a wilful state of alienation from God, and disobedience to his commands, that he may say, "I will not be enquired of by you."

What wringing of hands, what weeping of hearts as well as eyes if it were indeed true that prayer was denied to the people of God! It was a fair token for good when Ezekiel was bidden to say that God had now taken away the curse from his people, and though he had said aforetime, "I will not be enquired of by you," yet now, under the covenant of grace, having forgiven their sins, he mercifully proclaimed, "Thus saith the Lord, For this will I be enquired of by the house of Israel to do it for them."

As you would be struck with horror if you were forbidden to pray, so I beseech you use the privilege of prayer while you may. Since at this time you are all, if you be the people of God, made to be a royal priesthood, and the mercy-seat is open to every believer, take care that ye do not despise your birthright. To each one of you the promise is given, "He that seeketh findeth, and to him that knocketh it shall be opened," and is not this sufficient reason why we should arouse ourselves to use the privilege which the Lord accords to us?

Secondly, *prayer is also to be looked upon as a precious gift of the Spirit of God* as well as a great privilege. Wherever the spirit of prayer exists it is wrought in the heart by the Holy Spirit himself; and when the text says, "For this will I be enquired of," it is a promise that men shall enquire. It is by virtue of covenant promise and covenant grace that men are made to pray: for the Lord has said, "I will pour out upon the house of David, and upon the inhabitants of Jerusalem, the spirit of grace and of supplications." Every child of God who understands anything knows that real prayer is "the breath of God in man returning whence it came." It first comes from God, and then it goes back to God. The Spirit knows what the mind of God is, and then he writes the mind of God upon our mind, and thus the desire of the believer is the transcript of the decree of God: hence the success of prayer. If united, earnest, hearty enquiry of the Lord be a covenant gift and a work of the Spirit, we dare not despise it, but we would earnestly seek after it. When we obtain a measure of prayerfulness we ought to cultivate it, and seek to make it grow abundantly. Covenant gifts are always to be earnestly coveted, for they are "the best gifts." Remember what blood it was which sealed that covenant, and made it sure to all the seed: you cannot look upon one item of the inheritance which the covenant entails upon the saints without feeling that it cost the Redeemer his heart's blood. Forsake not then the assembling of yourselves together in prayer as the manner of some is, neither neglect the mercy-seat in private, nor fail to enquire at the Lord's hand, for supplication is a covenant gift, and must not be despised by any heir of heaven.

These are two forcible arguments, but here is another. In the third place we must pray, because *it is a needful work in order to the obtaining of the blessing*. The Church of God is to be multiplied; but "Thus saith the Lord God, I will yet for this be enquired of." Remember that this is virtually written at the bottom of every promise. God saith, "I will do this or that," but it is understood that for this he will be enquired of. Doubtless we receive many unasked for favours, but the rule of the kingdom is, "He that asketh receiveth." This rule applies even to the King of the kingdom himself,—"Ask of me," saith God to his own Son, "and I will give thee the heathen for thine inheritance, and the uttermost parts of the earth for thy possession." I must then exhort you to be much in enquiring at the Lord's hands, because countless blessings are suspended upon the exercise of prayer.

Imagine for a moment that these blessings should not come; suppose that month after month the particular blessing of the text should be withheld: into what a state of mind would every earnest Christian be brought. No increase—we come to the communion table but report no additions; no need to hold church-meetings, for there are no confessions of faith to be heard, and no converts are coming forward to tell of the power of love divine. Suppose that such a state of stagnation should continue month after month with us! *And why should it not?*

It has done so with many others. Up to this moment we have never had to sigh and cry because the Lord has left us without an increase; but only suppose that the benediction should be withdrawn. You can cause it to be withdrawn, if so you will, by restraining prayer. Only let the cry which goes up to God continually from thousands of earnest hearts cease for awhile, and it will be a token that the blessing has ceased also. Only as long as there shall be this enquiring at the hand of the Lord can we expect that he will do as he has done, namely, multiply us with men as with a flock. Enquire ye, therefore, eagerly, because the blessing is suspended on it.

Next, we ought to have much of this enquiry, because *it is a business which is above all others remunerative.* Look at the text: "I will yet for this be enquired of by the house of Israel, to do it for them; I will increase them with men like a flock." That is a beautiful idea of multitude. You have perhaps seen an immense flock, a teeming concourse of congregated life. Such shall the increase of the Church be. But then it is added, to enhance the blessing, "As the holy flock, as the flock of Jerusalem in her solemn feasts." This to the Jewish mind conveyed a great idea of number. At the three great feasts of Pentecost, the Passover, and the Feast of Tabernacles, the Israelites were accustomed to offer sacrifices in vast numbers; and therefore lambs and sheep were brought into Jerusalem in such enormous numbers that without a book before me I should not like to mention the figures which have been put down by Josephus and others. We read of Solomon's offering "an hundred and twenty thousand sheep," and of seventeen thousand sheep offered in a single day, in Hezekiah's time; we may therefore imagine what the need was in our Saviour's day that there should be a sheep market by the Pool of Bethesda, for there would be need of immense lairs for such numerous flocks. Then might the city be described in the language of Isaiah when he said, "All the flocks of Kedar shall be gathered together unto thee, the rams of Nebaioth shall minister unto thee; they shall come up with acceptance upon mine altar." Now, saith the Lord, I will not only multiply you as the sheep are multiplied upon Sharon and Carmel, but as the flocks in Jerusalem when they come together from every quarter on solemn feast days, by hundreds and by thousands. You shall ask, "Who are these that fly as a cloud and as the doves to their windows?" The Lord will multiply the people beyond all count. There is this additional beauty about the promise, that the sheep which were brought to Jerusalem on the solemn feasts were not only numerous, but they were the best sheep in the land, because no animal could be offered to God if it had any blemish. The priests were peculiarly careful to select the lambs for the passover and the sheep for the sacrifice, and they were always the pick of the flock, the choice sheep of all the flocks of Palestine. What a mercy when the Lord multiplies the Church with a holy flock, as the flock of Jerusalem on her solemn feast days! Then, in addition, not only were they the choice of the flock, but they were all consecrated to God, for they were brought to Jerusalem, on purpose to be sacrificed. O happy Church which receives a host of self-sacrificing members who do not come to the Church in name only, but to present their bodies a living sacrifice unto God: to place body, soul, and spirit at the feet of Jesus, and say, "Thine are we, thou Son of David, and all that we have."

See, then, what can be had by enquiring for it. "For *this* will I be enquired of." And what is the "this" which is spoken of? Why this, that God will give us a numerous people, a choice people, his own elect, and they shall be all consecrated unto himself. They shall give themselves first to the Lord, and afterwards to us by the word of God. This is to be had by praying for it. Ah, my Lord, how foolish are we not to pray more! To thee only can we look for this favour. My soul, wait thou only upon God, for my expectation is from him. The Lord is a man of war, the Lord is his name. His right hand and his holy arm hath gotten him the victory. Wherefore, O house of Israel, enquire at the hands of the Lord, and a boundless blessing shall come.

I need not stay, I think, to say that it is necessary for us to pray, because *the results of prayer as I have already described them are such as greatly glorify God.* Kindly read the last sentence of the text; it is important: "And they shall know that I am the Lord." When a Church is increased largely with choice persons thoroughly consecrated, then the Church knows anew that there is a God in Israel; the world also opens its eyes with wonder, and admits that there is something in prayer after all. When the kingdom of God is largely increased in answer to prayer, there is a wonderful power abroad to answer the arguments of sceptics, and put to silence the ribaldry of ungodly tongues. "This is the finger of God," say they. How bitterly they ridiculed Whitefield and Wesley when first they begun to preach the blessed Gospel. They were fanatics and enthusiasts, disturbing the peace of the land! They were Jesuits, Jacobites, and I do not know what they were not, but everything conceivable that is bad! But when the Lord put power into those men, and multiplied their adherents by tens of thousands, then presently the world changed its tone, and dreaded and feared those whom they had formerly despised. So it is now. If we do not pray, if we grow cold in heart, and the blessing is withdrawn, then the worldly wise begin to say, "It is an old, effete doctrine, proclaimed by the last of the Puritans —it is dying out"; but as soon as ever they see God blessing us, and the multitudes coming together, and the Church growing to be a power in the land, they like it none the better, but they are obliged to respect it. Oh, that the Lord would stir you up as a Church to pray, and do the like with all the churches of the land.

Secondly, let us answer the question—How SHOULD THIS DUTY BE PERFORMED? First, it should be *by the entire body of the Church.* Let us turn to our Bibles and read the text again: "For this will I be enquired of by"—By the ministers? By the elders? By the little number of good people who always come together to pray? Look! Look carefully! "By the house of Israel"; that is by the whole company of the Lord's people. To obtain a great increase there must be unanimous prayer, prayer from the whole house of Israel; every one must join, without exception. Where two or three are met together there will be an answer of peace; the prayer of one prevails; but if ever the house of Israel, the whole company of the faithful shall get together in prayer, ah, then we shall see the multiplication of saints as the flock of Jerusalem on her solemn feasts; and it will not be till then. When Israel was defeated at Ai, one of the reasons of their failure was that there was an abominable thing in the tent of Achan, but another cause of defeat was this, that they said "Let not all the people labour thither." A part of the people were to go and take Ai, and the rest were to lie at ease. The Church of God will always have ill times so long as a few people are left to do what should be done by all the redeemed. The whole house of Israel must besiege Ai if Ai is to be taken; the whole army of the living God must bend the knee together, and together plead with God if any great victory is to be achieved.

Next, the successful way to enquire of the Lord is for the Church to *take personal interest in the matter.* "Thus saith the Lord God; I will yet for this be enquired of by the house of Israel, to do it *for them.*" When the people feel that the conversion of souls is their own personal affair; when the Sunday School teachers feel that the multiplication of the Church would be something done for them, and each Christian labourer feels that he has a personal interest in the saving of souls, then will the Lord's work be done on a great scale. When the case of poor sinners becomes our case, and our heart cries, "I must break unless those souls are saved," then we are sure to succeed. If the sinner will not repent, let us break our heart about him. Let us go and tell the Lord his sins, and mourn over them as if they were our own. If men will not believe, let us by faith bring them before God, and plead his promise for them. If we cannot get them to pray, let us pray for them and intercede on their behalf, and in answer to our repentance they shall be made to repent, in answer to our faith they shall be led to believe, and in reply to our prayer they shall be moved to pray. The Lord says he will do it, but he will have us seek it as a personal favour, that thus our souls may be made earnest in his cause.

The blessing will come in the third place, to *the prayer of a dependent Church.* See how it is put: "I will yet for this be enquired of by the house of Israel, *to do it for them*"; that is to say, they will not dream of being able to do it for themselves, but will apply to God for it. Christian men should never speak of getting up a revival. Where are you going to get it up from? I do not know any place from which you can get it *up* except a place which it is better to have no connection with. We must bring a revival down, if it is to be worth having. We must enquire of the Lord to do it for us. Too often the temptation is to enquire for an eminent revivalist, or ask whether a great preacher could not be induced to come. Now, I do not object to inviting soul-winning preachers, or to any other plans of usefulness; but our main business is to enquire of the Lord, for after all he alone can give the increase. Suppose we collect a crowd of people, what of that? It is a fine thing to put in the papers; but what is the good of it, if it ends there? Suppose we have large services, and fierce excitement, and the whole thing ends in a pack of moonshine, where is the glory to God? On the contrary, his name is dishonoured, and his Church is discouraged from making special attempts; but when the holy work begins in prayer, continues in prayer, and everything is confessedly dependent upon the power of God, then the blessing is indeed worth having. Enquire of the Lord to multiply you, and you will be multiplied. We must wait upon God, conscious that we can do nothing of ourselves, and we must look to the Holy Spirit as the power alone for the conversion of souls. If we pray in this dependent way we shall obtain an overflowing answer.

Again, the way to obtain the promised blessing is that the prayer must be offered *by an anxious, observant, enterprising Church*. The expression used, "I will be enquired of," implies that the people must think and ask questions, must argue and plead with God. It is well to ask him why he has not given the blessing, and to urge strong reasons why he should now do so. We should quote his promise to him, tell him of our undesert and great need, and then come back again to asking, enquiring, and pleading our cause. Such a Church, pleading, will win a blessing beyond all doubt. It must be a Church which remembers the waste places; the text puts it in the promise, and it must not be forgotten in the prayer—"The waste cities shall be filled with flocks of men." A Church which anxiously remembers the departments of service which are not succeeding, casts a friendly eye over other churches which may be failing, and takes careful notice of those places where the Spirit of God does not seem to be at work, and mentions all those in prayer, is the Church to which the promise is made.

I pray the Lord to give you heartbreak over sinners whose hearts do not break, to give you painful anxiety for those who are not anxious; in fact, may God make all the members of this Church into anxious enquirers, and when the saved ones are anxious enquirers themselves there will be plenty of anxious enquirers brought from the world. The way to have enquiring sinners is for us to become enquiring saints. When the saints enquire of the Lord the sinners will ask their way to Zion with their faces thitherward. Every prayer meeting ought, as a matter of fact, to be an enquirers' meeting, where true hearts behold the beauty of the Lord and enquire in his temple.

If we are to obtain the blessing in answer to prayer, *that prayer must be offered by a believing Church.* Oh that we did believe God's promise. The Lord says, "I will be enquired of, to do it for them": but unbelieving enquiries are only a mockery of God. How few really believe in prayer! I was reading that the Chinese converts of the Inland Mission have shown a feature of piety which is not very common. When they learned that God would hear prayer, they wanted to be always praying, because, they said, "If it be so, that the great God hears prayer, let us ask for a great deal." We do not wonder, therefore, that they have received answers to their believing prayers so remarkable that the missionary scarcely cares to narrate them, lest to unbelievers they should seem to be as idle tales. Indeed, his fears are not at all unreasonable, for in other cases the written lives of praying men have been wretchedly mistrusted. Huntingdon's "Bank of Faith" has been called a bank of nonsense, yet I believe him to have been a thoroughly honest recorder of facts, and quite incapable of a lie. When they read the story of Sammy Hick, and his turning the wind by prayer, most persons are dubious; but why? Bread was needed for a religious meeting, and no flour could be had, for the mill could not go without wind. Hick took his bag of corn to the miller and bade him grind it. "But there is no wind, Sammy," said the miller. "Never mind, there will be if you only put the corn into the hopper." It was put in, the wind ground the wheat, and then it ceased. "Ah," people say, "that is a Methodist story." Yes, it is, and there are many others of the same kind; and some of us have had them happen to ourselves. Answers to prayer do not now appear to us to be contrary to the laws of nature; it seems to us to be the greatest of all the laws of nature that the Lord must keep his promises and hear his people's prayers. Gravitation and other laws may be suspended, but this cannot be. "Oh," says one, "I cannot believe that." No, and so your prayers are not heard. You must have faith, for if faith be absent you lack the very backbone and soul of prayer. Oh, for mighty faith! If we once behold a Church filled with real active faith, exercised in believing prayer to the living God, the God of Israel, we shall see the churches multiplied with men as with a flock.

We are now to seek comfort for you who do not come to prayer meetings, or otherwise wrestle in prayer. ON WHAT GROUND CAN ANYBODY BE EXCUSED FROM THE DUTY OF PRAYER? Answer: On no ground whatever. You cannot be excused on the ground of *common humanity*; for if it be so that God will save sinners in answer to prayer, and I do not pray, what am I? Souls dying, perishing, sinking to hell, while the ordained machinery for salvation is prayer, and the preaching of the word; and if I restrain prayer, what am I? Surely the milk of human kindness has been drained from my breast, and I have ceased to be human, and if so, it is idle to talk of communion with the divine. He who has no pity on a wounded man, and would not seek to relieve the hunger of one expiring of want, is a monster: but he who has no pity on souls who are sinking into everlasting fire, what is he? Let him answer for himself.

Next, can any excuse be found in *Christianity* for neglect of prayer? I answer, there is none to be found in Christianity any more than in humanity, for if Christ has saved us, he has given us of his Spirit; "If any man have not the Spirit of Christ, he is none of his." And what was the Spirit of Christ? Did he look upon Jerusalem and say, "I believe that the city is given up, predestined to be destroyed," and then coolly go on his way? No, not he. He believed in predestination, but that truth never chilled his heart. He wept over Jerusalem, and said, "O Jerusalem, Jerusalem, how often would I have gathered thy children together as a hen gathereth her chickens under her wings, and ye would not."

> *Did Christ o'er sinners weep,*
> *And shall our cheeks be dry?*

Shall there be no prayer in our hearts, when God has appointed prayer to be the channel of blessing to sinners as well as to ourselves? Then how can we say that we are Christians? In God's name, how can we make a profession of Christianity if our hearts do not ascend in mighty prayer to God for a blessing on the sons of men?

But perhaps an excuse is found in the fact that the Christian man does not feel that his prayer is of very much consequence, for his *heart is in a barren state*. Ah, well, this is no excuse, but an aggravation of the sin. If you feel you cannot pray, you are the man who ought to pray twice as much as anybody else.

Now, surely we ought to be much in prayer, because after all we owe a great deal to prayer. Those who were in Christ before me prayed for me: should I not pray for others? By a mother's prayers some of you when you were girls were brought to Christ; will you not pay back the debt to your mother by praying for your own children? By a father's prayers, young man, you were brought to the Saviour's feet; now pray for those who are younger than yourself that they may be brought to Jesus too.

I am afraid I shall have also to plead that I must suspect your soundness in the faith if you do not join in prayer. I know some who, if they are anything at all, are sound in the faith. This is their beginning and their ending. I used to know years ago a few people who were sound all over, and never cared whether souls were saved or not because they were so sound. That kind of soundness is empty sound, from which may the Lord deliver us. Correct opinions are a poor apology for heartlessness towards our fellow men. If we are orthodox, we believe that regeneration is the work of the Spirit of God. Then, dear friend, the natural inference is that those of us who are regenerated, should pray the Holy Spirit to regenerate others. If it be entirely his work, and we cannot depend upon the preacher at all, we must invoke the power divine. If you do not thus call in divine energy, where is your soundness? By your soundness in the faith, therefore, I would plead with you that you increase your earnestness in prayer.

You may say, "Well, I think I may be excused," but I must reply you cannot. "*I am very sick*," says one. Ah, then you can lie in bed and pray. None of us can fully estimate the blessings which have come down on this Tabernacle in answer to the pleadings of our friends who are constant invalids. I believe the Lord sets apart a certain section of the Church to keep up prayer through the night watches; and when you and I who are healthy are sound asleep the watchers do not slumber, or keep silence, but either in praise or prayer they make the hours holy with their devout exercises. I consider that I sustain great losses when dear Christian men and women who have for years sustained me by their prayers are taken home to glory. Who will fill the gaps?

"*I am so poor,*" says one. Well, you are not called upon to pay a shilling every time you pray to God. It does not matter how poor you are, your prayers are just as acceptable; only, remember, if you are so poor, you ought to pray all the more, because you cannot give your offering in the shape of gold. I should like you to say with the apostle, "Silver and gold have I none, but such as I have give I thee. My Master, I will be much in prayer."

"Ah," says another, "but *I have no talent.*" That is another reason why you should pray more, and not why you should be prayerless, because if you cannot contribute to the Church's public service from lack of talent, you should the more zealously contribute to her strength by the private exercise of prayer and intercession, and thus make those strong who are better fitted to go to the front.

"Ah," says one, "but *I am just converted*; I have hardly obtained peace myself: how can I pray?" If you want an answer to that question read the fifty-first psalm. David begins, "Have mercy upon me, O God, according to the multitude of thy tender mercies," and so on, but he does not continue long before he cries, "Do good in thy good pleasure unto Zion; build thou the walls of Jerusalem." He has hardly been washed himself from sin before he begins to pray to be useful—"Then will I teach transgressors thy ways, and sinners shall be converted unto thee." You new converts are the very people to pray with power.

So, from my inmost soul, I beg you to enquire of the Lord. Prove him now, and see if he does not pour you out a blessing, yea, if he does not increase you with men as with a flock, as the holy flock, as the flock of Jerusalem on her solemn feast days. God grant his blessing for Christ's sake.

IV

MAN'S EXTREMITY, GOD'S OPPORTUNITY

"For the Lord shall judge his people, and repent himself for his servants, when he seeth that their power is gone, and there is none shut up, or left."—Deut. 32: 36.

THE same event may happen alike to all, yet it may have a very different meaning to different individuals. Ungodly men are brought low by affliction or poverty, for sinners have no immunity from suffering. Saints also are led into trying circumstances, for the utmost holiness will not preserve any man from trial. But what a difference there is between the downfall of the prosperous sinner and of the man whom God loves! The wicked man, who continueth in his wickedness, falleth for ever; but the righteous man, though he may fall seven times, riseth up again, for he shall not fall finally. How dreadful is the language of Jehovah when speaking of the ungodly! "To me belongeth vengeance, and recompence; their foot shall slide in due time: for the day of their calamity is at hand, and the things that shall come upon them make haste."

The wicked man, who prospers in this world, carries his head very high; he is proud and conceited, and he treads the poor under his feet. His career seems to be one of uninterrupted prosperity; higher, and higher, and higher, and yet higher he mounts; he becomes more wealthy and famous, and, meanwhile, he also becomes more boastful, and more arrogant towards God. He asks, "Who is the Lord that I should obey his voice?" He breathes defiance against the Most High; his heart grows harder and harder, like the heart of Pharaoh. Do you see where he is now? He has climbed to the very mountain's brow; he is rejoicing that he has reached the topmost pinnacle of fame. Who can ever pull him down from that height? Who can even disturb his peace? Wait a while, tarry but a brief season. High places are full of danger, and the terrible

prophecy shall yet be fulfilled in his experience, and in that
of many others who are like him. Their feet shall slide in due
time"; and when men in such a position do begin to slip and
slide, their fall is irrevocable. Down, down they go, falling
from precipice to precipice, until they are utterly broken in
pieces. Am I addressing any man who thinks that he is beyond
the reach of the arrows of the Almighty? Ere another week
has passed over your head, sir, you may lie gazing into eternity,
and the joints of your loins shall be loosed as you begin to
realize that you must so soon stand before the judgment seat
of Christ. Vain, then, will be all your wealth and all your
wit. You may now deride the godly, who seek mercy at the
hands of God; but then, you will cry out worse than they have
ever done. I would not change places with the greatest man
who is living without the Saviour; if I could have the whole
world given to me, if I could be the possessor of a thousand
worlds, and yet live for a single moment without having my
sin forgiven, and without the love of God shed abroad in my
heart, it would be a living death to me.

I want you to think all the more of this solemn truth because
I am going to speak of others, who do fall very low, and suffer
very much, yet, after all, their descent is followed by an
ascent, their declining leads to a revival, for, according to our
text, "the Lord shall judge his people, and repent himself
for his servants, when he seeth that their power is gone, and
there is none shut up, or left."

I shall apply the text, first of all, to THE LORD'S OWN CHURCH.

It may relate to *any sorely-tried Church*. I may be addressing
some brethren, up from the country, who are members of
churches that are sadly declining. If that is the case, let me
remind you, dear friends, that God may have a true church
which is very severely tried. The track of the ship of the
Church has lain full often over very boisterous waters. Sometimes the sea has seethed and the billows have boiled through
the fury of persecution; the prow of the vessel has been crim-
soned with blood, but onward has she moved. The days of
persecution have not yet ceased, but when any churches are
brought very low through the attacks of cruel enemies, there
is still hope for them in this promise of the living God.

What is far worse for a church even than persecution, it may be minished and brought low through the folly of its own members. Mine eyes could weep day and night over some churches that I know, which seem to me to be determined to commit spiritual suicide. They fall to quarrelling, when they are weak enough already, and need what little strength they have for fighting against the common foe. Often, they divide into parties about nothing at all; and where there should be unbroken brotherhood, there is an absence of anything like Christian love, and therefore the Spirit of God departs from them.

Many churches are, alas! brought low through a faulty ministry. A ministry that does not ring out in tones as clear as a clarion, "Salvation by grace, through faith in the precious blood of Jesus Christ," is an impoverishing ministry. If there is no nourishing food for the soul, how can it be in spiritual health? If Christ be absent from the assembly, is not everything lacking that can build up a true Christian church? In many and many a place that I wot of, the members of the church have become few and feeble because the ministry has not fed their souls. And, sometimes, a church may get down so very low that it appears as if it would become altogether extinct. One is afraid that the doors of the chapel will have to be closed, that the altar-fire will go out, and that the testimony for God will cease in that particular hamlet, or village, or township.

Now, if any of you are members of such a church as that, what you have to make sure of is that *it* is a church of Christ, and that *you* are God's people and God's servants, for our text speaks of God's favour to "his people" and "his servants." This passage does not apply to every nominal church, nor to every conglomeration of merely moral men who call themselves Christians; but it does concern every real church of God, however low it may have been brought.

When you are in such a state as this, what you have to do is to lay the condition of the Church to heart, and *to cry unto God to raise it up again.* Use every possible and right means to bring a revival; but if your way is blocked up, and there seems to be no possibility of success attending your efforts, then fall back upon this text, and plead it with God in prayer: "For the Lord shall judge his people, and repent himself for his servants, when he seeth that their power is gone, and there is none shut up, or left."

For, next, *if you pray in faith, God will return to you.* I believe that half-a-dozen persons, with vital religion in their souls, and really in earnest, may pray a church right out of any ditch into which it may have fallen, or bring it up even from the sepulchre where it has been buried, and make it live again in fulness of life; only there must be an intense determination that it shall be so, and real anguish and travail of soul until the desired end is attained. The fact that the Church has come to her extremity of weakness should cheer you, rather than drive you to despair; for when a thing is so low that it cannot get any lower, there is some consolation in that fact. Now is the time to hope that the tide will turn, and that God will raise it up again.

You remember that, when John Huss was being burned to death, he said, "Within a hundred years, there will come a man whom the persecutors will not be able to burn." The name Huss signified goose, and he said, "there will come a swan that you will never be able to roast"; that was Martin Luther, who was many times in great peril, and yet was not killed by the persecutors. When he was converted, the world was as dark spiritually as it well could be; yet God then found, even in the monastery, a monk whose preaching of the Gospel shook the world. Never be afraid of the ultimate issue of the great battle; God will beat the devil yet. If ever this pulpit should cease to resound with the Gospel of Christ, do not give up hope, my brethren; still stick together, even if there are only a few of you left, and cry mightily unto God, pleading the promise of our text, for he will remember you, and will "repent himself for his servants," and his cause shall yet again revive.

Now, in the second place, I want to show you that our text is applicable to THE TRIED BELIEVER. I may be addressing someone to whom these words of Moses shall drop as the rain, and distil as the dew.

Beloved brethren, God may bring his people, in the order of his providence, into such a state that *"their power is gone."* Apparently, they are in such a condition that they are quite unable to help themselves. They have struggled against many difficulties; but, at last, the difficulties have proved more than a match for them. All earthly help has quite failed them; to quote the words of the text, "their power is gone, and there is none shut up, or left,"—no garrison left in the city, no soldier left in the field, no helper anywhere. You may be like Job, who had no friends left, except the miserable comforters, who spoke more like enemies than friends. You are not the first of God's servants whose power is gone, and whose friends are gone. The worst about your trial may be that it may seem to you, and seem truly, that *some of your suffering is the result of sin.* You may not have been walking with God as you ought to have done, your heart may have grown cold; so that which has come upon you may be a chastisement for your wandering, it may be a rod in the hand of your loving Father, smiting you because of your folly. But I beseech you, now that all human power is gone, do not run away from God, but fly to him. Do not give up your hope in him. However deplorable your circumstances may be, let them drive you to God, and not from him. Your only hope now lies in the compassion of your God. Let me read this text again to you, and I pray that your faith may enable you to grasp it: "for the Lord shall judge his people, and repent himself for his servants, when he seeth that their power is gone, and there is none shut up, or left." There is a gracious purpose behind your present trial, even though you do not yet perceive it.

It is possible that it was absolutely necessary that you should be brought as low as you are *in order to cure you of your sin.* You have come to your last shilling, have you? I have known a doctor to keep his patient almost without food, and bring the man down very low in order to starve out the complaint from which he was suffering; and in a surgical case, the knife has had to go in very deeply so as to get at the roots of the cancer. In like manner, it may be that it was necessary that your affliction should not be stopped midway, but should be allowed to proceed to the bitter end, in order that it might be the means of curing you of the evils which were rankling in your spirit.

Possibly, too, the affliction was permitted to develop to the uttermost *in order that you might be induced to return to your God.* It may be that, in your prosperity, you had grown so careless and so fond of the world, and you had so little delight in God, that it was necessary for you to have your gourds withered, and your flowers all made to decay, in order that you might, in your abject distress, turn again unto your God.

Or it may be that God intends that *you should for ever bear a testimony to his faithfulness such as no ordinary man can bear.* Those people who only sail in a little boat on a lake have no stories to tell of adventures at sea; but he who is to write a book describing long voyages must travel far out of sight of land, and behold the sea in the time of storm, as well as in a calm. You are to become, perhaps an experienced Christian, you are to bring great honour to God, by being the means of comforting others who will be tried in a similar way to yours, you are to be trained into a hero, and that cannot be done except by great and bitter griefs coming upon you. I believe that there are some of us whom God cannot trust with much joy. His head would turn dizzy if he were set upon a high pinnacle, and he would get proud, and self-sufficient, and so be ruined. God will not kill his children with sweets any more than he will destroy them with bitters. They shall have a tonic when they need it; but when that tonic is so bitter that they seem as if they could not drink it and live, their Lord will either take the tonic away, or give them some delicious sweetness to remove all the bitter taste.

I will read the text to you again; I cannot preach from it as I should like to do, but the text itself is full of comfort to the Lord's own chosen ones who are in sore straits: "For the Lord shall judge his people, and repent himself for his servants, when he seeth that their power is gone, and there is none shut up, or left." Tried child of God, I wish I could grasp thy hand in tenderest sympathy, and whisper in thine ear, "In thy lowest moments, do not despair. 'Hath God forgotten to be gracious? hath he in anger shut up his tender mercies?' Nay, verily, 'for the Lord will not cast off for ever: but though he cause grief, yet will he have compassion according to the multitude of his mercies.' 'Weeping may endure for a night, but joy cometh in the morning.' The Lord himself saith to thee, 'I have loved thee with an everlasting love: therefore with lovingkindness have I drawn thee;' 'when thou passest through the waters, I will be with thee; and through the rivers, they shall not over-flow thee: when thou walkest through the fire, thou shalt not be burned; neither shall the flame kindle upon thee.' Therefore, if thou walkest in darkness, and seest no light, trust in the Lord, and stay thyself upon thy God, for he will have compassion upon thee; he will take away his wrath, and smile again upon thy soul, and turn thy lamentation into singing, and thy mourning into dancing."

I want secondly to show that the text also applies to THE CONVICTED SINNER.

Are there any of you who cannot say that you are the children of God, but who wish that you were? I said to one, the other day, "Are you a Christian?" and he replied, "No, sir; but, oh! how I wish that I were!" When I heard with what emphasis he spoke, I thought that he must be not far from the kingdom; for is not he who wishes to be a Christian, almost one already? Is there not the beginning of a work of grace in his heart which the Holy Spirit will carry on to completion? So I will read the text now to you who wish to be saved, but fear that you shall not be, for you have such a dreadful sense of sin: "For the Lord shall judge his people, and repent himself for his servants, when he seeth that their power is gone, and there is none shut up, or left."

Do these words describe your present condition? First, *is your self-righteousness all gone?* A few months ago, you were a fine fellow according to your own estimate; you thought that there were few as good as you. But, you came slinking in as if you felt afraid even to sit down with the people of God. You remember that line of the hymn, "Then look, sinner,—look unto him, and be saved," and you feel that you would like to look to the Crucified One; you can go as far as that, but you cannot yet say that you have looked unto him, and that you are saved, for you have such an awful sense of your guilt in the sight of God. I know you, my friend; I "know the heart of a stranger"; for such was my heart in the time of my con-viction on account of sin. Oh, the heaviness of a guilty con-science! Oh, the long, dark, dreary winter of the soul, when sin blots out the sun, turns even mercy into misery, and sorrow makes the day into night! Ah! I know you, my brother; your self-righteousness is all gone, and I am glad of it.

Then, next, you say that *your power is all gone.* Not many
months ago, you thought that you could believe in the Lord
Jesus Christ whenever you liked, that it was the easiest thing
in all the world to become a Christian, and that you would trust
the Saviour, some fine day or other, whenever you pleased.
Yet, at this moment, you are sighing, "I would, but can't
believe. Lord, relieve my load of guilt. All my help must come
from thee." You are the gentleman who was going to conquer
his evil temper, and give up his bad habits, and be a saint, and
do it all yourself! Oh, yes, yes! then, you thought you could do
anything and everything, but now you have come to realize
that, apart from Christ, you can do nothing. Only the other
morning, when you got up, you prayed to God, and you thought
that you would lead a very good life throughout that whole
day, yet you were out of temper before breakfast was over.
You went to your business, and you were going to be quite an
example there; and a pretty example you were! You felt that,
as you went home at night, all your attempts to be better, and
to do right, had failed. I am glad you have learnt your weakness,
and I hope that your consciousness of weakness will become
deeper and more painful still; for, until every bone in your body
is broken, I am afraid that you will not turn to God.

Is my text true concerning any of you? "Their power is
gone, and there is none shut up, or left." Are you brought to
such a pass that *you have not anything in the whole world that
you dare to rely upon?* You look back upon all your church-
going and your chapel-going, but you dare not rely upon them,
for you feel that you have been a hypocrite in the house of God,
and that your heart has not been right towards him. You look
back upon your attempts to pray,—for you have been trying
to pray lately,—but you feel as if you could not pray aright,
the words stuck in your throat, and the very desires were dead
within your spirit. Have you come to such a pass that, when
you read the Bible, it condemns you; and when you hear the
Gospel, the preacher seems as if he excluded you from its
provisions? Is it so? Is there no ray of hope for you anywhere? You used to have some kind of hope in reserve, some
secret, mysterious confidence that still buoyed you up: is that
all gone? Do you realize that you are lost? Do you know that
the sentence of death has been pronounced against you? Do

you seem to feel in your heart the working of the Spirit, as if even now he would take you away, and cast you into hell? Blessed be the Lord if you have come to such a pass as that!

Your extremity is God's opportunity. The difficulty all along has been to get to the end of you; for when a man gets to the end of himself, he has reached the beginning of God's working. When you are cleaned right out, and have not anything at all left, then all the mercy of the covenant of grace is yours. I may have doubts about whether God's grace will be exercised in certain cases; but I cannot raise any question about the freeness of divine grace to a soul that is empty, to a soul that is ready to perish, and to a soul that is enquiring after God, to a soul that is hungering and thirsting after righteousness. When once your soul is so conscious of your sin that every hope of salvation by your own works is entirely abandoned, and you feel that you are utterly condemned, then is Jesus Christ yours, for he came, not to call the righteous, but sinners. So, accept him as yours; take him, receive him now. He is made of God fulness to our emptiness, righteousness to our unrighteousness, life to our death, salvation to our condemnation, all in all to our poverty, our wretchedness, our sin.

Now let me read the text to you yet once more, and see if God the Holy Spirit does not press it home upon your conscience and heart: "For the Lord shall judge his people, and repent himself for his servants, when he seeth that their power is gone, and there is none shut up, or left." There is no hope for you except in the pity of God, no hope except in his mercy, and no hope of mercy except in the freeness of his mercy; and no hope even of the freeness of mercy except in the sovereignty of God, who hath mercy on those upon whom he will have mercy, and who gives his grace to the most unworthy, that it may be proved to be all the greater grace because it saves the very chief of sinners. If there is one of you who says, "I am the most unlikely man in all the world ever to be saved; I have the least claim upon God of any man that lives; the only claim I have is the right to be damned, for I have so grievously transgressed against God; I feel myself to be so guilty, that my only claim upon justice is the demand to be tried, condemned, and executed";—if you really mean what you say, then you are the man to whom the Gospel of the grace of God is specially sent, for it is written, "when we were yet without strength, in due time Christ died for the ungodly. For scarcely for a righteous man will one die: yet peradventure for a good (a benevolent) man some would even dare to die. But God commendeth his love toward us, in that, while we were yet sinners, Christ died for us." He gave himself for our sins, not for our righteousness; and he himself said, "They that are whole have no need of the physician, but they that are sick: I came not to call the righteous, but sinners to repentance." Trust Christ, thou who darest not trust thyself. Fling thyself, all broken to pieces, at the feet of the broken-hearted Saviour, and he will turn again, and have compassion upon you. Yea, look unto him, and live, for—

There is life for a look at the Crucified One:
There is life at this moment for thee.

Give but one believing glance at that dear dying Son of God, and thou shalt hear him say to thee, "Go thy way; thy sins, which are many, are all forgiven thee." The Lord grant it, for his name's sake! Amen.

V

AN ANTIDOTE FOR MANY ILLS

"Turn us again, O Lord God of hosts, cause thy face to shine; and we shall be saved."—Ps. 80: 19.

THIS seems to be the only prayer the Psalmist puts up in this Psalm, as being of itself sufficient for the removal of all the ills over which he mourned. Though he sighs over the strife of neighbours and the ridicule of foes; and lamenting the ill condition of the goodly vine, he deplores its broken hedges, and complains of the wild beasts that waste and devour it, yet he does not petition the Most High against these evils in detail; but gathering up all his wishes into this one prayer, he reiterates it o'er and o'er—"Turn us again, O Lord God of hosts, cause thy face to shine; and we shall be saved." The reason is obvious. He had traced all the calamities to one source, "O Lord God, how long wilt thou be angry—?" And now he seeks refreshing from one fountain. Let thy face no longer frown, but let it beam upon us with a smile and all shall then be well.

THE BENEFITS OF REVIVAL TO ANY CHURCH IN THE WORLD WILL BE A LASTING BLESSING.

God's revivals, whilst they are attended with a great heat and warmth of piety, yet have with them knowledge as well as life, understanding as well as power. The revivals that we may consider to have been genuine, were such as those wrought by the instrumentality of such men as President Edwards in America, and Whitefield in this country, who preached a free-grace Gospel in all its fulness. Such revivals I consider to be genuine, and such revivals, I repeat again, would be a benefit to any church under heaven. There is no church, however good it is, which might not be better; and there are many churches sunken so low, that they have abundant need, if they would prevent spiritual death, to cry aloud, "Lord, revive us."

Among the blessings of the revival of Christians, we commence, by noticing *the salvation of sinners*. When God is pleased to pour out his Spirit upon a church in a larger measure than usual, it is always accompanied by the salvation of souls. And oh, this is a weighty matter, to have souls saved. Some laugh, and think the salvation of the soul is nothing; but I trust you know so much of the value of souls that you will ever think it to be worth the laying down of your lives, if you might but be the means of the saving of one single soul from death. The saving of souls, if a man has once gained love to perishing sinners, and love to his blessed Master, will be an all-absorbing passion to him. It will so carry him away, that he will almost forget himself in the saving of others. He will be like the stout, brave fireman, who careth not for the scorch or for the heat, so that he may rescue the poor creature on whom true humanity hath set his heart. He must, he will pluck such an one from the burning, at any cost and expense to himself. Oh the zeal of such a man as that Whitefield to whom I have alluded! He says in one of his sermons, "My God, I groan day-by-day over the salvation of souls. Sometimes," he says, "I think I could stand on the top of every hackney-coach in the streets of London, to preach God's Word. It is not enough that I can do it night and day, labouring incessantly by writing and by preaching; I would that I were multiplied a thousand-fold, that, I might have a thousand tongues to preach this Gospel of my blessed Redeemer."

Ah, you find too many Christians who do not care about sinners being saved. The minister may preach, but what heed they the results? So long as he has a respectable congregation, and a quiet people it is enough. I trust, my friends, we shall never sink to so low a state as to carry on our services without the salvation of souls. I have prayed my God many a time, and I hope to repeat the prayer, that when I have no more souls to save for him, no more of his elect to be gathered home, he may allow me to be taken to himself, that I may not stand as a cumberground in his vineyard, useless, seeing there is no more fruit to be brought forth.

I know you long for souls to be converted. I have seen your glad eyes when, at the church-meetings, night after night, sinners have told us what the Lord has done for them. I have marked your great joy when drunkards, blasphemers, and all kinds of careless persons have turned with full purpose of heart unto God, and led a new life. Now, mark you, if these things are to be continued, and above all, if they are to be multiplied, we must have again a revival in our midst. For this we must and will cry, "O Lord our God, visit thy plantation, and pour out again upon us thy mighty Spirit."

Another effect of a revival in a church is generally *the promotion of true love and unanimity in its midst*. An active church will be a united church; a slumbering church will be sure to be a quarrelsome one. If any minister desires to heal the wounds of a church, and bring the members into unanimity, let him ask God to give them all enough to fill their hands; and when their hands are full of their Master's work and their mouths are full of his praise, they will have no time for devouring one another, or filling their mouths with slander and reproach. Oh that Christ would give us that spirit that loveth all, hopeth for all, and will bear burdens for all, passing by little things, and differences of judgment and opinion, that so we may be united with a threefold cord that cannot be broken.

A revival is also necessary *in order that the mouths of the enemies of the truth may be stopped*. Do they not open wide their mouths against us? Ay, and not only against us, but against the truth we preach, and against the God we honour. How shall their mouths be stopped? By our replying to them? No; foul scorn we think it to utter one single word in our own defence. If our conduct be not sufficiently upright to commend itself, we will not utter words in order to commend it. But the way we can shut our adversaries' mouths is this: by seeking a revival in our midst. What! do they rail against our ministry? If more souls are saved, can they rail against that? Ay, let them if they will. Do they speak against the doctrines? Let them; but let our lives be so holy that they must lie against us when they dare to say that our doctrines lead any into sin. Let us seek of God that we may be so earnest, so eminently holy, so God-like, and so Christlike, that to all they say their own consciences may tell them, "Thou utterest a falsehood whilst thou speakest against him." This was the glory of the Puritans: they preached doctrines which laid them open to reproach. I am bold to say I have preached the doctrine of the Puritans; and I am bold to say, moreover, that those parts which have been most objected to in my discourses, have frequently been quotations from ancient fathers, or from some of the Puritans. I have often smiled when I have seen them condemned, and said, "There now, sir, thou hast condemned Charnock, or Bunyan, or Howe, or Doddridge," or some other saint of God whom it so happened I quoted at the time. The word condemn was theirs, and therefore it did not so much affect me. They were held up to reproach when they were alive; and how did they answer their calumniators? By a blameless and holy life. They, like Enoch, walked with God; and let the world say what they would of them, they only sought to keep their families the most rigidly pious, and themselves the most strictly upright in the world; so that while it was said of their enemies, "They talk of good works," it was said of the Puritans, that "They did them"; and while the Arminians, for such they were in those days, were living in sin, he who was called Calvinist, and laughed at, was living in righteousness, and the doctrine that was said to be the promoter of sin was found afterwards to be the promoter of holiness. We defy the world to find a holier people than those who have espoused the doctrines of free-grace, from the first moment until now. Their faith let us follow, and their charity let us emulate. Let us seek a revival here.

Above all, we want a revival, *if we would promote the glory of God.* The proper object of a Christian's life is God's glory. The Church was made on purpose to glorify God; but it is only a revived Church that brings glory to his name. Think you that all the churches honour God? I tell you nay; there are some that dishonour him—not because of their erroneous doctrines, nor perhaps because of any defect in their formalities, but because of the want of life in their religion. There is a meeting for prayer; six people assemble beside the minister. Does that proclaim your homage to God? Does that do honour to Christianity? Go ye to the homes of these people; see what is their conversation when they are alone; mark how they walk before God. Go to their sanctuaries and hear their hymns; there is the beauty of music, but where is the life of the people? Listen to the sermon; it is elaborate, polished, complete, a master-piece of oratory. But ask yourselves, "Could a soul be saved under it, except by a miracle? Was there anything in it adapted to stir men up to goodness? It pleased their ears; it instructed them in some degree, perhaps, but what was there in it to teach their hearts?" Ah, God knows there are many such preachers. Notwithstanding their learning and their opulence, they do not preach the Gospel in its simplicity, and they draw not near to God our Father. If we would honour God by the Church, we must have a warm Church, a burning Church, loving the truths it holds, and carrying them out in the life. Oh that God would give us life from on high, lest we should be like that Church of old of whom it was said, "Thou hast a name to live, and art dead."

WHAT ARE THE MEANS OF REVIVAL? They are two-fold. One is, "Turn us again, O Lord God of hosts"; and the other is, "Cause thy face to shine." There can be no revival without both of these. "Turn us again, O Lord God of hosts." Your minister feels that he needs to be turned more thoroughly to the Lord his God. His prayer shall be, God helping him, that he may be more fearless and faithful than ever; that he may never for one moment think what any of you will say with regard to what he utters, but that he may only think what God his Master would say concerning him;—that he may come into the pulpit with this resolve—that he cares no more for your opinion with regard to the truth than if you were all stones, only resolving this much:—come loss or come gain by it, whatsoever the Lord God saith unto him, that he must speak; and he desires to ask his Master that he may come here with more prayer himself than heretofore, that whatever he preaches may be so burnt into his own soul that you may all know, even if you do not think it true yourselves, that at any rate he believes it, and believes it with his inmost soul. And I will ask of God that I may so preach to you, that my words may be attended with a mighty and a divine power. I do forswear all pretence to ability in this work. I forswear the least idea that I have aught about me that can save souls, or anything which could draw men by the attractions of my speech. I feel that if you have been profited by my preaching, it must have been the work of God, and God alone, and I pray to him that I may be taught to know more my own weakness. Wherein my enemies say aught against me, may I believe what they say, but yet exclaim,

Weak though I am, yet through his might,
I all things can perform.

Will you ask such things for me, that I may be more and more turned to God, and that so your spiritual health may be promoted?

But there are some of you who are workers in the Church. Large numbers are actively engaged for Christ. In the Sabbath School, in the distribution of tracts, in preaching the Word in the villages, and in some parts of this great city—many of you are striving to serve God. Now what I ask and exhort you to is this: cry unto God—"Turn us again, O God." You want, my dear working friends, more of the Spirit of God in all your labours. I am afraid we forget him too much; we want to have a greater remembrance of him. Sunday School teachers, cry unto God that you may attend your classes with a sincere desire to promote God's glory, leaning wholly on his strength. Do not be content with the ordinary routine, gathering your children there, and sending them home again; but cry, "Lord, give us the agony which a teacher ought to feel for his child's soul." Ask that you may go to the School with deep feelings, with throes of love over the children's hearts, that you may teach them with tearful eyes, groaning before heaven that you may be the means of their salvation and deliverance from death. And you who in other ways serve God, I beseech you do not be content with doing it as you have done. You may have done it well enough to gain some approval of your fellows: do it better, as in the sight of the Lord. I do not mean better as to the outward form, but better as to the inward grace that goeth with it. Oh! seek from God that your works may be done from pure motives, with more simple faith in Christ, more firm reliance on him, and with greater prayer for your success. "Turn us again," is the cry of all, I hope, who are doing anything for Jesus.

Others of you are intercessors; and here I hope I have taken in all who love the Lord in this place. Oh! how much the strength of a church depends upon these intercessors! I had almost said we could do better without the workers than the intercessors. We want in every church, if it is to be successful, intercessors with God—men who know how to plead with him and to prevail.

We do want more prayer. Your prayers, I am sure, have been more earnest at home than ever they were, during the last three weeks; let them be more earnest still. It is by prayer we must lean on God; it is by prayer that God strengthens us. I beseech you, wrestle with God. I know your love to one another, and to his truth. Wrestle with God, in secret and in public, that he would yet open the windows of heaven, and pour out a blessing upon us, such as we shall not have room enough to receive. There must be a turning again to God of the intercessors in prayer.

Again: we want a turning again to God of all of you who have been accustomed to hold communion with Jesus, but who have in the least degree broken off that holy and heavenly habit. Beloved, are there not some of you who were accustomed to walk with God each day? Your morn was sanctified with prayer, and your eventide was closed in with the voice of praise. You walked with Jesus, in your daily business; you were real Enochs; you were Johns; you did lay your head on the bosom of your Lord. But ah! have not some of you known suspended communion of late? Have not we ourselves held less communions with Jesus? Have not our prayers been fewer to him, and his revelations less bright to us? It will never do for us to live without communion; we cannot, we must not, we dare not live without constant hourly fellowship with Jesus. I would stir you up in this matter. Seek of God that you may return, and experience the loveliness of Jesus in your eyes, that you may know more and more of your loveliness in his eyes.

And once more, beloved, "Turn us again" must be the prayer of you all, not only in your religious labours, but in your daily lives. Oh! how I do groan over each one of you, especially those of you who are my children in Christ, whom God has granted me to be the means of bringing from nature's darkness into marvellous light; that your lives may be an honour to your profession. Oh! my dear hearers, may none among you who make a profession, be found liars to God and man. There are many who have been baptized, who have been baptized into the waters of deception; there are some who put the sacramental wine between their lips, who are a dishonour and a disgrace to the church in which they assemble. Some who sing praises with us here can go and sing the songs of Satan elsewhere. You have crept into our number, you have deceived us, and there you are, like a cancer in our midst. God forgive you, and change your hearts; God turn you to himself! And one and all of us, though we hope we have the root of the matter in us, yet how much

room there is for improvement and amendment! How are your
families conducted? Is there as much of that true and earnest
prayerfulness for your children as we could desire? How is your
business conducted? Are you above the tricks of trade? Do you
know how to stand aloof from the common customs of other
men, and say, "If all do wrong it is no reason why I should—I
must, I will do right?" Do you know how to talk? Have you
caught the brogue of heaven? Can you eschew all foolishness, all
filthy conversation, and seek to bear the image of Jesus Christ
in the world? Cry out, ye Christians, "Turn us again, O God!"
If others sin, I beseech you, do not you sin; remember how God
is dishonoured by it. What! will you bring shame on Christ,
and on the doctrines we profess? There is enough said against
them without our giving cause of offence; lies enough are made
up, without our giving any cause that men should truthfully
speak ill of us. Oh! if I thought it would avail, methinks I would
go down upon my knees, my brethren and sisters in Christ
Jesus, to beg of you, as for my very life, that you would live close
to Jesus. I do pray the Holy Spirit that he may so rest on you
in every place, that your conversation may be "such as becometh
the gospel of Christ."

To be personal with each other again, are we where we want to
be just now, many of us? Can we put our hands to our hearts,
and say "O Lord, I am, in spiritual things just where I desire
to be?" No; I don't think there is one of us that could say that.
Are we now what we should desire to be if we were to die in our
pews? Come now, have we so lived during the past week, that
we could wish this week to be a specimen-week of our whole
lives? I fear not. How is your heart?—is it wholly set on Jesus?
How is your faith?—doth it dwell on God alone? Is your soul
sick, or is it healthy? Are you sending forth blossoms and
bearing fruit, or do you feel dry and barren? Remember, blessed
is the man who is planted by the rivers of water, that bringeth
forth his fruit in his season. But how about yourselves? Are
not some of you so cold and languid in prayer, that prayer is a
burden to you? How about your trials? Do they not break your
heart more, almost, than ever they did? That is because you
have forgotten how to cast your burden on the Lord. How about
your daily life? Have you not cause to grieve over it, as not
being all you could desire it? Ah! beloved, do not reckon it a

light matter to be going backwards; do not consider it a small thing to be less zealous than you used to be. Ah! it is a sad thing to begin to decline. But how many of you have done so! Let our prayer be now,—

Lord, revive us, Lord, revive us,
All our help must come from thee.

The other means of revival is a precious one—"Cause thy face to shine." Ah! beloved, we might ask of God, that we might all be devoted, all his servants, all prayerful, and all what we want to be; but it would never come without this second prayer being answered; and even if it did come without this, where would be the blessing? It is the causing of his face to shine on his Church that makes a Church flourish. Do you suppose that, if to our number there were added a thousand of the most wealthy and wise of the land, we should really prosper any the more without the light of God's countenance? Ah! no, give us our God, and we could do without them; but they would be a curse to us without him. Do you imagine that the increase of our numbers is a blessing, unless we have an increase of grace? No, it is not. It is the crowding of a boat until it sinks, without putting in any more provision, for the food of those who are in it. The more we have in numbers, the more we need have of grace. It is just this we want every day: "Cause thy face to shine." Oh! there have been times in this house of prayer, when God's face has shone upon us. I can remember seasons, when every one of us wept, from the minister down almost to the child; there have been times, when we have reckoned the converts under one sermon by scores. Where is the blessedness we once spoke of? Where is the joy we once had in this house! Brethren, it is not all gone; there are many still brought to know the Lord; but oh! I want to see those times again, when first the refreshing showers came down from heaven. Have you never heard that under one of Whitefield's sermons there have been as many as two thousand saved? He was a great man; but God can use the little, as well as the great to produce the same effect; and why should there not be souls saved here, beyond all our dreams? Ay, why not? We answer, there is no reason why not, if God does not cause his face to shine.

If he makes bare his arm,
Who can his cause withstand?
When he his people's cause defends,
Who, who can stay his hand?

Children of God, I need not enlarge on the meaning of this. You know what the shining of God's face means; you know it means a clear light of knowledge, a warming light of comfort, a living light poured into the darkness of your soul, an honourable light, which shall make you appear like Moses, when he came from the mountain—so bright, that men will scarce dare to look upon you. "Cause thy face to shine." Shall we not make this our prayer, dearly beloved? Have I one of my brethren in the faith, who will not this day go home to cry out aloud unto his God, "Cause thy face to shine?" Let us give no rest unto our God, until he hear this our prayer, "Turn us again, O Lord God of hosts, cause thy face to shine; and we shall be saved."

Come, now, let me stir you all up, all of you who love the Saviour, to seek after this revival. Some of you, perhaps, are now resolving in your hearts that you will at once, when you reach your homes, prostrate yourselves before your God, and cry out to him that he would bless his church; and oh! do so I beseech you. You have often said, when you left the house of God, "I will carry out that injunction of my pastor, and will be much in prayer." You thought to do it so soon as you arrived at home, but you did not, and so there was an untimely end of the matter—it accomplished not what was designed. Pray to God that you, as a soldier of the Cross, may never disgrace the banner under which you fight. Ask of him that you may not be like the children of Ephraim, who turned back in the day of battle, but that you may stand fast in all weathers, even as good old Jacob, when "in the day the drought consumed him and the frost by night,"—so may you serve that God who has called you with so high a calling. Perhaps others of you think there is no need of a revival, that your own hearts are quite good enough; I hope but few of you think so. But if thou dost think so my hearer, I warn thee. Thou fanciest thou art right, and therein thou dost prove that thou art wrong. He who says within himself, "I am rich and increased with goods," let him know that he is "poor, and naked and miserable." He who says he needs no revival knoweth not what he says. Beloved, you shall find that those who are noted as best among God's people need to write themselves the worst; and those who fancy all goes well in their hearts oft-times little know that an under-current of evil is really bearing them away as with a tide where they would not wish to go, whilst they fancy they are going on to peace and prosperity.

Oh! beloved, carry into effect the advice I have just given.

But oh! ye who come here and approve the truth with your judgment but yet have never felt its power in your hearts or its influence in your lives, for you we sigh and groan; for your sake I have stirred up the saints among us to pray. Oh how many of you there are that have been pricked in your consciences and hearts many a time. Ye have wept, ay, and have so wept that you have thought with yourselves "Never souls wept as we have done!" But ye have gone back again. After all the solemn warnings ye have heard, and after all the wooings of Calvary, ye have gone back again to your sins. Sinner! thou who heedest little for thyself, just hear how much we think of thee. Little dost thou know how much we groan over thy soul. Man! thou thinkest thy soul nothing; yet morning, noon, and night, we are groaning over that precious immortal thing which thou despisest. Thou thinkest it little to lose thy soul, to perish, or mayhap to be damned. Dost thou account us fools that we should cry over thee? Dost thou suppose we are bereft of reason, that we should think thy soul of so much concern, whilst thou hast so little concern for it? Here are God's people; they are crying after thy soul; they are labouring with God to save thee. Dost thou think so little of it thyself, that thou wouldst fool away thy soul for a paltry pleasure, or wouldst procrastinate thy soul's welfare beyond the limited domain of hope; Oh! sinner, sinner, if thou lovest thyself, I beesech thee, pause and think that what God's people love must be worth something; that what we labour for, and strive for, must be worth something; that what was reckoned worth a ransom so priceless as Jesus paid must have its sterling value in the sight of heaven. Do, I beseech thee, pause. Think of the value of thy soul; think how dreadful it will be if it is lost; think of the extent of eternity; think of thine own frailty; bethink thee of thine own sin, and of thy deserving. May God give thee grace to forsake thy wicked ways, turn unto him and live; for he "hath no pleasure in the death of him that dieth, but rather that he should turn unto him and live!" Therefore, saith he, "Turn thee, turn thee, why wilt thou die?"

And now, O Lord God of hosts, hear our ardent appeal to thy throne. "Turn us again." Lighten our path with the guidance of thine eye; cheer our hearts with the smiles of thy face. O God of armies, let every regiment and rank of thy militant church be of perfect heart, undivided in thy service. Let great grace rest upon all thy children. Let great fear come upon all the people. Let many reluctant hearts be turned to the Lord. Let there now be times of refreshing from thy presence. To thine own name shall be all the glory.

VI

CONVERSIONS DESIRED

"And the hand of the Lord was with them: and a great number believed, and turned unto the Lord."—Acts 11: 21.

THE brethren who had dwelt together in church fellowship at Jerusalem were scattered abroad by persecution which arose about Stephen. Their Master had told them that when they were persecuted in one city they were to flee to another. They obeyed his command, and in the course of escape from persecution they took very long journeys—very long journeys indeed for that age of the world, when locomotion was exceedingly difficult: but wherever they found themselves they began at once to preach Jesus Christ, so that the scattering of the disciples was also a scattering of good seed in broader fields. The malice of Satan was made the instrument of the mercy of God.

Learn from this, every one of you, that wherever you are called to go you should persevere in making known the name and Gospel of Jesus. Look upon this as your calling and occupation. You will not be scattered now by persecution, but should the demands of business carry you into different climes, employ your distant travel for missionary purposes. Providence every now and then bids you remove your tent; take care that wherever it is pitched you carry with you a testimony for Jesus. At times the necessities of health require relaxation and change of air, and this may take you to different places of public resort: seize the opportunity to encourage the Churches in such localities by your presence and countenance, and also endeavour to spread the knowledge of Jesus among those to whom you may be directed. The position which you occupy in society is not an accidental one; it has not been decreed to you by a blind, purposeless fate; there is predestination in it, but that predestination is wise, and looks towards a merciful end: you are placed where you are that you may be a preserving salt to those around, a sweet savour of Christ to all who know you. The methods of divine grace have ordained a happy connection between you and the people with whom you associate; you are a messenger of mercy to them, a herald of good tidings, an epistle of Christ. The surrounding darkness needs you, and therefore it is written, "Among whom ye shine as lights in the world." You are intended to warn and rebuke some, to entreat and encourage others.

These good people of the early Church, however, with all their zeal, were somewhat narrow-minded and hampered by their national prejudices, for they preached at first to the Jews only, and it was very hard to make them see that the Gospel was meant for the whole race of man, Gentiles as well as Jews. Their Master had said "Go ye into all the world, and preach the gospel to every creature," and yet they began with preaching to the Jews only. Words could not have been plainer, and yet they missed their meaning. It is not to be wondered at that some in our day are still unable to preach to men as men when we see how slow the early saints were to learn the lesson. If there be any narrowness about our spirit, let us pray the Lord to take it away. We shall not, of course, be shackled as these Jews were by boasting our nationality, but perhaps there may be classes of society of whom we despair, and therefore for whom we make no effort. We say, "It would be useless to attempt the conversion of such characters. I feel myself quite able to talk to other persons; but although I am placed in the midst of these people I cannot bring my mind to speak with them about spiritual things, for I feel hopeless of success." Beloved, may you be delivered from this snare, and learn to sow beside all waters.

The Gentiles, though they were for awhile passed over by the brethren, turned out to be the most hopeful of all classes; from the Gentile fields they reaped harvests such as were never gathered in Judea. Antioch with its Grecians became famous among Christian Churches—there the Church of Christ first took its name amid a revival of religion, when great multitudes believed and turned unto the Lord. God had from of old intended that the great majority of the election of grace should be gathered out of those very Gentiles whom even the apostles themselves scarcely ventured to address.

Now then, in the light of this incident begin to work where as yet you have done nothing: begin to hope where hitherto you have despaired, throw out your best energies in that very direction in which you have felt most hampered, for there awaits you, to your own intense surprise, a success which will amply reward you. You need not restrict yourselves to lands familiar with the plough, invade the primeval forest, fell the ancient trees, and clear the broad acres: that virgin soil will yield you harvests a hundredfold such as you will never find in fields where others have laboured before you. If your spiritual mining is becoming a failure, open fresh lodes of the precious metal, for veins of treasure lie concealed in the un-broken ground. Launch out into the deep, and let down your nets for a draught, and multitudes of fish shall crowd the net. It seems to me to be the obvious teaching of the text that wherever we are cast we should try to do good, and that we may hope for the largest success among the most neglected portions of society.

Let us first speak upon THE END WHICH WE DESIRE. It may seem very commonplace, but it is in fact one of the grandest designs under heaven: he who contemplates it has a higher aim than philosopher, reformer, or patriot. He aims at that for which the Son of God both lived and died. We desire that men may believe, that is to say, first, *that they may believe the testimony of Jesus Christ to be true,* for there are some who have not reached as far as that; they reject altogether the inspired Word, and to them the incarnation, the redemption, the resurrection, the glory, the second advent, are so many old wives' fables. You to whom these truths are the light of your lives can scarcely realise the power of unbelief of this kind, and yet some men live and die in its gloom. We pray that they may be taught better, and that the evidence of these great facts may be forced home upon them. Alas, there are many who profess to believe these things, but their only reason for so doing is that they have been taught so from their child-hood, and it is the current religion of the nation. They regard the inspiration of Scripture, and so on, as matters about which it is not expedient to trouble themselves,—they do not care one way or the other, but find it the easier and more respect-able plan to admit the truth of the Gospel, and think no more about it. Such a vain complimentary belief is rather an ins to our holy faith than a thing to be rejoiced in.

But, dear friends, we want more than this faith of indifference, which is little more than dishonest unbelief; we want men to believe for themselves, because they are personally convinced and have felt in themselves the saving power of Christ Jesus. We pray that nominal believers may treat the doctrines of revelation, not as dogmas, but as facts; not as opinions, but as verities; as surely facts as the events of history, as much verities as the actual incidents of everyday life; for, alas, the grand doctrines of eternal truth are frequently treated as venerable nonentities, and have no effect whatever upon the conduct of those who profess to receive them, because they do not realise them as matters of fact, or see their solemn bearings. It is shocking to reflect that a change in the weather has more effect on some men's lives than the dread alternative of heaven or hell. A woman's glance affects them more than the eye of God. We, therefore, desire to see men really and truly believing the facts of the Gospel, in an honest, practical manner.

We cannot, however, be content with this; we labour *that those around us may savingly believe by putting their trust in the Lord Jesus Christ.* This is the grand saving act: the man brings his soul and commits it to Christ for safe keeping, and that entrusting of the soul to Jesus saves him. He makes the Saviour trustee of his spiritual estates, and leaves himself and all his eternal interests in those dear hands which once were nailed to the cross. Oh, how we long to see the Holy Spirit bringing men to this, that they may believe in Jesus Christ by resting in him and trusting upon him. For this we live, for this we would be content to die, that many might believe.

The end we aim at is that men may so believe in Jesus that they may be altogether changed in their relation towards God, for "many believed *and turned unto the Lord.*" What does that mean? It means that these heathen gave up their idols and began to worship the only living and true God. When a man believes in Jesus Christ he puts away his false gods, and worships the great Father of spirits; he makes no inferior object the aim of his being, but henceforth lives for the glory of God.

This is a glorious turning, a complete conversion of the man's heart and soul.

To turn to God means not merely to forsake the false god for the true, but to turn from the love of sin. Sin lies that way, but God's glory lies in the opposite quarter. He who looks sinward has his back to God—he who looks Godward has his back to sin. It is blessed conversion when men turn from the folly of sin to the glory of God. Precious in the sight of the Lord are the tears of penitence and the sighs of contrite hearts. We can never be satisfied with the results of our ministry unless faith leads men to hearty repentance towards God, an intense loathing of their sins, and an actual forsaking of them.

To turn to God means that henceforth God shall be sought in prayer. "Behold he prayeth" is one of the indications of a true convert. The man who lives without prayer lives without God, but the man who has turned to God is familiar with the mercy-seat. To turn to God means to yield yourself obediently to his sway, to be willing to do what he bids, to think what he teaches, and to be what he commands. Faith is nothing unless it brings with it a willing and obedient mind. Wilful rebellion is the child of unbelief, sincere obedience is the offspring of humble believing. "They believed, and turned unto the Lord." We want men, indeed, so to turn that their whole life shall be a going towards God, a growing more like him, a closer communing with him, leading on to the soul's becoming perfectly like him, and dwelling for ever where he is.

Now, dear friends, when I speak thus of believing and turning unto God some will say, "Well, but that must be a very easy matter, only to believe and turn." Yes, it appears simple, but it is none the less vitally essential. "He that believeth on the Lord Jesus hath everlasting life; but he that believeth not is condemned already because he hath not believed." You say, "Why make all this stir about it?" Just because upon this apparently little matter depends the present and eternal condition of the sinner. To believe and to turn to God is to be delivered from the present dominion of sin, and from the future punishment of it: to be without faith and without God is to be without joy here and without hope hereafter. Brothers and sisters in Christ, this is what you and I must aim at in all our attempts to influence our fellow men. It may be useful to reform them, but it is far better that grace should regenerate them. God speed every effort to promote sobriety, chastity, thrift, honesty, and morality; but you and I are sent for something more than this, our work goes deeper and is more difficult; we do not so much pray that the lion may be tamed as that he may be turned into a lamb. It may be well to lop the branches of the tree of sin, but our business is to lay the axe at the root of the trees by leading men to turn to God. This is a change, not of the outward conduct merely, but of the heart; and if we do not see this result, if men do not believe and turn to God, we have laboured in vain, and spent our strength for naught and in vain.

There is the object—aim at it, saying, "This one thing I do." Praying in the Holy Ghost, and depending upon his power, push on with this one sole object. Drive at it, you teachers in the Sabbath School; do not be satisfied with instructing the children, labour to have them converted. Drive at it, you preachers; do not believe that you have done your work when you have taught the people, you must never rest till they believe in Jesus Christ. Pursue this end in every sermon or Sabbath School address; throw your whole soul into this one object. Yours must not be a cold inculcation of an external morality, but a warm enthusiasm for an inward regeneration. You are not to bring men to believe in themselves and so become self-made men, but to lead them to believe in Jesus, and to become new creatures in him. There is our end and aim—are we all alive to it?

Secondly, let us consider THE POWER BY WHICH THIS CAN BE ATTAINED. "The hand of the Lord was with them." None ever believe in Jesus except those in whom God's arm has been revealed, for Jesus says, "No man can come to me except the Father which hath sent me draw him." But in answer to prayer that power has been revealed among his people, and is with them still. His arm is not shortened that he cannot save, neither has he withdrawn it from his Church.

Be encouraged while I suggest to you a few thoughts. The hand of God is upon many of our friends before we speak to them. It is most pleasant to me when I am seeing inquirers, to observe how God makes ready the hearts of my hearers. I am studying a certain subject, and praying to God for a blessing on it, and upstairs in a chamber, which I have never seen, one of my hearers is being made ready for my message; he is smitten with a sense of sin, or troubled with uneasy thoughts, or rendered hopeful of better things, and thus he is being made ready to accept the Christ whom I shall preach to him; yes, and ready to accept that particular form of the Gospel message which the Spirit of God gave me when I preached. There on a sick bed will lie a woman painfully exercised with the sad memory of her sinful life, in order that when she comes up to the house of God every word may have power over her. Sickness and pain, shame and poverty, often produce a condition of mind most hopeful for the reception of the Gospel.

A man well to do in circumstances has been ruined in business, he despairs of happiness below, and therefore comes to hear the Gospel, made willing to seek his happiness above. Another has lately felt failures of bodily strength, and so has been warned that life is frail, and thus he is prepared to listen to the admonitions which speak of eternity. Courage, minister of God: you are nothing, but the Almighty God is with you. When you lift your hand to build the house of the Lord omnipotence works with you, and makes your labour a success. "The hand of the Lord was with them." What more do we want? Sow, for God has ploughed. Go up and build, for God has prepared the stones and made ready the foundation.

Moreover, the hand of the Lord is with his people in helping the teachers and preachers themselves. There are strange impulses which come over us at times, which make us think and say what otherwise had never crossed our minds, and these work with power upon men's minds. If you will live to win souls it shall be given you in the self-same hour what ye shall speak. My experience teaches me that we are often wise in our ignorance, and as often foolish in our wisdom. We have frequently done best when we felt that we did but badly. If we will but trust God and be whole-hearted in the winning of souls we shall have a power assisting us in our speech of which the greatest orator in the world is not aware. Think of this, ye workers, and be encouraged.

Besides providence and the gracious help by which good men speak, there is a distinct work of the Spirit of God upon the

hearts of men where the Gospel is preached. Not only is the
Spirit in the Word, but over and above that, in his own elect
God worketh most effectually, so the truth is rendered irresistible. Let us never forget where our great strength lieth, for
in this matter we must rely alone upon the *Spirit* of God. How
often has God wrought in the power of his grace by making
men feel the majesty of the word. They come, perhaps, to hear
the preacher out of the idlest curiosity, they look for something which shall amuse them; but the truth comes home to
them and searches their heart. Simple as the language is,
"as if an angel spake they hear the solemn sound"; it goes
through them like a dart, and they cannot help feeling, "Surely
God was there, and he spoke with me."

The Spirit of God makes men recollect their sins: they try
to forget them, but sometimes they cannot; sad memories
steal over them, and wholesome regrets thrill their very souls.
Men who have been giddy and careless, and forgetful, have on
a sudden found themselves turning over the pages of their old
diaries, and with thoughtfulness reviewing the past: all this
leads to repentance and faith. That same Spirit makes men see
the beauty of holiness; they cannot help admiring it, though
they are far from it. They are charmed with the loveliness of
the character of Jesus, and begin to feel that there is something
about it which they would wish to imitate. When the preacher
proclaims the way of salvation the same Spirit leads men to
admire it, and to say within themselves, "There is something
here which human wisdom could never have devised," and they
begin to long for a share in it. Sometimes also the Spirit
blows like a hurricane through men's hearts, and they have
been borne along by its power without the will to resist. Glory
be to God when this is the case, for then the soul is driven to
cling to Jesus.

Yes, it is not the preacher, and it is not altogether what
the preacher says, but there is a power abroad, as potent as
that by which the worlds were made. Unbelievers sometimes
ask, "Where is your God?" If you once felt the power of the
great Spirit you would never ask that question. "Since the
fathers fell asleep," say they, "all things continue as they
were"; but this they willingly are ignorant of, that new creations
are being wrought every day, that there are men and women

alive in this world who are neither liars nor enthusiasts, who can declare that upon their spirit the eternal power and God-head has operated and changed them, conquering them, and holding them henceforth as willing captives to its supreme majesty. Yes, there is a hand of the Lord, and that hand of the Lord is with his people still. If it be not, then we shall see no believing and no turning to God; but since it is still at work among us, let us work on, for as surely as we live we shall see great numbers converted to God, and God will be glorified.

Thirdly, let us now dwell upon THE DESIRABLENESS OF CON-VERSIONS. It is no new thing to you and to me to see many believing and turning to God. Month by month, I think I might say Sabbath by Sabbath, souls have been saved, and the Church has grown exceedingly, and God has been glorified. What we have enjoyed we desire to retain—yea, we would have more. The Lord says to us what he said to the Church at Philadelphia, "Hold fast what thou hast, that no man take thy crown," and our crown is the crown of soul-winning, which we must hold fast, for we cannot endure to lose it. We desire this because, first of all, we desire to see truth, godliness, virtue, and holiness extended. Who among you does not? Does not every good man wish others to be good, every honest man wish others to be honest? Does not every man who loves his family desire that other families should be well-ordered? Oh, then, if there were no nobler reason, you may desire that men may be converted, since conversion is the root of everything that is pure, and lovely, and of good report.

You desire, too, that your fellow-creatures should be happy, but there is no such happiness as that which springs out of reconciliation to God. The peace which you yourselves enjoy through pardoned sin must surely make you desire that others may possess the same. If religion be indeed a source of perennial joy to yourself, you are inhuman if you do not wish others to drink of it. As you would make eyes sparkle, as you would make countenances radiant with delight, as I know you would spread gladness on all sides, desire above all things that your children, your relations, your neighbours, your friends, should be converted to God. Thus shall thorns and briars give place to myrtles and roses, and deserts shall be turned into gardens of the Lord.

You also desire conversion, I am sure, because you feel the dreadful hazard of unconverted men. You have not yet subscribed to the modern doctrine that these men and women around you are only two-legged cats and dogs and horses, and will ultimately die out and cease to be. You believe in the God-given immortality of human souls, a heritage from which no man can escape, the noblest of all man's endowments; in itself the highest of all boons, though sin may pervert it into the direst of all necessities. You would have scant motives for desiring men's conversion if you did not believe that there is another and everlasting state; but, believing that men live hereafter, and exist for ever, you must, I am sure, be eager that men may escape from the wrath to come. Knowing the terrors of the Lord, you would persuade men; judging that there is one of two things for them all, either "These shall go away into everlasting punishment", or else "The righteous into life eternal," you can never rest until you feel convinced that those about you are partakers of life eternal. Look at any unconverted person, and your sympathies should be aroused. If I saw tokens of fever or marks of consumption in the face of any one I loved, I should be struck with alarm; what, then, must I feel when I see damnation—as I do see it—in the face of every unbeliever? How is it that we are not more distressed than we are when men are perishing in their sins? Why are we not more intent upon the conversion of men? Let these questions humble us and cause great searchings of heart. It is a shame to us that we have so little of the mind of Christ, so little compassion for men's souls.

Moreover, self-preservation is a law of nature, and the Church can never preserve herself except by increasing from the world by conversion. Where are the preachers for the next generation? To-day they are amongst the ungodly, and we must labour to bring them to God. Who will fill our places? Who will bear the banner? Who will blow the trumpet? Who will wield the sword? We must find new champions in the ranks of the foe; they must be born unto God, and we must pray that this may be accomplished by our instrumentality.

Seek conversions *for Christ's sake*. You know the agony and bloody sweat; shall these be spent in vain? You know the nailing to the Cross and the shriek of "Why hast thou forsaken

me?"; shall these be unrewarded? You have thought over
and trusted in the bitter pangs of your Redeemer's death;
shall he not see of the travail of his soul? Shall he not be
satisfied? These lost sheep are *his* sheep, for whom he shed his
precious blood; these lost pieces of money are *his* money, and
they bear his image and superscription; shall they not be
found? These lost sons, away there spending their living in
riotousness, are *his* brothers, children of *his* Father; do you
not desire for Jesus' sake that they should be brought home?

Dear friends, what joy it will be to yourselves if men believe
and turn to the Lord by your means. I put that motive last,
and hope it will not be the strongest, but it may yet be one of
the liveliest. What joy it will be to yourselves if you see many
converted! Somebody has asked, "If the heathen are not
evangelized, what will become of them?" I will put another
question of a far more practical character. If you do not
try to evangelise the heathen, *what will become of you?* Do not
so much inquire about *their* destiny as your own, if you have
no care for their salvation. He who never seeks the conversion
of another is in imminent danger of being damned himself. I
do not believe in any man's salvation who is wrapped up in
self, assuredly he is not saved from selfishness. I cannot
believe in any man's possessing the Spirit of God who is indifferent to the condition of others, for one of the first fruits
of the Spirit is love. Even as flowers at their very first blooming
shed their perfume, so do the saved ones in their earliest days of
grace desire the good of their fellows. I know that one of my
earliest impulses when I first looked to Christ and lost the
burden of my sin was to tell everybody around me of the
blessings I had received, for I longed to make others as happy
as I was. I do fear me that you who never try to win souls
lack an essential part of the Christian character. I leave the
question with your own consciences.

Fourthly, let us enquire WHAT WE CAN DO TO PROMOTE CON-
VERSIONS. Conversion is God's work; it cannot be wrought
without his hand. Without him we can do nothing. Our hand
is far too puny for such a work; the power of the first disciples
and our own lies in the fact mentioned in the text, "The hand
of the Lord was with them." Still, there are certain circumstances
under which that hand will work, and there are hindrances

which will restrain it. Let us think awhile. First, then, if sinners are to be converted *we must distinctly aim at it*. As a rule, a man does what he tries to do, and not that which is mere by-play. The conversion of sinners is not one of those things which a man is likely to accomplish without intending it. Sometimes in the sovereignty of God a preacher who does not aim at conversion may nevertheless be made useful, for God works as he wills; but largely, and as a rule, men do not win souls if they do not eagerly desire to do so. Fishing for men cannot be carried out by throwing in the net anyhow, without caring whether fish be caught or no. Few traders become rich by accident, they generally have to plod and work hard for money: and to be rich in treasures of saved souls you must aim at it and labour for it. Ah, if you want men to come to Christ you must preach Christ to them with all your heart, with this design, that immediately they may close in with Christ, and at once give their hearts to Jesus. Yes, and you are to pray that they may do so through the present effort which you are making for their good. There is the target, and if you continue to shoot into the air long enough an arrow may perhaps strike it; but, man alive, if you want to win the prize of archery you had better fix your eye upon the white and take your aim distinctly and with skill. If an individual would win souls he must bend his whole soul to it and make it the object of his whole energy.

Next to that we must take care if we would have souls won that we *press upon them the truths which God usually blesses*. Shall I read to you the verse before my text? Here it is · "They spake unto the Grecians, preaching the Lord Jesus, and the hand of the Lord was with them." Now, if we do not preach Jesus Christ we shall not see souls saved. There are certain forms of doctrines which condemn themselves by working out their own extinction. Did you ever hear of a minister whose preaching leaned towards Unitarianism but what the congregation sooner or later began to diminish? Though many such preachers have been men of great ability, they have not as a rule been able to keep the dead thing on its feet.

If we want souls saved we must equally avoid the modern intellectual system in all its phases. "Oh," cries somebody, "you should hear the great Mr. Bombast. It is—— Oh, I cannot tell you what it is, but something very wonderful; it is an intellectual treat." Just so; but how many conversions are wrought by this wonderful display of genius? How many hearts are broken by fine rhetoric? How many broken hearts are healed by philosophy? So far as I have observed, I find that God does not save souls by intellectual treats.

Certain views as to man's future are equally to be kept clear of, if you would be the means of conversion. Diminish your ideas of the wrath of God and the terrors of hell, and in that proportion you will diminish the results of your work. I could not conceive a Bunyan or a Baxter, or any other great soul-winner, falling into these new notions, or if he did there would be an end to his success. Other crotchets and novelties of doctrine are also to be let alone, for they are not likely to promote your object, but will most probably divert men's attention from the vital point.

Dear brothers and sisters, if you want a harvest, look well to your seed. Time was when gardeners threw all the little potatoes on one side for seed, and then they had bad crops; but now I have seen them pick out the very best and put them by. "We must have good seed," say they. If I had to sow my fields with wheat I would not take the tail corn. I should grudge no expense about seed, for it would be false economy to buy any but the very best. Go preach, teach, and instruct with the best doctrine, even that of God's word; for depend upon it though the result is not in your hands, yet it very much depends upon what you teach. O, eternal and ever blessed Spirit, guide thy servants into all truth!

Next to this, if you want to win souls for Christ, *feel a solemn alarm about them.* You cannot make them feel if you do not feel yourself. Believe their danger, believe their helplessness, believe that only Christ can save them, and talk to them as if you meant it. The Holy Spirit will move them by first moving *you.* If you can rest without their being saved *they* will rest too; but if you are filled with an agony for them, if you cannot bear that they should be lost, you will soon find that they are uneasy too. I hope you will get into such a state that you will dream about your child, or about your hearer perishing for lack of Christ, and start up at once and begin to cry, "O God, give me converts or I die." Then you will have converts;

there is no fear about that. God does not send travail pangs
to his servants without causing them to abound in spiritual
children. There will be new births to God when you are
agonising for them.

But, let me add, *there must be much prayer.* I delight to be at
prayer meetings where the brethren will not let the Lord go
except he bless them, when a brother prays, choking as he
speaks, tears rolling down his cheeks as he pleads with God to
have mercy on the sons of men. I am always certain that
sinners are ordained to be blessed when I see saints thus compelled to plead with God for them. In your closets alone, at
your family altars, and in your gatherings for prayer be importunate, and the hand of the Lord must and will be with you.
Cry aloud and spare not, plead as for your lives, and bring
forth your strong arguments, for only by prevailing with God
will you be enabled to prevail with men.

Then there must be added to prayer *direct personal effort
on the part of all of you.* Great numbers may be saved by my
preaching if the Holy Spirit blesses it, but I shall expect larger
numbers if you all turn preachers, if every brother and sister
here becomes a witness for Christ. Are you indolent? Are
any of you beginning to sleep? I charge you, wake up. By the
love you bear to Jesus, and by the love you bear to your fellow
men, begin at once to seek the conversion of those who dwell
around you. O my beloved, do not become lukewarm. My
heart fails me at the very thought. If you are earnest, I live;
if you grow slothful, my spirit dies within me.

Last of all, if you want to see many converts, *expect them.*
"According to your faith so be it unto you." Look out for
them; believe that God will bless every sermon, and go a-
hunting after the sermon to see where the converts are. Speak
with the young converts, cheer the broken hearts, comfort the
seekers, and bring into his palace trophies for your Lord. God
bless you, beloved, and may we have a larger increase to this
church than we have had for years past, that our God may
have greater praise.

VII

A REVIVAL PROMISE

"For I will pour water upon him that is thirsty and floods upon the dry ground: I will pour my spirit upon thy seed, and my blessing upon thine offspring: and they shall spring up as among the grass, as willows by the water courses. One shall say, I am the Lord's; and another shall call himself by the name of Jacob; and another shall subscribe with his hand unto the Lord, and surname himself by the name of Israel."—Isa. 44: 3-5.

IN the Christian Church at this moment there is a very general desire for a revival of religion. You may go where you may among Christian people, and you will find that they are mourning over the present state of things, and saying the one to the other, "When will a greater blessing come? How can we obtain it? When shall we make some impression upon the masses of the ungodly? When shall our houses of prayer be filled with attentive hearers? When will the Lord's kingdom come, and his right arm be made bare in the eyes of all the people?" I am delighted to hear the inquiry; my soul magnifies the Lord as I discern tokens of growing anxiety about the cause and kingdom of Jesus and the perishing sons of men. This is an omen of better times. "As soon as Zion travailed, she brought forth her children." Searchings of heart, anguish, groanings which cannot be uttered, and abounding intercession, are the heralds of blessing; they are that sound in the tops of the mulberry trees which calls upon believers to bestir themselves in hope of victory. May the movement among the saints continue and deepen, till it brings forth a movement among sinners far and wide. Our prayers must go up incessantly that God will be pleased to send forth his saving health among the people of this great city of London, and turn many to righteousness, to the praise of the glory of his grace. Our growing anxiety for Christ's glory, and our faith in the energy of his Spirit will be two hopeful signs of a coming blessing.

As a Church we have always felt a delight in any work of this kind which has to be done for God, and we have enjoyed for many years a continuous visitation of grace. That which would be a revival anywhere else has been our ordinary condition, for which we are thankful. By the space of these twenty years, almost without rise or fall, God has continued to increase our numbers with souls saved by the preaching of his truth. Unto him be all the praise! But now we are anxious to take a part in a yet further advance; we want a greater blessing. What we have had has not decreased, but rather stimulated our appetite. Oh, for more conversions! more hearts for Jesus! Would God that the dews of heaven would fall in sevenfold abundance upon us, and our fellow Christians, and the past be put to the blush by the future! That this desire may be fanned to a flame in all our hearts is my earnest prayer. I have taken this text as one which is full of encouragement, that we may be all moved with hope and excited with expectation.

In our text we have THE GREAT COVENANT BLESSING OF THE CHURCH. It is the gift of the Holy Ghost. Whatever metaphor is used, this is the meaning of it. He is the refreshing, life-giving, fertilising water, the living water of which Jesus spake. The first promise of the text, "I will pour water upon him that is thirsty, and floods upon the dry ground," is explained by the second, "I will pour my spirit upon thy seed, and my blessing upon thine offspring."

While speaking upon this, it is well for us to remember, first, that *this blessing has been already given*. We must never underrate the importance of the ascension of our Lord, and the gift of the Spirit which followed thereupon. God forbid that we should think lightly of Pentecost: the Holy Ghost then descended, and we have no record that the Spirit has since ascended and departed from the Church. He is the church's perpetual heritage, and abideth with us for ever. I like to sing—

> *The Holy Ghost is here,*
> *Where saints in prayer agree,*
> *As Jesus' parting gift he's near*
> *Each pleading company.*

Not far away is he,
To be by prayer brought nigh,
But here in present majesty,
As in his courts on high.

He is permanently resident in the midst of the Church. But when we have received that truth, we may still go on to use the language which is very frequent among us, and pray for the outpouring of the Spirit. If the language be not exactly accurate, the meaning is most excellent. So far as any one assembly or person is concerned, we may request the Holy Spirit to be poured forth upon us in his gracious operations; we desire to see the Spirit of God working more mightily in the Church; we long each one of us to be more completely subject to his influences, and more filled with his power, so that we may be full of faith and of the Holy Ghost. We want to see the Holy Spirit poured upon those who have it not; upon the dead in sin that they may be quickened, upon the desponding that they may be consoled, upon the ignorant that they may be illuminated, and upon seekers that they may find him who alone is our peace. We, being evil, give good gifts unto our children, and therefore we are persuaded that our heavenly Father will give the Holy Spirit to them that ask him. We do but enlarge upon the prayer of the apostolic benediction when we cry for the blessing peculiar to the Holy Spirit.

Notice that this *great* covenant blessing of the Spirit is in our text *the subject of a promise.* "I will pour water upon him that is thirsty, and floods upon the dry ground; I will pour my Spirit upon thy seed, and my blessing upon thine offspring." We may always be confident of receiving those blessings which are promised by the Lord. The general promise, "No good thing will I withhold from them that walk uprightly," is very comforting, and under its broad cover we are encouraged to plead for many favours for which we have no special note of promise; but when we can put our finger upon a plain and specific word, by which a certain good thing is guaranteed to us, our faith rises to full assurance, and we feel confident of receiving an answer to our prayer. "Thou hast said, 'I will pour my spirit upon thy seed,' therefore, O Lord, fulfil this word unto thy servant, in which thou hast caused him to hope." You have

God's word for it; place your finger upon it, and on your knees beseech the Lord to do as he has said. He cannot lie, he never will revoke his word. Has he said, and shall he not do it? He has spontaneously made the promise, and he will divinely make it good. Upon every promise the blood of Jesus Christ has set its seal, making it "yea and amen" for ever. Prove him, then, herewith, and you shall find him faithfulness itself. A promise of God is the essence of truth, the soul of certainty, the voice of faithfulness, and the substance of blessing.

What a right royal promise it is! How lofty and full of assurance is the language! "I will pour water upon him that is thirsty." It is for God to say, "I will." We may venture as far as declaring, "I will if I can;" but there are no limits to his power. Our wisdom is to say, "I hope I shall be able to do as I desire;" but there are no impossibilities with the Almighty. When the season for spring has arrived, the Lord does not ask man to help him to remove the ice from the streams, or the snow from the hills, or the damps from the air. He asks no human aid in quickening the seeds, and arousing the plants, so that the sleeping flowers may open their lovely eyes and smile on all around. He does it all. His mystic influences, as omnipotent as they are secret, come forth, and the work is done. And so, glory be to God, we have a promise here which is the word of omnipotence, and when we plead it we need not be at all dismayed by the question, "Can such a thing be?" We hear the double "I will, I will," and we are certain that the Lord can and will "pour water upon him that is thirsty, and floods upon the dry ground."

It becomes us also to notice that this gift, which is the subject of a promise, is *a most needful blessing*. I have sometimes heard it sneeringly remarked that we know very well we want the Holy Spirit, and there is no need to be everlastingly talking about it. But we need to make frequent acknowledgment of this truth; it is due to the Holy Spirit himself that we should do so. If we do not honour the Holy Spirit we cannot expect him to work with us; he will be grieved and leave us to find out our helplessness. Moreover, I fear that, however generally the doctrine of the necessity of the Spirit's work may be believed as a matter of theory, it is not acted upon; and what is not believed in practice is in fact not believed at all. I am very suspicious of a man who

tires of a truth so vitally important, and dares to call it a plati-
tude. We shall not hesitate to repeat the doctrine again and
again, and we feel persuaded that God's people will not tire of it.
Without the Spirit of God we can do nothing we are as ships
without wind, or chariots without steeds; like branches without
sap, we are withered; like coals without fire, we are useless; as
an offering without the sacrificial flame, we are unaccepted. I
desire both to feel and to confess this fact whenever I attempt
to preach. I do not wish to get away from it, or to conceal it,
nor can I, for I am often made to feel it to the deep humbling
of my spirit. I pray that you who teach in the Sunday School,
you who visit the poor, you who work in any way for God, may
own your impotence for good, and look for power from on high.
To our hand the Holy Ghost is the force, to our eye he is the
light. We are but the stones and he the sling, we are the arrows
and he the bow. Confess your weakness, and you will be fit to
be strengthened; own your emptiness, and it will be a preparation for receiving the divine fulness. For, observe, the promise
of the living water is to "him that is thirsty," or, as it may be
better rendered, and the figure would be more clear, "I will pour
water upon it (the land) that is thirsty, and floods upon the dry
ground." The blessing is to come where it is needed, upon the
desert, the parched places which are as the valley of death till
the rain comes. If you think yourself to be as the well-watered
plain of Sodom, God will pour no floods upon you; it is upon the
thirsty land, upon the heart which laments its barrenness, and
confesses its own unworthiness, that the Spirit of God shall come.
I do pray that as a church we may never imbibe the idea that
we have an entail of God's blessing, or a monopoly of his benediction; so that he is sure to append his approval to any one
particular ministry, or any form of church government. The
Lord might leave us, and will, unless we lie low before him and
own our nothingness.

It should be very comfortable to us to reflect that, while we
need the Spirit of God, *his working is most effectual* to supply all
our needs when he comes upon us. In the East, you can generally
tell where there is a stream or a river by the line of emerald
which marks it. If you stood on a hill, you could see certain
lines of green, made up of grass, reeds, rushes, and occasional
trees, which have sprung up along the water-courses. Nothing

is required to make the land fertile but to water it. We are told by travellers that they have seen plains looking completely barren, apparently covered with dry dust and powder; yet a heavy shower has fallen, and in a space of time which seems incredible in our colder climate, the most lovely flowers and the most refreshing verdure have clothed the plains, till the wilderness and the solitary places have been glad, and the desert has rejoiced and blossomed as the rose; yea, it has blossomed exceedingly, and an excellency as of Carmel and Sharon has been upon it. Even thus let the Spirit of God come upon any church, and it is all that it needs to make it living and fruitful. Church machinery, apart from the Spirit of God, lacks the motive power; the motive power coming, your machinery will do its work. Of course, if it is an imperfect machinery, the Holy Ghost will not make it do all the work which a better organisation would have done; still, even the most imperfect shall accomplish so much as to astonish all who behold it. What a blessing it is when the Church does really receive the Spirit of God abundantly! Her ministry may be slow in utterance; like Moses, the leader of the people may be a man of stammering speech; or, like Paul, his personal appearance may be mean, and his speech contemptible; but this matters nothing when the Spirit of God is upon the man and in the people. The Church may be very small, and the members may be very poor, and many of them illiterate, too; but, where the Spirit of God is, there is the majesty of omnipotence.

I here call your attention to the fact that the promise in our text is *liberal and unstinted*. "I will *pour* water upon the thirsty land, and *floods* upon the dry ground." The Lord does not need to stint his gifts. When he gives a blessing he gives it like a king. His treasury will not be exhausted by giving, or replenished by withholding. I have seen in Italy the fields watered by the processes of irrigation: there are trenches made to run along the garden, and smaller gutters to carry the lesser streams to each bed, so that each plant gets its share of water; but the husbandman has to be very careful, for he has but little water in his tank, and only an allotted share of the public reservoir. No plant must have too much; no plot of ground must be drenched. How different is this from the methods of the Lord! He pours the water; he deluges the land. "The parched ground shall become a pool, and the thirsty land springs of water; in the habitation of dragons, where each lay, shall be grass with reeds and rushes." Oh that he would pull up the sluices now, and let a torrent of grace rush through this Tabernacle. He is able to do exceeding abundantly above what we ask, or even think. He giveth liberally, and upbraideth not. Our abounding sin and death need abounding life and power. Let us open our mouths wide, that he may fill them. The Lord is illimitable in his wealth of grace, and boundless in his goodness and power. Let us take the promise as it stands, and plead it at the throne, "Hast thou not said, 'I will pour water upon him that is thirsty, and floods upon the dry ground'?" Lord, do it, to the praise of the glory of thy grace.

This covenant blessing is, in our text, *peculiarly promised to a certain class of persons who are especially dear to us.* "I will pour my Spirit upon thy seed, and my blessing upon thine offspring." Parents, lay hold greedily upon these points of the promise. I am afraid we do not think enough of the promise which the Lord has made to our children. Grace does not run in the blood; we have never fallen into the gross error of birthright membership, or the supposition that the child of godly parents has a right to Christian ordinances. We know that religion is a personal matter, and is not of blood nor of birth; we know also that all children are heirs of wrath till the grace of God regenerates them; but still there is some meaning in that gracious saying, "The promise is unto you and your children, even to as many as the Lord your God shall call." Paul was assuredly not wrong, but sweetly right, when he said to the jailer, in answer to his question, "What must I do to be saved?" "Believe on the Lord Jesus Christ and thou shalt be saved, and thy house." Lay hold of those words, Christian parents, and do not be content to get half the promise. Pray to God to fulfil it all. Go to him this very day, you mothers and fathers, and implore him to have pity upon your offspring. Cry unto him, and say, "Thou hast said, 'I will pour my Spirit on thy seed, and my blessing on thine offspring:' do it, Lord, for Jesus Christ's sake."

We are now to consider THE GLORIOUS RESULT OF THIS COVENANT BLESSING. The certain result of the outpouring of the Spirit is the upspringing of spiritual life. Wherever the water comes in Palestine, as I said before, the grass will be sure to follow it, and vegetation becomes lively at once. Wherever the Spirit of God comes, there will be life in the church and life in the ministry, life in prayer, life in effort, life in holiness, life in brotherly love.

The next effect will be seen in the calling out of numerous converts by the Holy Spirit. "They shall spring up as among the grass, and as willows by the water courses." Who can count the blades of grass? They are a fine symbol of the greatness of number, and might as justly be used for that purpose as the sands of the seashore. Where the Spirit of the Lord comes, converts are not few as the cedars of Lebanon, but they flourish like the grass of the earth. Can we be satisfied with having in a year a dozen or so added to the Church? Yet do I meet with some of my brethren—and far be it from me to judge them— who say they have had a happy year, and are very comfortable though they have had only three or four persons added to the Church. Surely, however small the congregation, that must be a very unsatisfactory reward for a twelvemonth's ministry. My brethren, where at this day do we see results attending the Gospel which should satisfy us? Hundreds may be added to the Church in a year, as has been our common blessing, but what are hundreds? If four hundred were brought into our fellowship last year, what is that out of four millions? What are these saved ones among so many? The headway made by the Church is next to nothing; it hardly keeps pace with the growth of the population. We want more of the Spirit of God, and if we had it, I have no doubt whatever the converts would at once be counted by thousands and tens of thousands; and there is no reason whatever why the Church of God, which is now in a pitiful minority, should not become in many a district a triumphant majority, and the influences of the grace of God be felt far and near.

Observe that the text tells us that the converts called out by the Spirit of God are vigorous and lively. "They shall spring as the grass." Now the grass in the East springs up without any sowing, cultivating, or any other attention: it comes up of itself from the fruitful soil. There is the water, and there is the grass. So where the Spirit of God is with a Church there are sure to be conversions, it cannot be otherwise. True, we are bound to use all agencies that are fit and right for the promotion of the good end; but where the Spirit of God is we shall often be astonished to find that far beyond the usual result of agencies the life has extended. The willows also are mentioned, to indicate great vitality. How rapidly the willow grows! There is a proverb in Cambridgeshire that a willow will buy a horse, where an oak won't buy a saddle; because the willow grows so quickly and yields such frequent boughs to the cutter. You may cut it this year, and in a short time you may remove its pliant boughs again, for they will come anew. So truly saved ones will bear discouragement and trial, and still spring up. We may expect then, if the Spirit of God shall work among us, that there will be an abundance of converts, and those of the most vigorous kind.

These conversions will come from all quarters. The text says, one shall say, and another shall call, and another shall subscribe. Here is one who is the son of a deacon—we expected him to give his heart to Jesus. There is another, he is not the child of a religious professor, but comes right out from an ungodly family. Ah, here is another, he had grown up and come to ripe years, having followed after folly, and confirmed himself in sin, yet he comes forward, for the grace of God has called him. One comes from the wealthy, another comes from the poor, a third comes from nobody knows where; but they will and must come, for God knows his own, and will call them. They shall come from all trades and occupations, from all churches and denominations. We shall be wonderstruck as we hear from all corners, and parts, and places, "I am the Lord's;" and again, "I am called by the name of Jacob;" and again, "I am surnamed this day by the name of Israel." The work of divine grace does not run in a groove, but breaks out where it seems least likely to do so. At one time it creates a revival at Samaria, at another time it saves a widow at Joppa, or the eunuch on the road to Gaza. Lord, call whomsoever thou wilt, but do call many, for Jesus' sake.

One memorable thing about the conversions wrought by the Holy Ghost is this, that these converted people shall be led to avow their faith. They shall not, like Nicodemus, come to Jesus by night; they shall not hope to go to heaven creeping all the way behind the hedge; but they shall avow their allegiance. "One shall say, I am the Lord's; and another shall call himself by the name of Jacob, and another shall subscribe with his hand

unto the Lord, and surname himself by the name of Israel."
The God of Israel shall be their God, and the people of Israel
shall be their people. I love to see both these things in young
converts. Some appear to dedicate themselves to God, but they
feel themselves such superior beings that they do not join with
any Church, but hold themselves in the isolation which practically means, "Stand by, I am holier than thou." They do not
think any Church good enough for them, but my private opinion
is that they are not good enough for any Church. On the other
hand, some will join a church, but do not seem to have had
enough respect to the inward, vital part of religion in giving
themselves up to the Lord, and therefore no church will find
them to be any great gain. There must be the two together, a
surrender to God and then a union with the people of God.
Consider the first of these points:—One shall say, "I am the
Lord's." He shall confess that from head to foot, body, soul and
spirit, he is not his own but Christ's. He will feel, "I have been
washed in his blood; I have been pardoned all my sins, and been
renewed in heart; and now I am the Lord's, and I desire to live
to his praise. Tell me what I can do, and how I can serve the
Lord, for I am his, and mean to be his for ever." This is delightful. Oh, to hear hundreds of you saying this. I would give
my life to see it.

Another convert is said to subscribe with his hand to the God
of Jacob. He gives himself over to God, and he does it delib-
berately; as deliberately as a person who signs a deed by which
he makes over an estate. He writes his name, and places his
finger on the seal, and calmly says, "This is my act and deed."
We do not recommend persons to write out covenants with God
and sign them, they are apt to gender unto bondage; but we do
recommend them to make such a covenant in their hearts before
the Most High, saying,

'Tis done, the great transaction's done;
I am my Lord's and he is mine:
He drew me, and I followed on,
Charmed to obey the voice divine.

The text may have another rendering, for, if you notice, the
word "*with*" in the text is in italics, to show that it was inserted

by the translators. It might run thus: "Another shall subscribe his hand unto the Lord." This alludes to the custom which still exists, but which was more common in those days, of a servant being marked or tattooed in the hand with his master's name. So was it with soldiers; frequently when they were enthusiastic for a leader they would print his name on some part of their body, and very often upon the palms of their hands. There are constant allusions to this in the classics. We know that devout worshippers dedicated themselves to the god they worshipped, and were stamped with a secret mark. Paul alludes to this when he says, "Henceforth let no man trouble me, for I bear in my body the marks of the Lord Jesus;" as much as to say, "I am Christ's: I have had his name branded upon me." When he suffered from being scourged and beaten with rods, he called it bearing the marks of the Lord Jesus, and did as good as say, "Flog away, you will only engrave his name into my flesh, for I am Christ's." Now it would be a very superstitious and foolish thing for any man to be tattooed with the name of the Lord, or with a cross; but all that such an act meant in those who did it of old we ought to mean, namely, that we are for ever, and beyond recall, the property of Jesus. Who shall separate us from the love of God?

> High heaven that heard the solemn vow,
> That vow renewed shall daily hear,
> Till in life's latest hour I bow,
> And bless in death a bond so dear.

There was dedication to God of the fullest kind, but side by side with it went unity with the Church, for the declaration, "I am the Lord's," was parallel with "calling himself by the name of Jacob." Now the name of Jacob was the first, the lower, the common name of God's people, they were the seed of Jacob. "Ah," says the man who is converted, "I do not care what they call Christian people, they may call *me* by the same title if they will, and I will not complain. They may call us Puritans, Methodists, Ranters, Quakers, or whatever they like, I am one of them." I have read of a certain nobleman who was also a saint, that when he heard religious persons scoffed at as Puritans, he was accustomed at once to declare, "I am a Puritan too. I glory in being one of them." They felt that it was of little use to mock at him, he was too stout a soldier and too bold a speaker.

It is mentioned, also, that one surnamed himself by the name of Israel. That was the grand name of the Church in those days—Israel, the prevailing prince. We ought to feel that to be a Christian is to possess a patent of nobility second to none. Duke, earl, knight, esquire—we covet none of these; call us by the name of Christ and we have honour enough. The name of Caesar is a poor thing compared with the name of Christ. Better be owned as a disciple of Jesus than as an emperor of emperors. Oh, may the Spirit of God be poured out upon this place, that many of you may be savingly converted, and then say, "I will give myself to the Lord, and will also cast in my lot with his people; where they dwell I will dwell; where they die there would I die; their people shall be my people, since their God has become my God." Pray, that the promise before us may be fulfilled in this church, and in all the churches of our Lord Jesus Christ.

Now, lastly, I have to speak upon THE CONDUCT SUITABLE IF WE OBTAIN THIS BLESSING. First, O my brethren in Christ, if we would obtain these floods of blessing we must confess how dry, how thirsty, how wilderness-like we are. Humble yourselves, therefore, under the hand of God, and he will exalt you in due time. "He hath filled the hungry with good things, but the rich he hath sent empty away." Oh, for the spirit of humiliation throughout the Church!

Next to that let us cultivate prayer. "For this will I be enquired of by the house of Israel to do it for them." If you have a man's cheque for a thousand pounds, it would be very wicked of you to say, "I cannot get my money, this paper is not paid," if you have never taken it to the bank; and so, if you have God's promise, and have never pleaded it, it is your own fault if you have not obtained the blessing. The very least thing God can ask of us is that we shall ask of him, "Ask and it shall be given you: seek and ye shall find: knock and it shall be opened unto you." Plead more earnestly in private, make your prayer meetings more energetic, attend them more numerously, throw your hearts more fully into them, and God's Spirit will be surely given.

Next to that, if we want the blessing we must put forth our own personal effort. It would be a most absurd thing for a man to pray for a harvest, and neither plough nor sow. I cannot conceive anything more insulting to the majesty of God than for us to pray, and meanwhile fold our arms. It is not thus that we prove our sincerity. I desire to preach to you as if the conversion of these sinners around us depended wholly upon me, and then I delight to fall back upon the truth that it wholly depends upon the Lord God. Sunday School teachers, use the means for the conversion of your children! Try and speak personally to every one of them; if you can find opportunity, pray with them one by one alone. You will win young hearts for Jesus in that way. Try, dear friends, to get hold of individuals. You who come here continually, look out for individuals in the congregation, and endeavour to tell them what you have experienced of the love of Christ. If you cannot speak to them, write letters to them; an earnest letter is as good as a sermon. Do anything, do everything, to bring souls to Jesus. While we are working we shall find God working with us, for he is never slower than his people. If we are building, he will be the Master Builder, and will build through us. For a man to pray that he may have a safe journey, and then to go to bed, and not start from home, would be wickedness; and to pray to God to convert sinners, and then not to preach or teach them the Gospel, would be a piece of impudent mockery of God. Beloved, see to this.

Once more, I have a word to say to those who are not the people of God. O beloved ones, who are not saved, all our concern is about your salvation. We are always preaching and praying about you. How can you obtain saving faith? I would urge you to labour after a clear idea of your real position. May I ask you when you get home to sit down and write, every one of you, on a piece of paper, "Saved," if you are saved, and "Condemned," if you are not a believer, for that is your condition? I want you to realise whose you are, and where you are going. When you have done so, I pray that a sense of your condition and prospects may be deepened upon your mind. Sinners, do you think enough? Do you consider enough? You are busy about a thousand things, but do you really think about your souls, death and judgment, and eternal perdition? Do you think enough about the Saviour's love? Do you ponder your sin, and the blessed fact that it may be pardoned? Oh, that you would reflect, consider, and turn your whole mind to God!

But I am beating the bush. I have a much more important precept to which to exhort you. Remember, the Gospel command is, "Believe in the Lord Jesus Christ, and thou shalt be saved." Every minute that you remain an unbeliever you are adding to your sin, you are increasing your iniquity and confirming yourself in condemnation. Oh, that you would believe the divine testimony concerning Jesus, for that is the object of faith! What you are asked to believe is true. He whom you are commanded to trust in is able to save you; and the promise that you shall be saved if you trust is a sure and certain one. Do not, therefore, fling away your souls, and despise the mercy of God. May it please the Eternal Spirit to lead you at this very moment to put your trust in Jesus Christ, and to be saved; then you will be one of those who spring as the grass, and as the willows by the watercourse. May God bless you, every one of you, for Jesus Christ's sake. Amen.

VIII

APOSTOLIC EXHORTATION

"Repent ye therefore, and be converted, that your sins may be blotted out, when the times of refreshing shall come from the presence of the Lord."—Acts 3: 19.

AFTER the notable miracle of healing the lame man, when the wondering people clustered round about Peter and John, they were not at all at a loss for a subject upon which to address them. Those holy men were brimful of the Gospel, and therefore they had but to run over spontaneously, speaking of that topic which laid nearest to their hearts. To the Christian minister it should never be difficult to speak of Christ; and in whatever position he may be placed, he should never have to ask himself, "What is an appropriate subject for this people? for the Gospel is always in season, always appropriate, and if it be but spoken from the heart, it will be sure to work its way. Turning to the assembled multitude, Peter began at once to preach to them the Gospel without a single second's hesitation. Oh! blessed readiness of a soul on fire with the Spirit, Lord, grant it to us evermore. Observe how earnestly Peter turns aside their attention from himself and his brother John to the Lord Jesus Christ. "Why look ye so earnestly on us, as though by our own power or holiness we had made this man to walk?" The object of the Christian minister should always be to withdraw attention from himself to his subject, so that it should not be said, "How well *he* spake!" but, "Upon what weighty matters he treated!"

It is noteworthy that Peter, in addressing this crowd, came at once to the very essence of his message. He did not beat the bush; he did not shoot his arrow far afield, but he hit the very centre of the target. He preached not merely the Gospel of good news, but Christ, the person of Christ; Christ crucified—crucified by them, Christ risen, Christ glorified of his Father. Depend upon it, this is the very strength of the

Christian ministry, when it is saturated with the name and person and glory of the Lord Jesus Christ. If there was ever an occasion when a preacher of the Gospel might have forgotten to speak of Christ, it was surely the occasion on which Peter spake so boldly of him. For, might it not have been said, "Talk not of Jesus; they have just now haled him to the death: the people are mad against him; preach the truth, but do not mention his name. You will scarcely do good while they are so prejudiced, and you may do much mischief." But, instead of this, let them rage as they would, Peter would tell them about Jesus Christ, and about nothing else but Jesus Christ. He knew this to be the power of God unto salvation, and he would not flinch from it; so to them, even to them, he delivered the Gospel of our Lord Jesus Christ, with a pungency as well as a simplicity scarcely to be rivalled. Notice how he puts it: "*Ye*" have slain him; "*ye*" have crucified him; "*ye*" have preferred a murderer. He is not afraid of being personal; he does not shirk the touching of men's consciences; he rather thrusts his hand into their hearts and makes them feel their sin; he labours to open a window into the darkness of their spirits, to let the light of the Holy Ghost shine into their soul. Even thus, when we preach the Gospel, must we do; affectionately but graciously must we deal with men.

Nor did Peter fail, when he had enunciated the Gospel, to make the personal application by prescribing its peculiar commands. Grown up among us is a school of men who say that they rightly preach the Gospel to sinners when they merely deliver statements of what the Gospel is, and of the result of dying unsaved, but they grow furious and talk of unsoundness if any venture to say to the sinner, "Believe," or "Repent." To this school Peter did not belong—into their secret he had never come, and with their assembly, were he alive now, he would not be joined. For, having first told his hearers of Christ, of his life and death and resurrection, he then proceeds to plunge the sword, as it were up to the very hilt in their consciences by saying, "Repent ye therefore, and be converted that your sins may be blotted out." There, I say, in that promiscuous crowd, gathered together by curiosity, attracted by the miracle which he had wrought, Peter felt no hesitation, and asked no question; he preached the same Gospel as he would have preached to us today if he were here, and preached it in the most fervent and earnest style, preached the angles and the corners of it, and then preached the practical part of it, addressing himself with heart, and soul, and energy, to every one in that crowd, and saying, "Repent ye therefore, and be converted, that your sins may be blotted out."

First of all THE APOSTLE BADE MEN REPENT AND BE CON-VERTED. Of this our text is proof enough without our going afield for other instances. Repent signifies, in its literal meaning, to change one's mind. It has been translated "after-wit," or "after-wisdom;" it is the man's finding out that he was wrong, and rectifying his judgment. But although that be the meaning of the root, the word has come in scriptural use to mean a great deal more. Perhaps there is no better definition of repentance than that which is given in our little children's hymn-book:

> *Repentance is to leave*
> *The sins we loved before,*
> *And show that we in earnest grieve,*
> *By doing so no more.*

Repentance is a discovery of the evil of sin, a mourning that we have committed it, a resolution to forsake it. It is, in fact, a change of mind of a very deep and practical character, which makes the man love what once he hated, and hate what once he loved. Conversion, if translated, means a turning round, a turning from, and a turning to—a turning from sin, a turning to holiness—a turning from carelessness to thought, from the world to heaven, from self to Jesus—a complete turning. The word here used, though translated in the English, "Repent and be converted," is not so in the Greek; it is really, "Repent and convert," or, rather, "Repent and turn." It is an active verb, just as the other was "Repent and turn." When the demoniac had the devils cast out of him—I may compare that to repentance; but when he put on his garments, and was no longer naked and filthy, but was said to be clothed and in his right mind, I may compare that to conversion. When the prodigal was feeding his swine, and on a sudden began to consider and to come to himself, that was repentance. When he set out and left the far country, and went to his father's house, that was conversion. Repentance is a part of conversion. It is, perhaps, I may say, the gate or door of it. It is that Jordan through which we pass when we turn from the desert of sin to seek the Canaan of conversion. Regeneration is the implanting of a new nature, and one of the earliest signs of that is, a faith in Christ, and a repentance of sin, and a consequent conversion from that which is evil to that which is good.

The apostle Peter, addressing the crowd, said to them, "Change your minds; be sorry for what you have done; forsake your old ways; be turned; become new men." That was his message as I have now put it into other words.

Now, it has been said, and said most truly, that repentance and conversion are the work of the Holy Spirit of God. You do not need that I should stop to prove that doctrine. We have preached it to you a thousand times, and we are prepared to prove that if anything be taught in Scripture, that is. There never was any genuine repentance in this world which was not the work of the Holy Spirit. For this purpose our Lord Jesus has gone on high: "He is exalted on high to give repentance and remission of sins." All true conversion is the work of the Holy Ghost. You may rightly pray in the words of the prophet, "Turn thou us, and we shall be turned;" for until God turn us, turn we never shall; and unless he convert us, our conversion is but a mistake. Hear it as a gospel summons:

> *True belief and true repentance,*
> *Every grace which brings us nigh;*
> *Without money*
> *Come to Jesus Christ and buy.*

"And yet," say you, "and yet the apostle Peter actually says to us, 'Repent, and be converted!' That is, you tell us with one breath that these things are the gift of the Holy Spirit, and then with the next breath you read the text 'Repent, and be converted.'" Ay, I do, I do, and thank God I have learned to do so. But you will say, "How reconcile you these two things?" I answer, it is no part of my commission to reconcile my Master's words: my commission is to preach the truth as I find it—to deliver it to you fresh from his hand.

I not only *believe* these things to be agreeable to one another, but I think I see wherein they do agree, but I utterly despair of making the most of men see the agreement. It shall be enough for you and for me to find what is written in Scripture, and to accept it all, whether we can see the agreement of the two sets of truths or no—to accept them both because they are both revealed. With that hand I hold as firmly as any man living, that repentance and conversion are the work of the Holy Spirit, but I would sooner lose this hand, and both, than I would give up preaching that it is the duty of men to repent and to believe, and the duty of Christian ministers to say to them, "Repent and be converted, that your sins may be blotted out." If men will not receive truth till they understand it, there are many things which they never will receive. Ay, there are many facts, common facts in nature, which nobody would deny but a fool, which yet must be denied if we will not believe them till we understand them. There is a fish fresh taken from the sea: you take it to the cook to serve it on the table. You eat salt with it, do you? What for? You will have it dried and salted, but what for? Did not it always live in the salt sea? Why then is it not salt? It is as fresh as though it had lived in the purling brooks of the upland country—not a particle of salt about it—yet it has lived wholly in the salt sea! Do you understand that? No, you cannot. But there it is, a fresh fish in a salt sea!

Do you understand it? So there may be two great truths in Scripture, which are both truths, and yet all the wise men in the world might be confounded to bring those two truths together. I do not understand, I must confess, why Moses was told to cut down a tree and put it in the bitter waters of Marah; I cannot see any connection between a tree and the water, so that the tree should make it sweet, but yet I do believe that when Moses put the tree into the water the bitterness of Marah departed, and the stream was sweet. I do not know why it is that Elisha, when he went to Jericho and found the water nauseous, said "Bring me a cruse of salt;" I do not know why his putting the salt into the stream should make it sweet— it looks to me as if it would operate the other way; but I believe the miracle, namely, that the salt was put in, and that it was sweetened.

So I do not understand how it is that my bidding impenitent sinners to repent should in any way be likely to make them do so, but I know it does—I see it every day. I do not know why a poor weak creature, saying to his fellow men, "Believe," should lead them to believe, but it does so, and the Holy Spirit blesses it, and they do believe and are saved; and if we cannot see how, if we see the fact, we will be content and bless God for it. Perhaps you may be aware that an attempt has been made by ingenious expositors to get rid of the force of this text. They have said that the repentance to which men here are exhorted is but an outward repentance. But how is it so, when it is added, "Repent and be converted, *that your sins may be blotted out*"? Does a merely outward repentance bring with it the blotting out of sin? Assuredly not. The repentance to which men are here exhorted is a repentance which brings with it complete pardon—"that your sins may be blotted out." And, moreover, it seems to me to be a shocking thing to suppose that Peter and John went about preaching up a hollow, outward repentance, which would not save men. It was a soul-saving repentance, and nothing less than that, which Peter commanded of these men.

Now, let us come to the point. We tell men to repent and believe, not because we rely on any power in them to do so, for we know them to be dead in trespasses and sins; not because we depend upon any power in our earnestness or in our speech to make them do so, for we understand that our preaching is less than nothing apart from God; but we find that, if we speak in faith, God the Holy Ghost operates with us, and while we bid the dry bones live, the Spirit makes them live—while we tell the lame man to stand on his feet, the mysterious energy makes his ankle-bones to receive strength—while we tell the impotent man to stretch out his hand, a divine power goes with the command, and the hand is stretched out and the man is restored. The power lies not in the sinner, not in the preacher, but in the Holy Spirit, which works effectually with the Gospel by divine decree, so that where the truth is preached the elect of God are quickened by it, souls are saved, and God is glorified. Go on preaching the Gospel boldly, and be not afraid of the result, for, however little may be your strength, and though your eloquence may be as nought, yet

God has promised to make his Gospel the power to save, and so it shall be down to the world's end.

In the second place, THERE WAS GOOD REASON FOR THIS COMMAND.

The text says, "Repent ye *therefore.*" The apostle was logical: he had a reason for his exhortation. It was not mere declamation, but sound reasoning. "Repent ye therefore." What, then, was the argument? Why, first, because you, like the Jews, have put Jesus Christ to death. This was literally true of the people to whom he spoke: they had had a share in Christ's execution. And this is spiritually true of you today. Every sin in the essence of it is a killing of God. Do you comprehend me? Every time you do what God would not have you do, you do in effect, so far as you can, put God out of his throne, and disown the authority which belongs to his Godhead; you do in intent, so far as you can, kill God. That is the drift of sin—sin is a God-killing thing. When our Lord Jesus Christ was nailed to the tree by sinners, sin only did then literally and openly what all sin really does in a spiritual sense.

Suppose the principle of thy disobedience were carried out to the full, would not all laws be disregarded, and moral government subverted? And why not, since what one may do another has clearly the same right to do? What, then, if the authority of God should be no more owned in the universe—where should we all be? What a hell above ground would this world become! Do you not see what a mischievous thing, then, your iniquity has been? Repent and turn from it. If you can really believe that though you did not nail Christ to the cross, nor plait the crown of thorns and put it on his head, nor stand and mock him there, yet that every sin is a real crucifixion of Christ, and a mockery of Christ, and a slaughter of Christ. Then, truly, there is abundant reason why you should repent and turn from it.

The apostle also used another argument, namely, that he whom they had slain was a most blessed person—one so blessed that God the Father had exalted him. Jesus Christ came not into this world with any selfish motive, but entirely out of philanthropy, full of love to men; and yet men put him to death? Now, every sin is an insult against the good and kind God. God does not deserve that we should rebel against him. If he were a great tyrant domineering over us, putting us to misery, there might be some excuse for our sin, but when he acts like a tender father to us, supplying our wants day by day, and forgiving our offences, it is shame, a cruel shame that we should live in daily revolt against him. You who have not believed in Christ, have mighty cause for repenting that you have not believed in him, seeing he is so good and kind. What hurt has he ever done you that you should curse at him? What injury has Jesus done to any of you that you should despise him?

Moreover, Peter used another plea, that while they had rejected the blessed Christ they had chosen a murderer. Sinner, thou hast despised Christ, and what is it thou hast chosen? Has it been the drunkard's cup? Oh, what a bestial thing to prefer to Christ! Or has it been thy lust? What a devilish thing to set in the place of Christ! Man, what have thy sins done to thee that thou shouldst prefer them to Jesus? Have you lived in them for years? then what wages have you had? what profit have you had? Tell me now, you that have done the farthest in sin, tell me now, are you satisfied with the service? Would you wish to go over again the days you have lived, and to reap in your own bodies the fruit of your misdeeds? Nay, but you serve a hard master; a murderer from the beginning is that devil to whom you surrender your lives. Oh, then, this is a thing to be repented of—that you have cast Christ away, but have chosen a murderer. "Not this man," say you, "but Barabbas." You will take this murderous world, this killing sin, but the blessed Saviour, you let him go. Is not there good argument here for repentance and conversion? Surely there is.

Peter clinches his reasoning with another argument, bringing down, if I may so say, the big hammer this time upon the head of the nail. It is this, that the Lord Christ, whom you have hitherto despised, is able to do great things for you. "His name through faith in his name hath made this man strong, whom ye see and know." Christ then, by faith in him, is able to do for you all that you want. If you will trust Jesus today, all your iniquities shall be blotted out; the past shall not be remembered; the present shall be rendered safe, and the future blessed. If thou trustest in Christ, there is no sin which he will not forgive thee, no evil habit the power of which he will not break, no foul propensity the weight of which he cannot remove. Believing in him, he can make thee blessed beyond a dream. And is not this cause for repentance, that thou shouldst have slighted one who can do thee so much good? With hands loaded with love he stands outside the door of your heart. Is not this good reason for opening the door and letting the Heavenly Stranger in, when he can bless you to such a vast extent of benediction? What, will you reject your own mercies? Will you despise the heaven which shall be yours if you will have my Master? Will you choose the doom from which none but he can rescue you, and let go the glory to which none but he can admit you?

There was one other plea which he used, which I would employ now. He said, "Brethren, I wot that through ignorance ye did it." As if he would say, "Now that ye have more light, repent of what you did in the dark." So might I say to some here present. You had not heard the Gospel, you did not know that sin was so bad a thing, you did not understand that Jesus Christ was able to save to the uttermost them that came unto God by him. Well, now you do understand it. The times of your ignorance God winks at, but now, "commandeth all men everywhere to repent." Greater light brings greater responsibility. Do not go back to your sin, lest it become tenfold sin to you; for if you do in the light what once you did in the darkness, he who winked at you when you knew no better, may lift his hand, and swear that you shall never enter into his rest, because you sinned presumptuously, and did despite to the Spirit of his grace. I charge every unconverted man here to mind what he is at in future. If he did not know that Jesus was able to save him before, he knows it now; if he was in the dark till today, he is not in the dark any longer. "Now ye have no cloak for your sin." Therefore, because the cloak is pulled away, and you sin against the light, I say as Peter did, "Repent and be converted, that your sins may be blotted out."

But now, our third remark shall be given with brevity, and it is this, THAT WITHOUT REPENTANCE AND CONVERSION, SIN CANNOT BE PARDONED.

The expression used in the text, "blotted out," in the original may be better explained in this way. Many Oriental merchants kept their accounts on little tablets of wax. On these tablets of wax, they indented marks which recorded the debts, and when these debts were paid, they took the blunt end of the stylus or pencil, and just flattened down the wax, and the account entirely disappeared. That was the form of "blotting out" in those days. Now, he that repents and is pardoned, is, through the precious blood of Christ, so entirely forgiven, that there is no record of his sin left. It is as though the stylus had levelled the marks in the wax, and there was no record left. What a beautiful picture of the forgiveness of sin! It is all gone, not a trace left.

But rest assured it cannot be removed except there be repentance and conversion as the result of faith in Jesus. This must be so, for this is most seemly. Would you expect a great king to forgive an erring courtier unless the offender first confessed his fault! Where is the honour and dignity of the throne of God, if men are to be pardoned while as yet they will not confess their sin? In the next place, it would not be moral; it would be pulling up the very sluices of immorality to tell men that they could be pardoned while they went on in their sins and loved them. What, a thief pardoned and continue to thieve! Truly, then, the Gospel would be the servant of unrighteousness, and against us who preach it morality should make a law. But it is not so, impenitent sinners shall be damned, let them boast what they will about grace. Thou must hate thy sin, or God will hate thee. Thou must turn or burn. Thou canst not have thy sins and go to heaven. Which shall it be? Wilt thou leave thy sins and go to heaven, or hold thy sins and go to hell? Which shall it be, for it must be one or the other; there must be a divorce between us and sin, or there cannot be a marriage between us and Christ. Does not conscience tell us this? There is not a conscience here that will say to a man, "You can hope to be saved and yet live as you list." Some have said this—I query if any have believed it. No, no, no, blind as conscience is, and though its voice be often very feeble, yet there is enough of sight about conscience to see that continuance in sin and pardon cannot consist, and that there must be a forsaking of iniquity if there is to be a forgiving of it. Whether your conscience shall say so or not, God says it; "He that confesseth and forsaketh his sin shall find mercy," but there is no promise for the unrepenting.

If you loathe your sins, if God's Holy Spirit has made you hate your past lives, if you are anxious to be made new men in Christ Jesus, I have nothing but notes of love for you. Believe in Jesus, cast yourself on him, for he has said, "Him that cometh unto me I will in no wise cast out." "Though your sins be as scarlet, they shall be as white as snow; though they be red like crimson, they shall be as wool."

The last remark is this—REPENTANCE AND CONVERSION WILL BE REGARDED AS PECULIARLY PRECIOUS IN THE FUTURE, for my text says, "That your sins may be blotted out, *when the times of refreshing shall come from the presence of the Lord.*"

A very difficult passage indeed. Its meaning is scarcely known. Three or four meanings have been attached to it. In the first place, I think it means this—he that repents and is converted, shall enjoy the blotting out of sin in that season of sweet peace which always follows pardon. After a man has been thoroughly broken down on account of sin, God deals with him very tenderly. Amongst the very happiest parts of human life are the hours immediately after conversion. You know how we sing:

> *Where is the blessedness I knew*
> *When first I saw the Lord?*

When the broken bone begins to heal, David puts it, "Thou makest the bones which thou has broken to rejoice." When the prisoner first gets out of prison, when the fetters for the first time clank music as they fall broken to the ground! When the sick man leaves the sick chamber of his convictions to breathe the air of liberty, and to feel the health of a pardoned sinner! Oh, if you did but know what a bliss it is to be forgiven, you would never stay away from Christ! O "repent and be converted that your sins may be blotted out, when the times of refreshing shall come from the presence of the Lord."

Perhaps these "times of refreshing" may also relate to times of revival in the Christian Church. The only way in which you, dear friends, can share in the refreshment of a revival, is by your own repenting and being converted. A revival is a great refreshment to the Church. I pray that a mighty wave may sweep over Great Britain, for much we need it. But of what use is a revival to an unpardoned sinner? It is like the soft south wind blowing upon a corpse—it can bring no genial warmth therewith. If you repent, and be converted, then amidst the general joy of the revival, you shall have this joy, that your sins have been blotted out. What a mournful cry is that, "The harvest is past, the summer is ended, and we are not saved!" Ah! I have been praying to God that you may yet be saved now; I would fain have more conversions. It is hard preaching, it is dull working, unless there be results. We must have conversions. As that woman of old said, "Give me children or I die," so is it with the preacher: he must have sinners saved, or he prays to die. Dear hearer, if these times of refreshing may come, our prayer is that you may repent and be converted, that your sins may be blotted out, and so may partake to the full in the priceless blessings of the season.

Once more, the text means, according to the context, the Second Advent. Jesus is yet to come a second time, and like a mighty shower flooding a desert shall his coming be. His Church shall revive and be refreshed; she shall once again lift up her head from her lethargy, and her body from her sepulchre. But woe unto you who are not saved when Christ cometh, for the day of the Lord will be darkness and not light to you. When Christ cometh to the unconverted, "the day shall burn as an oven; and all the proud, yea, and all that do wickedly, shall be stubble." "But who may abide the day of his coming? and who shall stand when he appeareth? for he is like a refiner's fire, and like fullers' soap: and he shall sit as a refiner and purifier of silver: and he shall purify the sons of Levi." Oh, if ye repent and be converted, ye shall stand fully absolved in the day of his coming, when heaven and earth do reel, when the solid rock begins to melt, and the stars, like fig-leaves withered, fall from the tree, when the trumpet sounds exceeding loud and long, "Awake, ye dead and come to judgment," when the grand assize is sitting, and the Judge shall be there—the Judge of quick and dead, to separate the righteous from the wicked. The Lord have mercy upon you in that day; and so he shall if his grace shall make you obedient to the words of our text, "Repent and be converted, that your sins may be blotted out, when times of refreshing shall come from the presence of the Lord."

IX

SOUNDING OUT THE WORD OF THE LORD

"For from you sounded out the word of the Lord not only in Macedonia and Achaia, but also in every place your faith to God-ward is spread abroad; so that we need not to speak anything."—1 Thess. 1 : 8.

PAUL went to Thessalonica from Philippi with a sore back, but with a sound heart. He went resolved to spend and to be spent for his Lord in that city. On the first three Sabbaths he spake to the Jews in the synagogue, but he soon found that they were obstinately resolved to reject Jesus of Nazareth as the Messiah; and therefore he directed his attention to the heathen of Thessalonica, and among them he had wonderful success. Large numbers of persons, some of honourable rank, turned from their idols of worship to the living God, and he soon gathered about him an enthusiastic people.

During his stay at Thessalonica, he pretty nearly wore himself out; for he had determined that he would accept no help from the people, who appear to have been in great straits at that time. He toiled night and day at his trade of tent-making, and even then could not earn sufficient, and might have failed to maintain existence had not the believers at Philippi sent once and again to assist him. Thus, being affectionately desirous of winning them to Jesus, the apostle was willing to have given unto them, not the Gospel of God only, but even his own life. The Lord accepted the cheerful sacrifice, and gave the apostle the reward he sought. The Thessalonians not only received the word with joy of the Holy Ghost, but became zealous in making it known. Their intensity of faith helped to spread the Gospel, for their lives were notably affected by it; and for their earnestness and godliness, they were everywhere talked of.

Living in a trading town, to which many went, and from which many came, their singular devotion to the faith of the Lord Jesus became the theme of conversation all over Greece;

and thus enquiry was promoted, and the Gospel was sounded out far and wide. In their case, learners speedily became teachers. The Lord Jesus had thus not only given them to drink, but he had made them into a well overflowing, to refresh the thirst of thousands. They had heard the Gospel trumpet, and now they had become trumpeters themselves. In their lives the echoes of Paul's preaching were preserved. This was a very happy circumstance for the tried apostle, and greatly cheered his spirit.

These Thessalonians must have been specially gracious people for Paul to praise them so heartily. "As the fining-pot for silver, and the furnace for gold; so is a man to his praise." Many can bear slander better than they could endure praise. Many, when commended, become puffed up; but the Thessalonians were in such a happy spiritual condition that Paul could safely speak of them as "ensamples to all that believe in Macedonia and Achaia." That praise was all the more precious because it was not indiscriminate—"not laid on with a trowel," as the proverb puts it. The Thessalonians had faulty ones among them. The best Church that ever existed has had in it imperfect members; and the very virtues of the Thessalonians carried them into certain faults. They were notable for their expectation of the coming of the Lord, and certain of them became fanatical, and ceased from work, because of the speedy approach of the last day. The apostle was obliged to talk to them about this in his two epistles, and even to lay down the rule very strongly—"If any man will not work, neither let him eat." Under whatever pretence men might cease from their daily callings, they were not to be maintained by their brethren. These good people were too ready to be deceived by idle rumours of coming wonders. Even the Thessalonian Church had its spots. But, then, there are spots on the sun, and yet we do not speak of it as a dark body, since its light so much preponderates. Grave faults in the Thessalonian Church did not prevent our honest apostle from awarding praise where praise was due.

I entreat you, dear friends, practically to learn from these Thessalonians, by being led to imitate them. May it be truly said of us also, "From you sounded out the word of the Lord"! It is true even now in a measure; may it be far more so! The expression to which I would call your attention is this—"From you *sounded out* the word of the Lord." It reminds us of a trumpet and its far-sounding notes. Having heard the Gospel sounding within, they in return sounded it out.

First we begin by looking at THE TRUMPETERS, THE THESSALONIANS. Observe, at the outset, that *they were a people in whom the three cardinal graces were conspicuous.* Kindly look at the third verse: "Remembering without ceasing your work of faith, and labour of love, and patience of hope." The three divine sisters —Faith, Hope, Love—linked hands in their lives. These were with them in their best condition—faith working, love labouring, hope enduring. Faith without works is dead; faith performing her work with energy is healthily alive. Paul saw the Thessalonian believers to be fulfilling the life-work of a true faith. Nor was faith left to work alone; but at her right hand was love, sweetening and brightening all. Their love did not consist in words, or in mere amiability of temper; but it wrought with a will. They threw their whole hearts into the cause of God; they loved Jesus, and rapturously waited for his appearing; they loved one another, and shared the sufferings of their leaders in the time of persecution. They exhibited a labour of love: it was not work only, but in intensity it deserved to be called "labour." As for hope—that bright-eyed grace, which looks within the veil, and realizes things not seen as yet—it was peculiarly their endowment—this enabled them to bear with patience their suffering for Christ, whether it lay in false accusation, or in the spoiling of their goods. Thus of them it could be said, "Now abideth faith, hope, charity, these three."

Next, I note in these Thessalonian believers, that they were *a people whose election was clear.* Read the fourth verse:—"Knowing, brethren beloved, your election of God." Paul said the same of them in the second epistle (2: 13): "We are bound to give thanks alway to God for you, brethren beloved of the Lord, because God hath from the beginning chosen you to salvation, through sanctification of the Spirit and belief of the truth." They rejoiced in having been chosen of God from the beginning. They saw the practical nature of the election, for they perceived that they were chosen unto sanctification. Their lives were such as to prove that they were the Lord's chosen men, for they became choice men. They gave evidence of the secret choice of God by their holy lives. This, I hope, is true of us as a people:

we are old-fashioned enough to rejoice in the electing love of God, and free grace has a sweet sound to our ears. If it be so, we ought to bring forth fruits worthy of it. Gratitude for sovereign grace and eternal love should operate upon us mightily. None can show forth the praises of God like those who taste his special love, and know the unutterable sweetness of it.

These trumpeters *had received the word of God themselves in much assurance and with much power.* Note the fifth verse: "For our gospel came not unto you in word only, but also in power, and in the Holy Ghost, and in much assurance." The apostle also says, in the thirteenth verse of the second chapter, "For this cause also thank we God without ceasing, because, when ye received the word of God which ye heard of us, ye received it not as the word of men, but as it is in truth, the word of God, which effectually worketh also in you that believe." Beloved, it is a poor thing to receive the Gospel in word only. Then you say, "Yes, it is true, I believe it"; and there the matter ends. It is a far different matter to feel the power of the word as it comes from the omnipotent Lord, so as to have your heart broken by it, and then healed by it. To receive the Gospel not because you are of a certain way of thinking, but because it carries conviction with it, and bears you away by its irresistible force; this is to receive it in its power.

The Thessalonians were *a people whose constancy was proved.* They received the word "with much affliction." The apostle says, "For ye, brethren, became followers of the churches of God which in Judæa are in Christ Jesus: for ye also have suffered like things of your own countrymen, even as they have of the Jews." The assault by the mob, recorded in Acts 17, was, doubtless, only one of their many trials. They remained steadfast, enthusiastic under all their tribulations; and hence the Gospel was sounded out by them. Cowards hold their tongues, but brave men are not to be put down. Having already borne slander, reproach, and misrepresentation of every kind, we are not abashed, but rather are hardened to endurance, and publish our belief more unreservedly than ever. We have nothing to conceal, nothing to fear. Slander can say no more. Wherefore, we the more boldly sound forth the word of God. Unless you can hold on in rough weather, and bear up under opposition, you will do little in sounding out the word of God.

Hence, again, *these people really and lovingly served God.* Look at the ninth verse : " For they themselves shew of us what manner of entering in we had unto you, and how ye turned to God from idols to serve the living and true God." I have no doubt many of these folks had been great devotees of their idols, for it is amazing what idolaters will do for their deities! At this day the gifts of *Hindus* to idol shrines put to shame the offerings given by Christians to their Lord. Shall hideous deities of wood and stone command a zeal which is not shown in the service of the living God? I doubt not that these Thessalonians became as earnest worshippers of the living Jehovah as they had once been earnest votaries of their idols.

For one thing the Thessalonians were peculiarly notable : *they were enthusiastic expectants of the second coming of the Lord Jesus Christ.* Paul says of them, in the tenth verse, that they waited for the Son of God from heaven. They even carried this expectation beyond its proper bounds, for they grew impatient of the Lord's apparent delay. Some of their number died, and they laid it to heart as though in their case their hope had failed, insomuch that the apostle wrote : " But I would not have you to be ignorant, brethren, concerning them which are asleep, that ye sorrow not, even as others which have no hope." They would be no losers by death ; for those who remained alive till the Advent would have no preference over them which slept. In their case, there was no need to write "of the times and the seasons," for they well knew that the Lord would come as a thief in the night. They came so to accept the immediate coming of the Lord as to fall into unhealthy excitement about it ; and it was needful for Paul, to prevent their becoming fanatical, to say, " Now we beseech you, brethren, by the coming of our Lord Jesus Christ, and by our gathering together unto him, that ye be not soon shaken in mind, or be troubled, neither by spirit, nor by word, nor by letter as from us, as that the day of Christ is at hand."

Paul delighted to see them waiting for the coming of Christ ; but he also prayed, " The Lord direct your hearts into the *patient* waiting for Christ." He wishes rest to the troubled. But this unrest was a virtue carried to excess. We are not, many of us, in danger of exaggeration in that direction. I fear that we are more likely to forget the Lord's coming, or to treat it as an unpractical speculation. If any truth should arouse us, this should do it: yet even the wise virgins, as well as the foolish, are all too apt to slumber and sleep because the bridegroom delayeth his coming. Hear ye not the midnight cry? Does not this startle you? "Behold, the bridegroom cometh; go ye out to meet him." If you hearken to that call, you will be the men to sound out the word of the Lord in every place.

Secondly, let us notice THEIR TRUMPETS. "From you sounded out the word of the Lord." Their testimony was distinct, clear, resonant, and far sounding. We may find an illustration in the silver trumpets of the sanctuary which were sounded to gather the people together. Let your trumpets ring out the call to assemble to our Lord Jesus. Trumpets are blown in time of war: many are the allusions to this in Scripture. Oh, that the Church of God may boldly sound the war-trumpet, at this time, against impurity, intemperance, false doctrine, and loose living! Our Lord has come to send a sword upon earth, in these matters. Fain would we also earn the name given to the apostles, "They that turn the world upside down"; for at this present it is wrong-side up. A trumpet is also used simply for musical purposes, and the testimony of the Church to her Lord Jesus should be the most melodious sound the ears of man have ever heard. "How sweet the name of Jesus sounds!" Oh, to sound forth the glorious name, "with trumpet and sound of cornet," that multitudes might be compelled to hear it! Oh, to make all earth and heaven ring with that dear name!

What was the means by which these excellent people made the Gospel to sound out? It was made known by the *remarkable conversions* which happened among them. These men had been idolaters and had fallen into divers lusts common in those times. Paul's preaching had made a change which none could have looked for. They had been brought to worship the true God, and to look for his Son from heaven, and to walk worthy of their high calling. Everybody asked, "Why, what has happened to these Thessalonians? These people have broken their idols: they worship the one God; they trust in Jesus. They are no longer drunken, dishonest, impure, contentious." Everybody talked of what had taken place among these converted people. Oh, for conversions, plentiful, clear, singular, and manifest; that so the word of God may sound out! Our converts are our best advertisements and arguments. Have you not known a whole town startled by the conversion of one great sinner? A distinct, clear-cut conversion will often astound an entire parish, and compel the crowd to say, "What is this word of the Lord?"

The attention commanded by their conversion was further secured by *their unmistakable, unquestionable character.* They became such godly, honest, upright, sober, saintly people, that all who observed them took note of their excellence. They were Christians indeed, for they were Christians in their deeds. Their whole lives were affected by their faith, both at home and abroad. They were so admirable in character that they had become ensamples to those who were already saved. Notice, in the seventh verse, the remarkable expression, "Ye were ensamples to all that believe." It is not so difficult to become an example to the ungodly, for their level is a low one; but it is a high attainment to become an example to those who fear God. This needs great grace. If even saints may copy from you, you had need write a good hand.

The Thessalonians had attained to this, and it was by this that they were able to give such voice to the Gospel. Holy living is a grand pulpit. A godly character has a louder voice in it than the most eloquent tongue. The apostle says that their lives were so complete a publication of the Gospel, that he did not need to call attention thereto. He writes, "We need not to speak anything": as much as to say, "We have only to point to you." Shall I ever feel that I have little need to preach in words, since my people preach far better by their lives? Yes, there are many cases among you concerning which I might say—There, watch that friend's life, and see what the Gospel is: there is no need for me to tell you. Nobody stands, on a summer's day, and points upward, saying, "There is the sun." No, the great light sheds its radiance everywhere, and nobody mistakes him for the moon or a star. Oh, that all of us were of such a character that none should mistake us! Till we have more grace in the heart, and more holiness in the life, we shall lack the greatest means of making the Gospel known. We must shine by our works if men are to see our light. Oh, what a sounding forth of the Word will your holy lives be!

I have no doubt that the Thessalonians added to their character many *earnest efforts* for the spread of the truth. They

went about telling what they had heard, believed, and enjoyed.
Some of them became preachers of the Word at home, and others
went abroad to publish the glad tidings. Jesus would be made
known to the poor in the back slums of Thessalonica, and talked
of to the sailors on board the vessels, and to the merchants on
the quays. Are you, beloved, all of you, making Jesus known?
Are there none of you silent? Have we not among us some who
should now be working in foreign lands? Have we not in these
pews many whose voices should be heard in our streets? We
shall never be as we ought to be till every talent is utilized.
We must be all at it, always at it, and at it with all our might.
We have not come to this yet. May the love of Christ constrain
us thereto!

Meanwhile, it was by *their faith that their teaching was made so
clear and forcible*. They were intense believers, so that Paul
says, "Your faith to God-ward is spread abroad." They did
not half-heartedly teach what they half-heartedly believed.
They accepted the teaching of the apostle as being, not the
word of man, but the word of God; and so they spoke with the
accent of conviction. This was as a trumpet for the Gospel,
giving no uncertain sound. When holy constancy is to the front
under reproach and ridicule, the gospel is sounded as with a
bugle note, and men are compelled to hear it. You possess this
confidence. Have it more and more!

Third THERE IS NEED, AT THE PRESENT TIME, FOR A TRUMPET
BLAST OF THIS KIND. Oh, that the Holy Ghost would put fire
into my sermon, that its live coals may touch your hearts.

The Word of the Lord ought to be sounded out, *because it is
the Word of God*. If it is the word of man, let him spread it as he
can; we are not concerned to help him. The word of man comes
from a dying source, and it will return to it; but the Word of the
Lord endureth for ever.

> *Waft, waft, ye winds, his story!*
> *And you, ye waters, roll,*
> *Till, like a sea of glory,*
> *It spreads from pole to pole.*

The Word of the Lord is so all-important, that it should have
free course, run, and be glorified. When he gives the word, great

should be the company of them that publish it. If you believe the Gospel to be the divine word, you dare not withhold it. The stones would cry out if you were silent.

With many of us, *this is a matter of solemn obligation.* The Word of God has been to us life from the dead, deliverance out of bondage, food for our hunger, strength for our weakness, comfort for our sorrow, satisfaction for our hearts. Spread it then.

Can ye, whose souls are lighted
With wisdom from on high,
Can ye, to men benighted,
The lamp of life deny?

Seeing that God's Word has come to you with power and has saved you from all evil, you must sound it abroad.

Remember, too, that *this is salvation to the perishing.* You believe that men are diseased with sin, and that Christ is the only remedy: will you not tell them the remedy? You see men dying without hope; will you not tell them where there is hope as to the hereafter? You tremblingly feel that for souls to die without accepting the Saviour is eternal woe; will you not pray them, in Christ's stead, to be reconciled to God? O sir, by everything that is terrible in the doom of those who die in unbelief, I charge you, sound out the Word of the Lord! As you will shortly appear before the judgment-seat of Christ, be clear of the blood of all men. The Gospel has power to save today, and to save for ever: sound it out.

This is a time in which the word of the Lord is much abused. Many venture to say that it has lost its power, and has proved unsuitable to the age. They tell us that we need something in advance of it. O you that love it, avenge this insult by manifesting its power in your lives, and by sounding out the old Gospel with new vigour. By your holy characters, and by your incessant labours, force men to see the power of the divine word. Let its secret power be embodied in your practical consecration, and proclaimed in your incessant witness-bearing. If you have slept until now, "Awake, awake; put on strength"! for the enemy is at the gate. I beseech you, now that Christ's crown and throne are assailed by his adversaries, put on your armour, grasp the sword, and stand up for the sacred cause.

At this time *many other voices are clamouring to be heard.* The air is full of din. Men have devised new methods by which to elevate the race, and loud are the voices that proclaim the man-invented nostrums. "Shall we be heard?" cries one, "if we lift up our voices?" Yes, if you take the Gospel trumpet, you will enforce a hearing. It chanced one evening, when there was a large gathering of friends at the Orphanage, that our boys were sweetly discoursing a hymn-tune upon their bells, the American organ was being played as an accompaniment, and all the gathered company were singing at their best, making a rushing flood of music. Just then I quietly hinted to our friend Mr. Manton Smith to put in a few notes from his silver cornet; and when he placed it to his lips, and threw his soul into it, the lone man was heard above us all. Bells, organ, voices everything seemed to yield before that one clear blast of trumpet music. So will it be with the Gospel. Only sound it out as God's own word, and let the power of the Holy Ghost go with it, and it will "drown all music but its own." At any rate, you will have done your part, and will be no longer responsible, even if men do not hear it, if from your very soul you sound out the word of the Lord.

Finally I want to hint to the members of this church, and to those many friends far and near who are so generously associated with me in holy enterprises, that WE ARE THE PEOPLE TO GIVE FORTH THIS SOUND.

It is our duty, first, *because of our position.* Thessalonica was a well-chosen centre, because it was a place of great resort. Ships were always coming into that part and going out again. Whatever was done at Thessalonica would soon be known in all quarters. We are placed in a central position in London. Who does not know the Tabernacle? Hither the tribes come up, and here the multitudes continually assemble. Friends from the country flock to this spot; and on any Sabbath-day of summertide persons from all countries are in these pews and aisles. I state the simple truth when I speak of this house as known to some of all nations, and therefore what is done here is done in the heart of England, and in the centre of the world. If you, as a church, can sound forth by your character and exertions the word of God, you are in the fittest place for it. The position demands it of you; act not unworthily.

Providence has forced us into prominence. We have not desired it ; but we are known and observed by multitudes. If, beloved, we keep the fire burning here, it will be a beacon seen afar. If we are consecrated men and women, we have a great opportunity. If my helpers will see to it that nothing fails in this place, we shall encourage many ; but we shall dispirit thousands unless we carry on the work here with great vigour, the Lord being our helper.

Nor can I forget our numbers. There may have been churches of larger numbers than ours, but I have never heard of them. In this I do not glory, but I dare not conceal from you the anxiety which it causes me. If little is done by such an assembly, it will be a great disgrace to us. I am overwhelmed with the thought of more than five thousand souls united here in Church fellowship. Large numbers may be our weakness; we may become a mere horde of men, without discipline, without unity, without power; but I trust in the great Lord that it shall not be so. If God has caused us to be as large as almost any other ten churches put together, does he not call upon us to exert ourselves with tenfold energy to spread abroad the Gospel of our Lord Jesus Christ? I am sore burdened with this great host : will you allow it to be a burden? Will you not make it a joy? Will all these professed believers make up a crowded hospital? Shall not this house the rather be a barrack of soldiers? Shall not our voice be louder for our Lord than if we were but five hundred, instead of five thousand? How would I plead with you, if I knew how! Do not make this community a gigantic failure. God grant that, remembering our numbers, we may not be satisfied with a thin and feeble voice for Jesus. Our voice should be as the noise of many waters. Is it so? Is it so much so as it ought to be? Oh, for the Spirit of God among us as a rushing mighty wind!

Through our agencies we ought to sound out the word of the Lord very loudly. At this moment you have, by the College, sent out more than seven hundred preachers of the word, into all countries. Oh, that they were all as faithful as some are! Many are the churches presided over by those trained in your school of the prophets; pray that the Lord may be with them. Your orphan children are growing up: oh, that they may be a seed to serve the Lord! Your colporteurs are going from door to door with holy literature. Oh, for the power of God with their laborious efforts! Your evangelists are heard by tens of thousands; implore the unction from on high for them. The sermons preached in this place are not only printed in our own tongue, but many of them are translated into other languages, and are widely read. This is no mean agency for good. All this, and much more which I will not speak upon, I mention not to boast thereof, but that we may be humbled under our responsibilities, and may cry to God for his power. All this, if the Holy Ghost be with us, must accomplish great results; but without him—and we shall be without him unless we are a holy, godly, earnest, Christ-loving people—nothing will be accomplished. Our agencies will become burdens to us, until that which should be the armour of our warfare will become the sepulchre of our life. I feel this more than anyone else, since the very finding and using of funds for so great a work would crush me if the Lord were not my helper.

Beloved, I press home upon you the duty of sounding out the word of God because of *your prayers*. If there be a people under heaven that constantly meet in large numbers to pray, we are that people. Albeit, some of you are lax on this point, I am bound to say that I rejoice in your gatherings for prayer. In this you are my joy and crown. God be praised for it! But if any cry to God, and then do not work for him, what hypocrisy it is! What if we ask him to save souls, and never lift a finger to spread the Gospel! Is this truthful? Dare we hang the trumpet on the wall, and then pray, "Lord, let it be blown"? No. By the honesty of your hearts, set that trumpet to your lips, if you desire its sound to go forth. Give it your very life-breath. Lift up your voice with strength; lift it up; be not afraid.

Today, again, I lay the sacrifice upon the altar, by reasserting the old Gospel against the down-grade of the times. The God that answereth by fire, let him be God! On you may the tongues of fire descend and rest. May you, who are with me, whether in London or in the utmost parts of the earth, be inflamed with zeal, and fired with love. I have not preached to sinners; I leave that, for once, to you. I lay on you this burden, that you each one make the word of the Lord to sound out, "so that we need not to speak anything." God grant it may be so, for Jesus' sake!

X

"COME FROM THE FOUR WINDS, O BREATH"

"Then said he unto me, Prophesy unto the wind, prophesy, son of man, and say to the wind, Thus saith the Lord GOD; Come from the four winds, O breath, and breathe upon these slain, that they may live."—Ezek. 37 : 9.

ACCORDING to some commentators, this vision in the valley of dry bones may refer to three forms of resurrection. Holy Scripture is so marvellously full of meaning, that one interpretation seldom exhausts its message to us. The chapter before us is an excellent example of this fact; and supplies an illustration of several Scriptural truths.

Some think they see here a parable of the resurrection of the dead. Assuredly, Ezekiel's vision pictures what will happen in the day when "the trumpet shall sound, and the dead shall be raised." No matter how dry the bones may be, the bodies of those who sleep in the dust of the earth shall rise again. That which was sown shall spring up from the grave; and, in the case of the children of God, it shall wear a new glory. At the word of Christ it shall come to pass: "For the hour is coming, in the which all that are in the graves shall hear his voice, and shall come forth: they that have done good, unto the resurrection of life; and they that have done evil, unto the resurrection of damnation."

Others see here the resurrection of the almost destroyed host of Israel, which had been divided into two companies, and carried away captive to Babylon. Plague and pestilence and the sword of the Chaldean had gone far to cut off the chosen nation; but God promised to restore his people, thus mingling mercy with judgment, and again setting in the cloud the bow of his everlasting covenant. A partial fulfilment of this promise was given when, for a while, the Lord set up again the tribes of Israel at Jerusalem, and they had a happy rest before the coming of Christ. But Israel's full restoration is yet to be accomplished. The people shall be gathered out of the graves in which, as a nation, they have so long lain buried, and shall be placed in their own land, then will come to pass the word of Jehovah: "Then shall ye know that I the Lord have spoken it, and performed it, saith the Lord."

There are others who, looking beyond the literal for the spiritual teaching, see, and, I think, rightly see, that here is a picture of the recovery of ungodly men from their spiritual death and corruption—a parable of the way in which sinners are brought up from their hopeless, spiritually dead condition, and made to live by the power of the Holy Ghost. I shall, at any rate, use the text in this sense, for I am not now aiming at the interpretation of prophecy, nor concerned greatly with what is to happen in the future. Neither do I wish to conduct you into the deep things of God; but I am just now thinking of practical uses to which I can put this incident, in order to stir up God's people to deal with the Holy Spirit as he should be dealt with, and to urge the unconverted to seek the Lord, in the hope that some of them, as dead and dry as the bones in the valley of vision, may be made to live by his divine power.

Now, first, in using this text, as I have said, for practical purposes, I am going to make this remark upon it: WE ARE NOTHING WITHOUT THE HOLY SPIRIT. I speak now to you who love the souls of men. I know that there are some among you here who preach and teach with all earnestness, with broken-hearted love; and for the glory of Christ you try to bring men to believe in Jesus. In thus endeavouring to save the souls of lost and ruined men, you are engaged in a noble work. But I dare say that you have often felt, what I also fully realize, that you have not gone far in your holy service before you are brought face to face with the fact that, in itself, the work you propose to do is an utter impossibility. We begin our labour according to the Word of the Lord, and we prophesy. God helping us, we can do that; and, though the burden of the Lord be heavy, yet if we are told to prophesy again, we can, by his grace, do that also. We can prophesy to dry bones, or prophesy to the wind, according to God's commandment. We are not afraid of seeming to be foolish, since we know that, when "the world by wisdom knew not God, it pleased God by the foolishness of preaching to save them that believe." But when we preach the Word, and as the result of our preaching expect men to be saved, and so saved that we may know it, we come all of a sudden upon an iron-bound coast, and can get no further. We find that men are dead; what is wanted is that they shall be quickened; and *we* cannot quicken them. There are a great many things we can do—and God forbid that we should leave one of them undone!—but when we come to the creation of life, we have reached a mysterious region into which we cannot penetrate; we have entered the realm of miracles, where Jehovah reigns supreme. The prerogative to give life or to take it away must remain with the Most High; the wit and wisdom of man are altogether powerless to bestow life upon even the tiniest insect. We know of a surety, doctrinally, and we know it with equal certainty by experience, that we can do nothing towards the quickening of men apart from the Spirit of God. If he does not come, and give life, we may preach till we have not another breath left, but we shall not raise from the tomb of sin even the soul of a little child, or bring a single sinner to the feet of Christ.

How, then, should this fact affect us? Because of our power-lessness, shall we sit still, doing nothing, and caring nothing? Shall we say, "The Spirit of God must do the work, therefore I may fold my arms, and take things easily"? Beloved, we cannot do that. Our heart's desire and prayer for our fellow-men is that they might be saved; and we have sometimes felt that, for their sakes, we could almost be willing to be accursed, if we might bring eternal life to them. We cannot sit still: we do not believe that it was God's intent that any truth should ever lead us into sloth: at any rate, it has not so led us; it has carried us in quite the opposite direction. Let us try to be as practical in this matter as we are in material things. We cannot rule the winds, nor create them. A whole parliament of philosophers could not cause a capful of wind to blow. The sailor knows that he can neither stop the tempest nor raise it. What then? Does he sit still? By no means. He has all kinds of sails of different cuts and forms to enable him to use every ounce of wind that comes; and he knows how to reef or furl them in case the tempest becomes too strong for his barque. Though he cannot control the movement of the wind, he can use what it pleases God to send. Thus, though we cannot command that mighty influence which streams from the omnipotent Spirit of God; though we cannot turn it which way we will, for "the wind bloweth where it listeth," yet we can make use of it; and in our inability to save men, we turn to God, and lay hold of his power.

What, then, are we to do? Face to face with spiritual death, conscious of the fact that we cannot remove it, and fully aware that only the Holy Spirit can quicken dead souls, what shall we do? There are certain ways and means by which we can act properly towards this divine Person; certain attitudes of heart which it would be well for us to take up; and certain results which will follow from a clear apprehension of the true state of the case.

First, by this fact, *we must feel deeply humbled, emptied, and cut adrift from self.* Look you, you may study your sermon; you may examine the original of your text; you may critically follow it out in all its bearings; you may go and preach it with great correctness of expression; but you cannot quicken a soul by that sermon. You may go up into your pulpit; you may illustrate, explain, and enforce the truth; with a mighty rhetoric you may charm your hearers; you may hold them spellbound; but no eloquence of yours can raise the dead. Another voice than ours must be heard; other power than that of thought or suasion must be brought into the work, or it will not be done. You may organize your societies, you may have excellent methods, you may diligently pursue this course and that; but when you have done all, nothing can come of it if the effort stands by itself. Only as the Spirit of God shall bless men by you, shall they receive a blessing through you. Whatever your ability or experience, it is the Spirit of God who must bless your labour. Therefore, never go to this service with a boast upon your lip of what you can do, or with the slightest trace of self-confidence; else will you go in a spirit which will prevent the Holy Ghost from working with or through you. We are nothing: you are nothing. "Not by might, nor by power, but by my Spirit, saith the Lord of hosts," is a message that should make us lie in the dust, and utterly despair of doing anything in and of ourselves, seeing that all the power is of God alone.

Next, because of our absolute need of the Holy Spirit, *we*

must give ourselves to prayer before our work, in our work, and after our work. A man who believes that, do what he may, no soul will be quickened apart from the work of the Spirit of God, and who has a longing desire that he may save souls, will not venture to his pulpit without prayer. He will not deliver his message without a thousand groans and cries to God for help in every sentence that he utters; and when the sermon is done, his work will not be done; it will have scarcely begun. His sermons will be but a text for long-continued prayer. He will be crying to God continually to anoint him with the heavenly oil. His prayer will be "Let the Spirit of God be upon me, that I may preach deliverance to the captives; else men will still remain in the prisonhouse in spite of all my toil."

And you, beloved, as you believe that doctrine, will not allow the preacher to go to his work without your prayers. You will bear him up in your supplications, feeling that your attendances at the house of God will be all vanity, and the coming together of the people will be as nothing, unless God the Holy Ghost is pleased to bless the Word. This thought will drive you to besiege the throne of grace with strong crying and tears that God would quicken the dead sons of men. If any of you are working without prayer, I will not advise you to cease your work; but I will urge you to begin to pray, not merely as a matter of form, but as the very life of your labours. Let the habit of prayer be constant with you, so that you neither begin any service for God, nor carry it on, nor conclude it, without crying to the Lord for his Holy Spirit to make the work effectual by his almighty power.

But we must go a little further. Since everything depends upon the Spirit of God, *we must be very careful to be such men as the Spirit of God can use.* We may not judge others; but have you not met with men whom you could not think the Spirit of God would be likely to bless? If a man is self-sufficient, can the Spirit of God to any large degree bless him? If a man is inconsistent in his daily life, if there is no earnestness about him, if you cannot tell where he is in character or creed, if he contradicts one day what he said the day before, if he is vain-glorious and boastful, is it likely that the Spirit of God will bless him? If any of us should become lazy, indolent, or self-indulgent, we cannot expect the Spirit, whose one end is to glorify Christ, to work with us. If we should become proud, domineering, hectoring, how could the gentle Dove abide with us? If we should become despondent, having little or no faith in what we preach, and not expecting the power of the Holy Spirit to be with us, is it likely that God will bless us? Believe me, dear friends, that a vessel fit for the Master's use must be very clean. It need not be of silver or of gold; it may be but a common earthen vessel; but it must be very clean, for our God is a jealous God. He can spy a finger-mark where our eyes could not see it, even with a microscope; and he will not drink out of a vessel which a moment before was at the lips of Satan. He will not use us if we have been used by self, or if we have allowed ourselves to be used by the world. Oh, how clean should we be who expect the Holy Spirit to make use of us! How careful should we be in our private life as well as in our ordinary walk and conversation!

Next, since we depend wholly upon the Spirit, *we must be most anxious to use the Word, and to keep close to the truth,* in all our work for Christ among men. The Word of God is the Holy Spirit's sword; he will not wield our wooden weapon. Let us, then, set high value on the inspired Word; we shall defeat our adversaries by that sword-thrust, "It is written." So spake the Christ; and so he conquered Satan. So also the Holy Spirit speaketh. Be wise, therefore, and let your reliance be, not on your own wisdom, but on the word to which you can add, "Thus saith the Lord." If our preaching is of that kind, the Holy Ghost will always set his seal to it. Our Lord Jesus said to his disciples, in that memorable discourse, before he went out to Gethsemane, "The word which ye hear is not mine, but the Father's which sent me." Let us try to imitate him, being willing not to think our own thoughts, or to speak our own words, but those which God shall give to us. I would rather speak five words out of this Book than fifty thousand words of the philosophers. I had rather be a fool with God than be a wise man with the sagest scientist, for "the foolishness of God is wiser than men; and the weakness of God is stronger than men." You cannot work for Christ except by the Spirit of Christ, and you cannot teach for Christ except you teach Christ; your word will have no blessing upon it, unless it be

God's Word spoken through your lips to the sons of men. If we want revivals, we must revive our reverence for the Word of God. If we want conversions, we must put more of God's Word into our sermons; even if we paraphrase it into our own words, it must still be his Word upon which we place our reliance, for the only power which will bless men lies in that. It is God's Word that saves souls, not our comment upon it, however correct that comment may be. Let us, then, be scrupulously careful to honour the Holy Spirit by taking the weapon which he has prepared for us, believing in the full inspiration of the sacred Scriptures, and expecting that God will prove their inspiration by their effect upon the minds and hearts of men.

Again, since we are nothing without the Holy Spirit, *we must avoid in our work anything which is not of him.* We want these dead people raised, and we cannot raise them; only the Spirit of God can do that. Now, in our part of the work, for which God condescendingly uses us, let us take care that there is nothing which would grieve the Spirit, or cause him to go away from us. I believe that, in places where the work of conversion goes on largely, God is much more jealous than he is anywhere else. He watches this Church; and if he sees, in the officers of the Church, or in the workers, something unholy; if he beholds practices tolerated that are not according to his pure mind; and if, when they are noticed, these evils are winked at, and still further indulged, he will withdraw his blessing until we cease to have a controversy with him. Possibly he might give his blessing to a Church which was worse than this in many respects, while he might withdraw it from this Church, which has already been so highly favoured, if it countenanced anything contrary to his Word. We must be very sensitive in this divine employment in which we come nearest to Christ; we must be careful to co-operate with him in our work of seeking to pluck brands from the burning. We must mind how we do it, for we may, perhaps, be led to adopt ways and methods which may grieve him; and if we persevere in those ways and methods, after we have learned that they are not according to his will, the Spirit of God will leave us, lest he should seem to be setting his seal upon that of which he does not approve.

Moreover, *we must be ever ready to obey the Holy Spirit's*

gentlest monitions; by which I mean, the monitions which are in God's Word, and also—but putting this in the second place—such inward whispers as he accords to those who dwell near to him. I believe that the Holy Spirit does still speak to his chosen in a very remarkable way. Men of the world might ridicule this truth, and therefore we speak little of it; but the child of God knows that there are at times distinct movements of the Holy Spirit upon his mind leading in such and such ways. Be very tender of these touches of God. Some people do not feel these movements; but perhaps if they, with a more perfect heart, feared the Lord, his secret might be revealed to them. That great ship at sea will not be moved by a ripple; even an ordinary wave will not stir it; it is big and heavy. But that cork, out yonder, goes up and down with every ripple of the water. Should a great wave come, it will be raised to the crest of it, and carried wherever the current compels. Let your spirit be little before God, and easily moved, so that you may recognize every impulse of the Spirit, and obey it at once, whatever it may be. When the Holy Ghost moves thee to give up such and such a thing, yield it instantly, lest you lose his presence; when he impels thee to fulfil such and such a duty, be not disobedient to the heavenly vision; and when on thy knees he seems to direct thee in prayer, go in that direction; or if he suggests to thee to praise God for such and such a favour, give thyself to thanksgiving. Yield thyself wholly to his guidance. You who are workers, do ask for the wisdom of the Spirit carefully and believingly. Keep yourself before that valley of dry bones free to do just what the Spirit of God would have you do, that he, through you, may raise the dead.

Since, apart from the Spirit, we are powerless, *we must value greatly every movement of his power.* Notice, in this account of the vision in the valley, how the prophet draws attention to the fact of the shaking and the noise, and the coming of the sinews and the flesh, even before there was any sign of life. I think that, if we want the Spirit of God to bless us, we must be on the watch to notice everything he does. Look out for the first desire, the first fear! Be glad of anything happening to your people that looks as if it were the work of the Holy Spirit; and, if you value him in his earlier works, he is likely to go on to do more and more, till at last he will give the breath, and

the slain host shall arise, and become an army for God. Only
you cannot expect the Spirit of God to come and work by you
if you are half asleep. You cannot expect the Spirit of God to
put forth his power if you are in such a condition that, if he
saved half your congregation, you would not know it, and if he
saved nobody, you would not fret about it. God will not bless
you when you are not all awake. The spirit of God does not
work by sleepy men. He loves to have us alive ourselves, and
then he will make others alive by us. See to this, dear friends.
If we had more time at our disposal, I would speak longer on
this part of the subject; but I have said enough, now, if God
the Holy Spirit blesses it, upon this first great truth that we
are nothing without the Holy Spirit.

Now, secondly, we may learn, from the action of Ezekiel
on this occasion, that WE MAY SO ACT AS TO HAVE THE HOLY
SPIRIT. When he first saw the dry bones, there was no wind
nor breath; yet, obeying the voice of the Lord in the vision,
the breath came, and life followed. How, then, shall we act?
I will only give you in brief a few of the conditions to be
observed by us.

If we want the Holy Spirit to be surely with us, to give us a
blessing, *we must, in the power of the Spirit, realize the scene in
which we are to labour.* In this case, the Holy Spirit took the
prophet, and carried him out, and set him down in the midst
of the valley which was full of bones. This is just a type of what
will happen to every man whom the Spirit means to use. Do
you want to save the people in the slums? Then, you must go
into the slums. Do you want to have sinners broken down
under a sense of sin? You must be broken down yourself; at
least, you must get near to them in their brokenness of heart;
and be able to sympathize with them. I believe that no man
will command power over a people whom he does not understand. If you have never been to a certain place, you do not
know the road; but if you have been there yourself, and you
come upon a person who has lost his way, you are the man to
direct him.

Dear friends, we must have greater sympathy with sinners.
You cannot pluck the brand out of the burning if you are
afraid of being singed yourself; you must be willing to smut
your fingers on the bars of the grate if you would do it. If

there is a diamond dropped into a ditch, you must thrust your
arm up to your elbow in the mud, or else you cannot expect to
pick the jewel out of the mire. The Holy Spirit, when he
blesses a man, sets him down in the midst of the valley full of
bones, and causes him to pass by them round about until he
fully comprehends the greatness and the difficulty of the work
to be accomplished, even as the prophet said, "Behold, there
were very many in the open valley; and, lo, they were very
dry."

Next, if the Holy Spirit is to be with us, *we must speak in
the power of faith.* If Ezekiel had not had faith, he certainly
would not have preached to dry bones; they made a wretched
congregation; and he certainly would not have preached to
the wind, for it must have been but a fickle listener. Who but
a fool would behave in this manner unless faith entered into
the action? If preaching is not a supernatural exercise, it is a
useless procedure. God the Holy Ghost must be with us, or
else we might as well go and stand on the tops of the hills of
Scotland, and shout to the east wind. There is nothing in all
our eloquence unless we believe in the Holy Spirit making use
of the truth which we preach for the quickening of the souls
of men. Our prophesying must be an act of faith. We must
preach by faith as much as Noah built the ark by faith; and
just as the walls of Jericho were brought down by faith, men's
hearts are to be broken by faithful preaching, that is, preaching
full of faith.

In addition to this, if we desire to have the Spirit of God with
us, *we must prophesy according to God's command.* By prophesying, I do not mean foretelling future events; but simply uttering
the message which we have received from the Lord, proclaiming
it aloud so that all may hear. You will notice how it is twice
said, in almost the same words, "So I prophesied as he commanded me." God will bless the prophesying that he commands,
and not any other; so we must keep clear of that which is
contrary to his Word, and speak the truth that he gives to us
to declare. As Jonah, the second time he was told to go to
Nineveh, was bidden by the Lord to "preach unto it the
preaching that I bid thee," so must we do if we would have
our word believed even as his was. Our message is received
when it is the Word of God through us. When the Lord

describes the blessing that comes upon the earth by the rain and snow from heaven, he saith, "So shall my Word be that goeth forth out of my mouth." Let us see to it that, before the word goes forth out of our mouth, we have received it from the mouth of God. Then we may hope and expect that the people will receive it also from us. The Spirit of God, that is, the breath of God, goes with the Word of God, and with that alone.

Notice, next, that if we would have the Spirit of God with us, *we must break out in vehemency of desire.* The prophet is to prophesy to the bones; but he does not begin in a formal manner by saying, "Only the winds coming can bring breath to these slain persons." No, he breaks out with an interjection, and with his whole soul heaving with a ground-swell of great desire, he cries, "Come from the four winds, O breath, and breathe upon these slain, that they may live!" He has the people before him in his eye, and in his heart; and he appeals, with mighty desire, to the Spirit of God that he would come and make them live. You will generally find, in our service today, that the men who yearn over the souls of their fellow-men are those whom the Spirit of God uses. A man of no desire gets what he longs for; and that is nothing at all.

Then, if we would have more of the power of the Spirit of God with us, *we must see only the divine purpose, the divine power, and the divine working.* God will have his Spirit to go forth with those who see his hand. "When I have opened your graves, O my people, and brought you up out of your graves, and shall put my spirit in you, and ye shall live, and I shall place you in your own land: then shall ye know that I the Lord have spoken it, and performed it, saith the Lord." It is not my plan that God is going to work out; it is his own. It is not my purpose that the Holy Spirit is going to carry out; it is the purpose of the eternal Jehovah. It is not my power, or my experience, or my mode of thought, which will bring men from death to life; it is the Holy Spirit who will do it, and he only. We must apprehend this fact, and get to work in this spirit, and then God the Holy Spirit will be with us.

I want now to address unconverted persons, or those who are afraid they are still unsaved; and with the text before us, WE WOULD SPEAK HOPEFULLY TO OUR HEARERS.

You who are not yet quickened by the divine life, or are afraid you are not, *we would exhort you to hear the Word of the Lord.* Though you feel that you are as dead as these dry bones, yet if you want to be saved, be frequent in hearing the Word. "Faith cometh by hearing, and hearing by the Word of God." If you wish to find the divine life, thank God that you have that wish, and frequent those houses where Christ is much spoken of, and where the way of eternal life is very plainly set forth. When you mingle with the worshippers, listen with both your ears; try to remember what you hear; and pray all the while that God will bless it to you. "O ye dry bones, hear the Word of the Lord!"

Next, *we would remind you of your absolute need of life from the Spirit of God.* Put it in what shape you like, you cannot be saved except you are born again; and the new birth is not a matter within your own power. "Ye must be born again,"— "from above," as the margin reads, in the third chapter of John's Gospel. All the religion of which you are capable will not save you, do what you will; strive as you may with outward ceremonies, or religious observances, there is no hope for you but in the Holy Ghost. There is something to be done for you which you cannot do for yourself.

But *we would have you note what the Holy Spirit has done for others.* There are some of your friends who have been born again. They were as helpless and hopeless as you are; but they are now saved. You know they are, for you have seen their lives. Take note of them, for what the Holy Spirit can work in one he can work in another. Let the grace of God in others comfort you concerning yourself, especially when you hear of great drunkards, or great swearers, or very vicious persons, who have been transformed into saints. Say to yourself, "If the Holy Spirit could make a saint out of such a sinner as that, surely he can make a saint out of me." As you see the flesh and sinews on others who were once as dry as bare bones, be encouraged to hope that it may be even so with you ere long.

May I go a little further, and say that, *we would have you observe carefully what is done in yourself?* You cannot say yet that you have spiritual life; you are afraid that you have not. Still, you are not what you used to be. You have put away many things from you that were once a pleasure to you, and now you take a delight in many things which you once despised. There is some hope in that, though it may be nothing more than the sinews coming on the bones, and the flesh upon the sinews. Yet I notice that, where the Holy Ghost begins, he does not leave off till he has finished his work. God takes such a delight in his work, that, having begun it, he completes it. Well did Job say, "Thou wilt have a desire to the work of thine hands." Now, what he has done for you already, encourages me, and should encourage you, to hope that he will yet do much more, continuing his gracious work until life eternal is bestowed upon you.

Furthermore, *we would remind you that faith in Jesus is a sign of life.* If in your heart you can trust yourself to Christ, and believe in him that he can save you, you have eternal life already. "He that believeth on the Son hath everlasting life." If thou canst now, though it be for the first time, trust thyself alone on Christ, faith is the surest evidence of the work of the Holy Ghost. Thou "hast passed from death unto life" already. Thou canst not see the Spirit any more than thou canst see the wind; but if thou hast faith, that is a blessed vane that turns in the way the Spirit of God blows. "Whosoever believeth that Jesus is the Christ, is born of God." If thou believest, this is true of thee, and if thou dost cast thyself wholly upon Christ, remember that it is written, "He that believeth on him is not condemned;" wherefore be of good cheer.

We beg you not to be led aside to the discussion of difficulties. There are a great many difficulties. To tell dry bones to live, is a very unreasonable sort of thing when tried by rules of logic; and for me to tell you, a dead sinner, to believe in Christ, may seem perfectly unjustifiable by the same rule. But I do not need to justify it. If I find it in God's Word, that is quite enough for me; and if the preacher does not feel any difficulty in the matter, why should you? There is a difficulty, but you have nothing to do with it. There are difficulties everywhere. There is a difficulty in explaining how it is that bread sustains your body; and how that bread, sustaining your body, can be the means of prolonging your life. We cannot understand how the material can impinge upon the spiritual; and there are difficulties in almost everything connected with life. If a man will not do anything till he has solved every difficulty, we had better dig his grave. And you will be in hell if you will not go to heaven without having every difficulty solved for you. Leave the difficulties; there will be time enough to settle them when we get to heaven; meanwhile, if life comes through Jesus Christ, let us have it, and have done with nursing our doubts.

Further, *we would have you long for the visitation of God, the Holy Spirit.* Join with us in the prayer, "Come, Holy Spirit, come with all thy power; come from the four winds, O breath!" One wind will not do, it must come from all quarters. Your heart, filled with all sorts of evil, wants breaking; it wants throwing down like the house of Job's son when Job's children were in it, and "there came a great wind from the wilderness, and smote the four corners of the house, and it fell." Oh, for a wind from the four quarters of heaven, to smite the four corners of the house of your sin, and lay it low! "Come from the four winds, O breath!"

> *Lifeless in the valley,*
> *   Come, O breath, and breathe!*
> *New-create and rally!*
> *   Come, O breath, and breathe!*
> *Blowing where thou listest,*
> *Thou the word assistest,*
> *Thou death's power resistest,*
> *   Come, O breath, and breathe!*

Be willing to have the Holy Spirit as he wills to come. Let him come as a north wind, cold and cutting, or as a south wind, sweet and melting. Say, "Come, from any of the four winds, O breath! only come." He can come very mightily. There is a great deal about you that would shut him out. But it is hard to keep wind out when it blows in the fulness of its strength. You may fill up the crevices of the door as you please, but still the wind gets in. Thus, too, is it with the Spirit of God; he comes in might; and he can also come very sweetly. Be not afraid of the Holy Spirit. He can charm you to Christ, as well as drive you to Christ. May he enter your heart even now!

XI

A REVIVAL HARVEST

"Behold, the days come, saith the Lord, that the plowman shall overtake the reaper, and the treader of grapes him that soweth seed; and the mountains shall drop sweet wine, and all the hills shall melt."—Amos 9: 13.

GOD'S promises are not exhausted when they are fulfilled, for when once performed, they stand just as good as they did before, and we may await a second accomplishment of them. Man's promises even at the best, are like a cistern which holds but a temporary supply; but God's promises are as a fountain, never emptied, ever overflowing, so that you may draw from them the whole of that which they apparently contain, and they shall be still as full as ever.

Hence it is that you will frequently find a promise containing both a literal and spiritual meaning. In the literal meaning it has already been fulfilled to the letter; in the spiritual meaning it shall also be accomplished, and not a jot or tittle of it shall fail. This is true of the particular promise which is before us. Originally, as you are aware, the land of Canaan was very fertile; it was a land that flowed with milk and honey.

When, however, the children of Israel thrust in the ploughshare and began to use the divers arts of agriculture, the land became exceedingly fat and fertile, yielding so much corn, that they could export through the Phœnicians both corn, and wine, and oil, even to the pillars of Hercules, so that Palestine became, like Egypt, the granary of the nations. It is somewhat surprising to find that now the land is barren, that its valleys are parched, and that the miserable inhabitants gather miserable harvests from the arid soil. Yet the promise stands true, that one day in the very letter Palestine shall be as rich and fruitful as ever it was.

But while this promise will doubtless be carried out, and every word of it shall be verified, so that the hill-tops of that country shall again bear the vine, and the land shall flow with wine, yet,

I take it, this is more fully a spiritual than a temporal promise;
and I think that the beginning of its fulfilment is now to be
discerned, and we shall see the Lord's good hand upon us, so
that the ploughman shall overtake the reaper, the mountains
shall drop sweet wine, and all the hills shall melt.

First, I take the text as being A GREAT PROMISE OF SPIRITUAL
REVIVAL. And here, in looking attentively at the text, we shall
observe several very pleasant things.

In the first place, we notice a promise of *surprising ingather-
ing*. According to the metaphor here used, the harvest is to be
so great that, before the reapers can have fully gathered it in,
the ploughman shall begin to plough for the next crop—while
the abundance of fruit shall be so surprising that before the
treader of grapes can have trodden out all the juice of the vine,
the time shall come for sowing seed. One season, by reason of
the abundant fertility, shall run into another. Now you all
know, beloved, what this means in the Church. It prophesies that
in the Church of Christ we shall see the most abundant in-
gathering of souls. We read of such marvellous revivals a
hundred years ago, that the music of their news has not ceased
to ring in our ears; but we have seen, alas, a season of lethargy,
of soul-poverty among the saints, and of neglect among the
ministers of God. Now again God is about to send times of
surprising fertility to his Church. When a sermon has been
preached in these modern times, if one sinner has been converted
by it, we have rejoiced with a suspicious joy; for we have
thought it something amazing. But, where we have seen one
converted, we may yet see hundreds; where the Word of God
has been powerful to scores, it shall be blessed to thousands;
and where hundreds in past years have seen it, nations shall be
converted to Christ. There is no reason why we should not see
all the good that God hath given us multiplied a hundredfold;
for there is sufficient vigour in the seed of the Lord to produce a
far more plentiful crop than any we have yet gathered. God
the Holy Ghost is not stinted in his power. When the sower
went forth to sow his seed, some of it fell on good soil, and it
brought forth fruit, some twenty fold, some thirty fold, but it is
written, "*Some a hundred fold.*" Now, we have been sowing this
seed, and thanks be to God, I have seen it bring forth twenty
and thirty fold; but I do expect to see it bring forth a hundred

fold. I do trust that our harvest shall be so heavy, that while we are taking in the harvest, it shall be time to sow again; that prayer meetings shall be succeeded by the enquiry of souls as to what they shall do to be saved, and ere the enquirers' meeting shall be done, it shall be time again to preach, again to pray; and then, ere that is over, there shall be again another influx of souls, the baptismal pool shall be again stirred, and hundreds of converted men shall flock to Christ.

The promise then, seems to me to convey the idea of surprising ingatherings; and I think there is also the idea of *amazing rapidity*. Notice how quickly the crops succeed each other. Between the harvest and the ploughing there is a season even in our country; in the East it is a longer period. But here you find that no sooner has the reaper ceased his work, or scarce has he ceased it, ere the ploughman follows at his heels. This is a rapidity that is contrary to the course of nature; still it is quite consistent with grace. Among us all there is a tendency to imagine that conversion must be a slow work—that as the snail creeps slowly on its way, so must grace move very leisurely in the heart of man. We have come to believe that there is more true divinity in stagnant pools than in lightning flashes. We cannot believe for a moment in a quick method of travelling to the kingdom of heaven. Every man who goes there must go on crutches and limp all the way; but as for the swift beasts, as for the chariots whose axles are hot with speed, we do not quite understand and comprehend that. Now, mark, here is a promise given of a revival, and when that revival shall be fulfilled this will be one of the signs of it—the marvellous growth in grace of those who are converted. The young convert shall that very day come forward to make a profession of his faith; perhaps before a week has passed over his head you will hear him publicly defending the cause of Christ, and ere many months have gone you shall see him standing up to tell to others what God has done for his soul. There is no need that the pulse of the Church should for ever be so slow. The Lord can quicken her heart, so that her pulse shall throb as rapidly as the pulse of time itself.

A third blessing is very manifest here, and one indeed which is already given to us. Notice the *activity of labour* which is mentioned in the text. God does not promise that there shall be fruitful crops without labour; but here we find mention made of ploughmen, reapers, treaders of grapes, and sowers of seed; and all these persons are girt with singular energy. The ploughman does not wait, because, saith he, the season has not yet come for me to plough, but seeing that God is blessing the land, he has his plough ready, and no sooner is one harvest shouted home than he is ready to plough again. And so with the sower; he has not to prepare his basket and to collect his seed; but while he hears the shouts of the vintage, he is ready to go out to work.

Now one sign of a true revival, and indeed an essential part of it, is the increased activity of God's labourers. I meet with my brethren in the ministry who are able to preach day after day, day after day, and are not half so fatigued as they were; and I saw a brother minister this week who has been having meetings in his church every day, and the people have been so earnest that they will keep him very often from six o'clock in the evening to two in the morning. "Oh!" said one of the members, "our minister will kill himself." "Not he," said I, "that is the kind of work that will kill no man. It is preaching to a sleepy congregation that kills good ministers, but not preaching to earnest people." So when I saw him, his eyes were sparkling, and I said to him, "Brother, you do not look like a man who is being killed." "Killed, my brother," said he, "why I am living twice as much as I did before; I was never so happy, never so hearty, never so well." Said he, "I sometimes lack my rest, and want my sleep, when my people keep me up so late, but it will never hurt me: indeed," he said, "I should like to die of such a disease as that—the disease of being so greatly blessed." There was a specimen before me of the ploughman who overtook the reaper,—of one who sowed seed, who was treading on the heels of the men who were gathering in the vintage. And the like activity we have lived to see in the Church of Christ. Did you ever know so much doing in the Christian world before? There are grey-headed men around me who have known the Church of Christ sixty years, and I think they can bear me witness that they never knew such life, such vigour and activity, as there is at present. Everybody seems to have a mission, and everybody is doing it. There may be a great many sluggards, but they do not come across my path now. I used to be always kicking at them, and always being kicked for doing so. But now there is nothing to kick at—every one is at work—Church of

England, Independents, Methodists, and Baptists—there is not a single squadron that is behindhand; they have all their guns ready, and are standing, shoulder to shoulder, ready to make a tremendous charge against the common enemy. This leads me to hope, since I see the activity of God's ploughmen and vine dressers, that there is a great revival coming,—that God will bless us, and that right early.

We have not yet, however, exhausted our text. The latter part of it says, "The mountains shall drop sweet wine." It is not a likely place for wine upon the mountains. There may be freshets and cataracts leaping down their sides; but who ever saw fountains of red wine streaming from rocks, or gushing out from the hills? Yet here we are told that, "The mountains shall drop sweet wine"; by which we are to understand that conversions shall take place in unusual quarters. This day is this promise literally fulfilled to us. I have this week seen what I never saw before. It has been my lot these last six years to preach to crowded congregations, and to see many, many souls brought to Christ; it has been no unusual thing for us to see the greatest and noblest of the land listening to the word of God; but this week I have seen, I repeat, what mine eyes have never before beheld, used as I am to extraordinary things. I have seen the people of Dublin, without exception, from the highest to the lowest, crowd in to hear the Gospel. I have known that my congregation has been constituted in a considerable measure of Roman Catholics, and I have seen them listening to the Word with as much attention as though they had been Protestants. I have seen men who never heard the Gospel before, military men, whose tastes and habits were not likely to be those of the Puritanic minister, who have nevertheless sat to listen; nay, they have come again; they have submitted to be crowded, that they might press in to hear the Word, and I have never before seen such intense eagerness of the people to listen to the Gospel. I have heard, too, cheering news of work going on in the most unlikely quarters—men who could not speak without larding their conversation richly with oaths—have nevertheless come to hear the Word; they have listened, and have been convinced, and if the impression do not die away, there has been something done for them which they will not forget even in eternity. But the most pleasing thing I have seen is this, and I must tell it to

you. Hervey once said, "Each floating ship, a floating hell."
Of all classes of men, the sailor has been supposed to be the man
least likely to be reached by the Gospel. In crossing over from
Holyhead to Dublin and back—two excessively rough passages
—I spent the most pleasant hours that I ever spent. The first
vessel that I entered, I found my hands very heartily shaken by
the sailors. I thought, "What can these sailors know of me?"
and they were calling me "*brother*." Of course, I felt that I was
their brother too; but I did not know how they came to talk to
me in that way. It was not generally the way for sailors to call
ministers, brother. There was the most officious attention given,
and when I made the enquiry "What makes you so kind?"
"Why," said one, "because I love your Master, the Lord Jesus."
I enquired, and found that out of the whole crew there were but
three unconverted men; that though the most of them had been
before without God, and without Christ, yet by a sudden visitation of the Spirit of God they had all been converted. I talked
to many of these men, and more spiritual, heavenly minded men
I never yet saw. They have a prayer meeting every morning
before the boat starts, and another prayer meeting after she
comes to port; and on Sundays, when they lay-to off Kingstown
or Holyhead, a minister comes on board and preaches the Gospel; the cabins are crowded. Service is held on deck when it can
be; and said an eyewitness to me, "The minister preaches very
earnestly, but I should like you to hear the men pray; I never
heard such praying before," said he, "they pray with such
power, as only a sailor can pray." My heart was lifted up with
joy, to think of a ship being made a floating Church—a very
Bethel for God. When I came back by another ship I did not
expect to see the like; but it was precisely the same. The same
work had been going on. I walked among them and talked to
them. They all knew me. One man took out of his pocket an
old leather-covered book in Welsh—"Do you know the likeness
of that man in front?" said he. "Yes," I said, "I think I do:
do you read these sermons?" "Yes, sir," replied he, "we have
had your sermons on board this ship, and I read them aloud as
often as I can. If we have a fine passage coming over, I get a
few around me, and read them a sermon." Another man told me
a story of a gentleman who stood laughing when a hymn was
being sung; and one of the men proposed that they should pray

for him. They did, and that man was suddenly smitten down, and began on the quay to cry for mercy, and plead with God for pardon. "Ah! Sir," said the sailors, "we have the best proof that there is a God here, for we have seen this crew marvellously brought to a knowledge of the truth; and here we are, joyful and happy men, serving the Lord."

Now, what shall we say of this, but that the mountains drop sweet wine? The men who were loudest with their oaths, are now loudest with their songs; those who were the most darling children of Satan, have become the most earnest advocates of the truth: for mark you, once get sailors converted, and there is no end to the good they can do. Of all men who can preach well, sailors are the best. The sailor has seen the wonders of God in the deep; the hardy British Tar has got a heart that is not made of such cold stuff as many of the hearts of landsmen; and when that heart is once touched, it gives great big beats; it sends great pulses of energy right through his whole frame; and with his zeal and energy what may he not do, God helping him and blessing him?

This seems to be in the text, that a time of revival shall be followed by very extraordinary conversion. But, albeit that in the time of revival, grace is put in extraordinary places, and singular individuals are converted, yet these are not a bit behind the usual converts; for if you notice the text does not say, "the mountains shall drop wine" merely, but they "shall drop *sweet* wine." It does not say that the hills shall send forth little streams; but *all the hills shall melt.* When sinners, profligate and debauched persons, are converted to God, we say, "Well, it is a wonderful thing, but I do not suppose they will be very first-class Christians." The most wonderful thing is, that these are the best Christians alive; that the wine which God brings from the hills is sweet wine; that when the hills do melt they *all* melt. The most extraordinary ministers of any time have been most extraordinary sinners before conversion. We might never have had a John Bunyan, if it had not have been for the profanity of Elstow Green; we might never have heard of a John Newton, if it had not have been for his wickedness on shipboard. I mean he would not have known the depths of Satan, nor the trying experience, nor even the power of divine grace, if he had not been suffered wildly to stray, and then wondrously to be brought

back. These great sinners are not a whit behind those who have
been trained under pious influences, and so have been brought
into the Church. Always in revival you will find this to be the
case, that the converts are not inferior to the best of the converts of ordinary seasons—that the Romanist, and the men who
have never heard the Gospel, when they are converted, are as
true in their faith, as hearty in their love, as accurate in their
knowledge, and as zealous in their efforts, as the best of persons
who have ever been brought to Christ. "The mountains shall
drop sweet wine, and all the hills shall melt."

I must now go on to the other point very briefly—WHAT IS
THE DOCTRINAL LESSON WHICH IS TAUGHT IN OUR TEXT: AND
WHAT IS TAUGHT TO US BY A REVIVAL? I think it is just this,
that God is absolute monarch of the hearts of men. God does
not say here *if men are willing*; but he gives an absolute promise
of a blessing. As much as to say, "*I* have the key of men's
hearts; *I* can induce the ploughman to overtake the reaper; *I*
am master of the soil—however hard and rocky it may be *I*
can break it, and I can make it fruitful." When God promises to
bless his Church and to save sinners, he does not add, "if the
sinners be willing to be saved." No, great God! thou leadest
free will in sweet captivity, and thy free grace is all triumphant.
Man *has* a free will, and God does not violate it; but the free
will is sweetly bound with fetters of the divine love till it becomes
more free than it ever was before. The Lord, when he means to
save sinners, does not stop to ask them whether they mean to be
saved, but like a rushing mighty wind the divine influence
sweeps away every obstacle; the unwilling heart bends before
the potent gale of grace, and sinners that would not yield are
made to yield by God. I know this, if the Lord willed it, there is
no man so desperately wicked here that he would not be made
now to seek for mercy, however infidel he might be; however
rooted in his prejudices against the Gospel, Jehovah hath but to
will it, and it is done. Into thy dark heart, O thou who hast never
seen the light, would the light stream; if he did but say, "Let
there be light," there would be light. Thou mayest bend thy fist
and lift up thy mouth against Jehovah; but he is thy master
yet—thy master to destroy thee, if thou goest on in thy wickedness; but thy master to save thee now, to change thy heart and
turn thy will, as he turneth the rivers of water.

If it were not for this doctrine, I wonder where the ministry would be. The power of our preaching is nought—it can do nothing in the conversion of men by itself; men are hardened, obdurate, indifferent; but the power of grace is greater than the power of eloquence or the power of earnestness, and once let that power be put forth, and what can stand against it? Divine Omnipotence is the doctrine of a revival. We may not see it in ordinary days, by reason of the coldness of our hearts; but we *must* see it when these extraordinary works of grace are wrought. Have you never heard the Eastern fables of the dervish, who wished to teach to a young prince the fact of the existence of a God! The fable hath it, that the young prince could not see any proof of the Existence of a First Cause: so the dervish brought a little plant and set it before him, and in his sight that little plant grew up, blossomed, brought forth fruit, and became a towering tree in an hour. The young man lifted up his hands in wonder, and he said, "God must have done this." "Oh, but," said the teacher, "thou sayst, 'God has done this, because it is done in an hour: hath he not done it, when it is accomplished in twenty years?'" It was the same work in both cases; it was only the rapidity that astonished his pupil. So, when we see the Church gradually built up and converted, we lose the sense perhaps of a present God; but when the Lord causes the tree suddenly to grow from a sapling to a strong tall monarch of the forest, then we say, "This is God." We are all blind and stupid in a measure, and we want to see sometimes some of these quick upgoings, these extraordinary motions of divine influence, before we will fully understand God's power. Learn, then, O Church of God today, this great lesson of the nothingness of man, and the Eternal All of God. Learn, disciples of Jesus, to rest on him: look for your success to *his* power, and while you make your efforts, trust not in your efforts, but in the Lord Jehovah. If ye have progressed slowly, give him thanks for progress; but if now he pleases to give you a marvellous increase, multiply your songs, and sing unto him that worketh all things according to the counsel of his will.

I now desire, with great earnestness, as the Holy Ghost shall help me, to make the text A STIMULUS FOR FURTHER EXERTION.

The duty of the Church is not to be measured by her success. It is as much the minister's duty to preach the Gospel in adverse

times as in propitious seasons. We are not to think, if God with-
holds the dew, that we are to withhold the plough. We are not to
imagine that, if unfruitful seasons come, we are therefore to
cease from sowing our seed. Our business is with act, not with
result. The Church has to do her duty, even though that duty
should bring her no present reward. "If they hear thee not, Son
of man, if they perish they *shall* perish, but their blood will I
not require at thine hands." If we sow the seed, and the birds
of the air devour it, we have done what we were commanded to
do, and the duty is accepted even though the birds devour the
seed. We may expect to see a blessed result, but even if it did
not come we must not cease from duty. But while this is true
so far, it must nevertheless be a divine and holy stimulant to a
Gospel labourer, to know that God is making him successful.

And in the present day we have a better prospect of success
than we ever had, and we should consequently work the harder.
When a tradesman begins business with a little shop at the corner, he waits awhile to see whether he will have any customers.
By-and-by his little shop is crowded; he has a name; he finds
he is making money. What does he do? He enlarges his premises;
the back yard is taken in and covered over; there are extra men
employed; still the business increases, but he will not invest all
his capital in it till he sees to what extent it will pay. It still
increases, and the next house is taken, and perhaps the next; he
says, "This is a paying concern, and therefore I will increase it."

I am using commercial maxims, but they are common-sense
rules, and I like to talk so. There are, in these days, happy
opportunities. There is a noble business to be done for Christ.
Where you used to invest a little capital, a little effort, and a little
donation, invest more. There never was such heavy interest
to be made as now. It shall be paid back in the results cent. per
cent.; nay, beyond all that you expected you shall see God's
work prospering. If a farmer knew that a bad year was coming,
he would perhaps only sow an acre or two; but if some prophet
could tell him, "Farmer, there will be such a harvest next year
as there never was," he would say, "I will plough up my grass
lands, I will stub up those hedges: every inch of ground I will
sow." So do you. There is a wondrous harvest coming. Plough
up your headlands; root up your hedges; break up your fallow
ground, and sow, even amongst the thorns. Ye know not which

shall prosper, this or that; but ye may hope that they shall be alike good. Enlarged effort should always follow an increased hope of success.

And let me give you another encouragement. Recollect that even when this revival comes, an instrumentality will still be wanted. The ploughman is wanted, even after the harvest, and the treader of grapes is wanted, however plentiful the vintage; the greater the success the more need of instrumentality. You need not think that if better times should come, the world will do without you. You will be wanted. The ploughman shall never be so much esteemed as when he follows after the reaper, and the sower of seed never so much valued as when he comes at the heels of those that tread the grapes. The glory which God puts upon instrumentality should encourage you to use it.

And now I beseech and intreat you, inhabitants of this great City of London, let not this auspicious gale pass away without singular effort. I sometimes fear lest the winds should blow on us, and we should have our sails all furled, and therefore the good ship should not speed. Up with the canvas now. Oh! put on every stitch of it. Let every effort be used, while God is helping us. Let us be earnest co-workers with him. Methinks I see the clouds floating hither; they have come from the far west, from the shore of America; they have crossed the sea, and the wind has wafted them till the green isle received the showers in its northern extremity. Lo! the clouds are just now passing over Wales, and are refreshing the shires that border on the principality. The rain is falling on Oxfordshire and Gloucestershire; divine grace is distilling, and the clouds are drawing nearer and nearer to us. Mark, they tarry not for men, neither stay they for the sons of men. They are floating o'er our heads today. Shall they float away, and shall we still be left as dry as ever? 'Tis yours today to bring down the rain, though 'tis God's to send the clouds. God has sent this day over this great city a divine cloud of his grace. Now, ye Elijahs, pray it down! To your knees, believers, to your knees. *You* can bring it down, and only you. "For this thing will I be enquired of by the house of Israel to do it for them." "Prove me now herewith," said the Lord of hosts, "and see if I will not open the windows of heaven, and give you such a blessing that you shall not have room to contain it." Will you lose the opportunity, Christians? Will you let men be lost for want of effort? Will you suffer this all-blessed time to roll away unimproved? If so, the Church of one thousand eight hundred and sixty is a craven Church, and is unworthy of its time; and he among you, men and brethren, that has not an earnest heart today, if he be a Christian, is a disgrace to his Christianity. When there are such times as these, if we do not every man of us trust in the plough, we shall indeed deserve the worst barrenness of soul that can possibly fall upon us. I believe that the Church has often been plagued and vexed by her God, because when God has favoured her she has not made a proper use of the favour. "Then," saith he, "I will make thee like Gilboa; on thy mount there shall be no dew; I will bid the clouds that they rain no more rain upon thee, and thou shalt be barren and desolate, till once again I pour out the Spirit from on high."

I have done, when I have uttered a WORD OF WARNING to those of you who know not Christ. I cannot conceive a more doleful wail than that of the man who cries at last in hell, "The harvest is past—*there was a harvest*; the summer is ended—*there was a summer*—and I am not saved." Oh, may my Master smile into your face this day, and say, "I love thy soul; trust me with it. Give up thy sins; turn to me." O Lord Jesus, do it! and men shall not resist thee. Oh! show them thy love, and they must yield. Do it, O thou Crucified One, for thy mercy's sake! Send forth thine Holy Spirit now, and bring the strangers home; and grant thou, O Lord, that many hearts may be fully resigned to thy love, and to thy grace!

XII

GO HOME AND TELL OTHERS

"Go home to thy friends and tell them how great things the Lord hath done for thee, and hath had compassion on thee."— Mark 5: 19.

THE case of the man here referred to is a very extraordinary one: it occupies a place among the memorabilia of Christ's life, perhaps as high as anything which is recorded by either of the evangelists. This poor wretch being possessed with a legion of evil spirits had been driven to something worse than madness. He fixed his home among the tombs, where he dwelt by night and day, and was the terror of all those who passed by. The authorities had attempted to curb him; he had been bound with fetters and chains, but in the paroxysms of his madness he had torn the chains in sunder and broken the fetters in pieces. Attempts had been made to reclaim him; but no man could tame him. He was a misery to himself, for he would run upon the mountains by night and day, crying and howling fearfully, cutting himself with the sharp flints, and torturing his poor body in the most frightful manner. Jesus Christ passed by; he said to the devils, "Come out of him." The man was healed in a moment; he fell down at Jesus' feet; he became a rational being—an intelligent man, yea, what is more, a convert to the Saviour. Out of gratitude to his Deliverer, he said, "Lord, I will follow thee whithersoever thou goest; I will be thy constant companion and thy servant; permit me so to be." "No," said Christ, "I esteem your motive; it is one of gratitude to me; but if you would show your gratitude; 'go home to thy friends and tell them how great things the Lord hath done for thee, and hath had compassion on thee.'"

Now, this teaches us a very important fact, namely, this, that true religion does not break in sunder the bonds of family relationship. True religion seldom encroaches upon that sacred, I had almost said divine, institution called *home*; it does not

separate men from their families and make them aliens to their
flesh and blood. Superstition has done that; an awful superstition, which calls itself Christianity, has sundered men from
their kind; but true religion has never done so. Why, if I
might be allowed to do such a thing, I would seek out the hermit
in his lonely cavern, and I would go to him and say, "Friend,
if thou art what thou dost profess to be, a true servant of the
living God, and not a hypocrite, as I guess thou art—if thou art
a true believer in Christ, and would show forth what he has done
for thee, upset that pitcher, eat the last piece of thy bread,
leave this dreary cave, wash thy face, untie thy hempen girdle;
and if thou wouldst show thy gratitude, go home to thy
friends, and tell them what great things the Lord hath done for
thee. Canst thou edify the sere leaves of the forest? Can the
beasts learn to adore that God whom thy gratitude should
strive to honour? Dost thou hope to convert these rocks, and
wake the echoes into songs? Nay, go back; dwell with thy
friends, reclaim thy kinship with men, and unite again with thy
fellows, for this is Christ's approved way of showing gratitude."
And I would go to every monastery and every nunnery, and
say to the monks, "Come out brethren, come out! If you are
what you say you are, servants of God, go home to your friends.
No more of this absurd discipline; it is not Christ's rule; you
are acting differently from what he would have you; go home to
your friends!" And to the sisters of mercy we would say,
"Be sisters of mercy to your own sisters; go home to your
friends; take care of your aged parents; turn your own houses
into convents; do not sit here nursing your pride by a disobedience to Christ's rule, which says, "go home to thy friends."
"Go home to thy friends, and tell them how great things the
Lord hath done for thee, and had compassion on thee."

The first sure symptoms of a mind in health
Are rest of heart and pleasure found at home.

True religion cannot be inconsistent with nature. It never
can demand that I should abstain from weeping when my
friend is dead. "Jesus wept." It cannot deny me the privilege
of a smile, when providence looks favourably upon me; for
once "Jesus rejoiced in spirit, and said, Father, I thank thee."

It does not make a man say to his father and mother, "I am no longer your son." That is not Christianity, but something worse than what beasts would do, which would lead us to be entirely sundered from our fellows, to walk among them as if we had no kinship with them. To all who think a solitary life must be a life of piety, I would say, "It is the greatest delusion." To all who think that those must be good people who snap the ties of relationship, let us say, "Those are the best who maintain them." Christianity makes a husband a better husband, it makes a wife a better wife than she was before. It does not free me from my duties as a son; it makes me a better son, and my parents better parents. Instead of weakening my love, it gives me fresh reason for my affection; and he whom I loved before as my father, I now love as my brother and co-worker in Christ Jesus, and she whom I reverenced as my mother, I now love as my sister in the covenant of grace, to be mine for ever in the state that is to come. Oh! suppose not, any of you, that Christianity was ever meant to interfere with households; it is intended to cement them, and to make them households which death itself shall never sever, for it binds them up in the bundle of life with the Lord their God, and re-unites the several individuals on the other side of the flood.

"Go home to thy friends, and tell them how great things the Lord hath done for thee, and hath had compassion on thee." First, HERE IS WHAT THEY ARE TO TELL. It is to be a story of *personal experience*. You are not to repair to your houses and forthwith begin to preach. That you are not commanded to do. You are not to begin to take up doctrinal subjects and expatiate on them, and endeavour to bring persons to your peculiar views and sentiments. You are not to go home with sundry doctrines you have lately learned, and try to teach these. At least you are not commanded so to do; you may, if you please, and none shall hinder you; but you are to go home and tell not what you have believed, but what you have *felt*— what you really know to be your own; not what great things you have read, but what great things the Lord hath *done for you*.

Mark this: there is never a more interesting story than that which a man tells about himself. The Rhyme of the Ancient Mariner derives much of its interest because the man who told it was himself the mariner. He sat down, that man whose finger was skinny, like the finger of death, and began to tell that dismal story of the ship at sea in the great calm, when slimy things did crawl with legs over the shiny sea. The Wedding Guest sat still to listen, for the old man was himself a story. There is always a great deal of interest excited by a personal narrative. Virgil, the poet, knew this, and therefore he wisely makes Æneas tell his own story, and makes him begin it by saying, "In which I also had a great part myself." So if you would interest your friends, tell them what you felt yourself. Tell them how you were once a lost abandoned sinner, how the Lord met with you, how you bowed your knees, and poured out your soul before God, and how at last you leaped with joy, for you thought you heard him say within you, "I, even I, am he that blotteth out thy transgressions for my name's sake." Tell your friends a story of your own personal experience.

Note, next, it must be a story of *free grace*. It is not, "Tell thy friends how great things thou hast done thyself," but "how great things *the Lord* hath done for thee." The man who always dwells upon free will and the power of the creature, and denies the doctrines of grace, invariably mixes up a great deal of what he has done himself in telling his experience; but the believer in free grace, who holds the great cardinal truths of the Gospel, ignores this, and declares, "I will tell what the Lord hath done for me. It is true I must tell how I was first made to pray; but I will tell it thus,

> *Grace taught my soul to pray,*
> *Grace made my eyes o'erflow.*

It is true, I must tell in how many troubles and trials God has been with me; but I will tell it thus,

> *'Twas grace which kept me to this day,*
> *And will not let me go.*

He says nothing about his own doings, or willings, or prayings, or seekings, but he ascribes it all to the love and grace of the great God who looks on sinners in love and makes them his children, heirs of everlasting life. Go home, young man, and tell the poor sinner's story; go home, young woman, and open your diary, and give your friends stories of grace.

In the next place, this poor man's tale was a *grateful* story. I know it was grateful, because the man said, "I will tell thee how great things the Lord hath done for me"; and (not meaning a pun in the least degree) I may observe, that a man who is grateful is always full of the greatness of the mercy which God has shown him; he always thinks that what God has done for him is immensely good and supremely great. Perhaps when you are telling the story one of your friends will say, "And what of that?" And your answer will be, "It may not be a great thing to you, but it is to me. You say it is little to repent, but I have not found it so; it is a great and precious thing to be brought to know myself to be a sinner, and to confess it." Look them in the face and say, "If you had found him too you would not think it little. You think it little I have lost the burden from my back; but if you had suffered with it, and felt its weight as I have for many a long year, you would think it no little thing to be emancipated and free, through a sight of the Cross." Tell them it is a great story, and if they cannot see its greatness shed great tears, and tell it to them with great earnestness, and I hope they may be brought to believe that you at least are grateful, if they are not. May God grant that you may tell a grateful story. No story is more worth hearing than a tale of gratitude.

And lastly, upon this point: it must be a tale told by a poor sinner who feels himself *not to have deserved* what he has received. "How he hath had *compassion* on thee." It was not a mere act of kindness, but an act of free compassion towards one who was in misery. Oh! I have heard men tell the story of their conversion and of their spiritual life in such a way that my heart hath loathed *them* and their story too, for they have told of their sins as if they did boast in the greatness of their crime, and they have mentioned the love of God not with a tear of gratitude, not with the simple thanksgiving of the really humble heart, but as if they as much exalted themselves as they exalted God. Oh! when we tell the story of our own conversion, I would have it done with deep sorrow, remembering what we used to be, and with great joy and gratitude, remembering how little we deserve these things.

I was once preaching upon conversion and salvation, and I felt within myself, as preachers often do, that it was but dry work to tell this story, and a dull, dull tale it was to me; but on a sudden the thought crossed my mind, "Why, you are a poor lost ruined sinner yourself; tell it, tell it, as you received it; begin to tell of the grace of God as you trust you feel it yourself." Why, then, my eyes began to be fountains of tears; those hearers who had nodded their heads began to brighten up, and they listened, because they were hearing something which the man felt himself, and which they recognised as being true to him, if it was not true to them. "Go home, then, and tell your friends what great things the Lord hath done for you, and how he hath had compassion on you."

But now, in the second place, WHY SHOULD WE TELL THIS STORY? For I hear many of my congregation say, "Sir, I could relate that story to any one sooner than I could to my own friends; I could come to your vestry, and tell you something of what I have tasted and handled of the Word of God; but I could not tell my father, nor my mother, nor my brethren, nor my sisters." Come, then; I will try and argue with you, to induce you to do so, that I may send you home to be missionaries in the localities to which you belong, and to be real preachers, though you are not so by name.

First, for *your Master's sake*. Oh! I know you love him; I am sure you do, if you have proof that he loved you. You can never think of Calvary and his pierced hands and feet, without loving him; and it is a strong argument when I say to you, for his dear sake who loved you so much, go home and tell it. What! do you think we can have so much done for us, and yet not tell it? Our children, if anything should be done for them, do not stay many minutes before they are telling all the company, "such an one hath given me such a present, and bestowed on me such-and-such a favour." And should the children of God be backward in declaring how they were saved when their feet made haste to hell, and how redeeming mercy snatched them as brands from the burning? You love Jesus, young man! I put it to you, then, will you refuse to tell the tale of his love to you? Shall your lips be dumb, when his honour is concerned? Will you not, wherever you go, tell of the God who loved you and died for you? This poor man, we are told, "departed and began to publish in Decapolis how great things Jesus had done for him, and all men did marvel." So with you. If Christ has done much for you, you cannot help it —you must tell it. My esteemed friend, Mr. Oncken, a minister in Germany, told us that so soon as he was converted himself the first impulse of his new-born soul was to do good to others. And where should he do that good? Well, he thought he would go to Germany. It was his own native land, and he thought the command was, "Go home to thy friends and tell them." Well, there was not a single Baptist in all Germany, nor any with whom he could sympathise, for the Lutherans had swerved from the faith of Luther, and gone aside from the truth of God. But he went there and preached, and he has now seventy or eighty Churches established on the continent. What made him do it? Nothing but love for his Master, who had done so much for him, could have forced him to go and tell his kinsmen the marvellous tale of Divine goodness.

But in the next place, are your friends pious? Then go home and tell them, in order *to make their hearts glad*. I received a short epistle written with a trembling hand by one who is past the natural age of man, living in the county of Essex. His son, under God, had been converted by hearing the Word preached, and the good man could not help writing to the minister, thanking *him*, and blessing most of all, his God, that his son had been regenerated. "Sir," he begins, "an old rebel writes to thank you, and above all to thank his God, that his dear son has been converted." I shall treasure up that epistle. It goes on to say, "Go on! and the Lord bless you." And there was another case I heard some time ago, where a young woman went home to her parents, and when her mother saw her, she said, "There! if the minister had made me a present of all London, I should not have thought so much of it as I do of this —to think that you have really become a changed character, and are living in the fear of God."

Now let me tell you a story of Vanderkist, a city missionary, who toils all night long to do good in that great work. There had been a drunken broil in the street; he stepped between the men to part them, and said something to a woman who stood there concerning how dreadful a thing it was that men should thus be intemperate. She walked with him a little way, and

he with her, and she began to tell him such a tale of woe and
sin too—how she had been lured away from her parents' home
in Somersetshire, and had been brought up here in her soul's
eternal hurt. He took her home with him and taught her the
fear and love of Christ; and what was the first thing she did,
when she returned to the paths of godliness and found Christ
to be the sinner's Saviour? She said, "Now I must go home to
my friends." Her friends were written to; they came to meet
her at the station in Bristol, and you can hardly conceive what
a happy meeting it was. The father and mother had lost their
daughter, they had never heard from her; and there she was
brought back and restored to the bosom of her family. Woman!
hast thou strayed from thy family? Hast thou left them long?
"Go home to thy friends," I beseech thee. Tell mother thou art
penitent; tell her that God hath met with thee—that the young
minister said, "Go back to thy friends." And if so, I shall not
blush to have said these things, though you may think I ought
not to have mentioned them; for if I may but win one such
soul, I will bless God to all eternity. "Go home to thy friends.
Go home and tell them how great things the Lord hath done
for thee."

Cannot you imagine the scene, when the poor demoniac
mentioned in my text went home? He had been a raving mad-
man; and when he came and knocked at the door, don't you
think you see his friends calling to one another in affright,
"Oh! there he is again," and the mother running upstairs and
locking all the doors, because her son had come back that was
raving mad; and the little ones crying because they knew what
he had been before—how he cut himself with stones, because
he was possessed with devils. And can you picture their joy,
when the man said, "Mother! Jesus Christ has healed me;
let me in; I am no lunatic now!" And when the father opened
the door, he said, "Father! I am not what I was; all the evil
spirits are gone; I shall live in the tombs no longer. I want to
tell you how the glorious Man who wrought my deliverance
accomplished the miracle—how he said to the devils, 'Get ye
hence,' and they ran down a steep place into the sea, and I am
come home healed and saved." Oh! if such an one, possessed with
sin, were here now, and would go home to his friends, to tell them
of his release, methinks the scene would be somewhat similar.

I hear one of you say, "Ah! Sir, would to God I could go home to pious friends! But when I go home I go into the worst of places; for my home is amongst those who never knew God themselves and consequently never prayed for me, and never taught me anything concerning heaven." Well, young man, go home to your friends. If they are ever so bad they are your friends. I sometimes meet with young men wishing to join the Church, who say, when I ask them about their father, "Oh, sir, I am parted from my father." Then I say, "Young man, you may just go and see your father before I have anything to do with you; if you are at ill-will with your father and mother I will not receive you into the Church; if they are ever so bad they are *your parents*." Go home to them, and tell them, not to make them glad, for they will very likely be angry with you; but tell them *for their soul's salvation*. I hope, when you are telling the story of what God did for you, that they will be led by the Spirit to desire the same mercy themselves. But I will give you a piece of advice. Do not tell this story to your ungodly friends when they are all together, for they will laugh at you. Take them one by one, when you can get them alone, and begin to tell it to them, and they will hear you seriously. There was once a very pious lady who kept a lodging-house for young men. All the young men were very gay and giddy, and she wanted to say something to them concerning religion. She introduced the subject, and it was passed off immediately with a laugh. She thought within herself, "I have made a mistake." The next morning, after breakfast, when they were all going, she said to one of them, "Sir, I should like to speak with you a moment or two," and taking him aside into another room she talked with him. The next morning she took another, and the next morning another, and it pleased God to bless her simple statement, when it was given individually: but, without doubt, if she had spoken to them altogether, they would have backed each other up in laughing her to scorn. Reprove a man alone. A verse may hit him whom a sermon flies. You may be the means of bringing a man to Christ who has often heard the Word and only laughed at it, but who cannot resist a gentle admonition.

In one of the states of America there was an infidel who was a great despiser of God, a hater of the Sabbath and all religious institutions. What to do with him the ministers did not know.

They met together and prayed for him. But among the rest, one Elder B—— resolved to spend a long time in prayer for the man; after that he got on horseback, and rode down to the man's forge, for he was a blacksmith. He left his horse outside, and said, "Neighbour, I am under very great concern about your soul's salvation; I tell you I pray day and night for your soul's salvation." He left him, and rode home on his horse. The man went inside to his house after a minute or two, and said to one of his faithful friends, "Here's a new argument; here's Elder B—— been down here, he did not dispute, and never said a word to me except this, 'I say, I am under great concern about your soul; I cannot bear you should be lost.' Oh! that fellow," he said, "I cannot answer him"; and the tears began to roll down his cheeks. He went to his wife, and said, "I can't make this out; I never cared about my soul, but here's an elder, that has no connection with me, but I have always laughed at him, and he has come five miles this morning on horseback just to tell me he is under concern about my salvation. After a little while he thought it was time he should be under concern about his salvation too. He went in, shut the door, began to pray, and the next day he was at the deacon's house telling him that he too was under concern about his salvation, and asking him to tell him what he must do to be saved. Oh! that the everlasting God might make use of some of those now present in the same way, that they might be induced to

> *Tell to others round*
> *What a dear Saviour they have found;*
> *To point to his redeeming blood,*
> *And say, Behold the way to God!*

There is a third point, upon which we must be very brief. HOW IS THIS STORY TO BE TOLD?

First, *tell it truthfully*. Do not tell more than you know; do not tell John Bunyan's experience, when you ought to tell your own. Do not tell your mother you have felt what only Rutherford felt. Tell her no more than the truth. Tell your experience truthfully; for mayhap one single fly in the pot of ointment will spoil it, and one statement you may make which is not true may ruin it all.

In the next place, *tell it very humbly*. Do not intrude yourselves upon those who are older, and know more; but tell your story humbly; not as a preacher, not *ex-cathedra*, but as a friend and as a son.

Next, *tell it very earnestly*. Let them see you mean it. Do not talk about religion flippantly; you will do no good if you do. Do not make puns on texts; do not quote Scripture by way of joke: if you do, you may talk till you are dumb, you will do no good, if you in the least degree give them occasion to laugh by laughing at holy things yourself.

And then, *tell it very devoutly*. Do not try to tell your tale to man till you have told it first to God. When you are at home let no one see your face till God has seen it. Be up in the morning, wrestle with God; and if your friends are not converted, *wrestle with God for them*; and then you will find it easy work to *wrestle with them for God*. Seek, if you can, to get them one by one, and tell them the story. Do not be afraid; only think of the good you may possibly do. Remember, he that saves a soul from death hath covered a multitude of sins, and he shall have stars in his crown for ever and ever. Let your reliance in the Holy Spirit be entire and honest. Trust not yourself, but fear not to trust him. He can give you words. He can apply those words to their heart, and so enable you to "minister grace to the hearers."

To close up, by a short, and I think, a pleasant turning of the text, to suggest another meaning to it. Very soon with some of us, the Master will say, "Go home to thy friends." You know where the home is. It is up above the stars.

> *Where our best friends, our kindred dwell,*
> *Where God our Saviour reigns.*

And when we go home to our friends in Paradise, what shall we do? Why, first we will repair to that blest seat where Jesus sits, take off our crown and cast it at his feet, and crown him Lord of all. And when we have done that, what shall be our next employ? Why, we will tell the blessed one in heaven what the Lord hath done for us, and how he hath had compassion on us. And shall such a tale be told in heaven? Yes, it shall be; it has been published there before—blush not to tell it yet again

—for Jesus has told it before. "When he cometh home, he calleth together his friends and neighbours, saying unto them, Rejoice with me, for I have found my sheep which was lost." And thou, poor sheep, when thou shall be gathered in, wilt thou not tell how thy Shepherd sought thee, and how he found thee? Wilt thou not talk with thy brethren and thy sisters, and tell them how God loved thee and brought thee there? You will tell a long story there of God's sustaining, restraining, constraining grace, and I think that when you pause to let another tell his tale, and then another, and then another, you will at last, when you have been in heaven a thousand years, break out and exclaim, "Oh, saints, I have something else to say."

Oh! happy hour! Oh! blessed moment. "Go home," he will soon say, "go home to thy friends, and tell them how great things the Lord hath done for thee, and hath had compassion on thee." Wait awhile; tarry his leisure, and ye shall soon be gathered to the land of the hereafter, to the home of the blessed, where endless felicity shall be thy portion. God grant a blessing for his name's sake.

XIII

CONTINUE IN PRAYER

"Continue in prayer, and watch the same with thanksgiving."—Col. 4: 2.

HOW greatly do I rejoice that the Churches are aroused to prayer. First, in regard to prayer, the Apostle saith "CONTINUE." Be ye not, O ye intercessors with God for men— be ye not as those whose goodness is as the morning cloud and as the early dew. Do not begin to pray, and then suddenly cease your supplications. That will prove an ignorance as to the the value of the mercy which you seek, and a want of earnestness as to your obtaining it. How many there be who, under a powerful sermon or during a trying providence, have bent their knees suddenly in hasty prayer! They have risen from their knees, and they have forgotten what manner of men they were. Take away the whip from them and they have ceased to run; remove from them the tempest and they have ceased to fly before it. They have ceased to pray when God has ceased to smite. O Church of God! imitate not these heathen men and publicans.

There is a great distinction between the prayer of the real convert and the merely convinced sinner. The merely convicted sinner, terrified by the law, calls but once; the awakened heart, renewed of the Holy Spirit, never ceases to cry until the mercy comes. By the seaside, on the coast of the Isle of Wight, a woman thought she heard, in the midst of the howling tempest, the voice of a man. She listened; it was repeated; she strained her ear again, and she caught, amid the crack of the blast and the thundering of the winds, another cry for help. She ran at once to the beachmen, who launched their boat, and some three poor mariners who were clinging to the mast were saved. Had that cry been but once, and not again, either she might have doubted as to whether she had heard it at all, or else she could have drawn the melancholy conclusion that

they had been swept into the watery waste, and that help would
have come too late. So when a man prays but once, either we
may think that he cries not at all, or else that his desires are
swallowed up in the wild waste of his sins, and he himself is
sucked down into the vortex of destruction. If the Church of
God shall offer prayer, and then shall cease to be in earnest,
we shall think her never to have meant her prayers. The exhortation of my text, I think, stands in contrast, then, to the
transient prayer which is often offered by ungodly men. *Continue* in prayer; do not pray once and have done with it, but
continue in it.

I think further, that the exhortation to continue may be put in
opposition to the common dealings of many with God, who pray
and pause—are earnest and then cool, earnest and colder still.
There is a sharp frost—a rapid thaw, and then a frost again.
Their spiritual state is as variable as our own weather; a shower,
sunshine, mist, shower, sunshine again. They are everything
by turns, and nothing long. There are too many Churches which
are just of this character. See them one week, you would believe
they would carry all before them, and convert the town or
village in which they are located. See them next week, and they
are "As sound asleep as a church," which is a common proverb,
a church being too often the sleepiest thing in all the world.

Now, I am afraid our Churches have for a considerable period
been just in this state; have been sometimes hot and sometimes
cold. Look at our revivals everywhere—the American revival,
it is a great wave and then dry sand. Look at the Irish revival;
I fear that in the end it will come to the same amount. Almost
everywhere there have been great stirrings. As if a holy fire had
fallen, and was about to burn up all the stubble, all men stand
in wonder at it, but it ceases, and a few ashes remain. The fact
is, the Church is not healthy; she has intermittent fits of health,
she has starts of energy, she has paroxysms of agony; but she
does not agonize for souls, she is not always earnest, she is not
always busy. Well did Paul need to say to this age as to his
own, "*Continue* in prayer," not one week, but every week, not
for such a season, but at all seasons. Be ye always crying out
unto the Lord your God.

Why? Why should the Church always be in prayer? Understand, we do not mean by this that men ought to leave their

business, forsake their shops and neglect their household, to be always supplicating. There were some fanatics in the early Church who gave up everything that they might be always praying; we know what the apostle would have said to them, for did he not say, "If any man will not work, neither let him eat?" There are some lazy people who like praying better than working; let them learn that the Lord accepteth not this at their hands. Did not the Master, even when he was on earth, after he had preached a sermon in Simon Peter's boat—did he not as soon as ever he was done, say to Peter, "Launch out into the deep, and let down your nets for a draught?" to show that work, hard work, the hardest of work is quite in keeping with the hearing and the preaching of the Word; and that no man has any right to forsake his calling to which God has appointed him in his providence, under pretence of seeking the Lord. It is quite possible that you may continue in your labour, and yet continue in prayer. You may not always be in the exercise, but you may always be in the spirit of prayer. If not always shooting the arrow up to heaven, yet always keep the bow well stringed; so shall you always be archers, though not always shooting; so shall you always be men of prayer, though not always in the exercise of praying.

But why should the Church—to come to the question—why should the Church continue in prayer? For several reasons, and the first is, *God will answer her*. It is not possible that God should refuse to hear prayer. It is possible for him to bid the sun stand still, and the moon to stay her monthly march; it is possible for him to bid the waves freeze in the sea, possible for him to quench the light of the stars in eternal darkness, but it is not possible for him to refuse to hear prayer which is based upon his promise and offered in faith. The prayers of God's Church are God's intentions—you will not misunderstand me—what God writes in the book of his decree, which no eye can see, *that* he in process of time writes in the book of Christian hearts where all can see and read. The book of the believer's desire, if those desires be inspired of the Holy Spirit, is just an exact copy of the book of the divine decree. And if the Church be determined today to lift up her heart in prayer for the conversion of men, it is because God determined from before all worlds that men should be converted; your feeble prayer today, believer, can fly to heaven, and awake the echoes of the slumbering decrees of God. Every time you speak to God, your voice resounds beyond the limits of time, the decrees of God speak to your prayer, and cry, "All hail! brother, all hail! thou, too, art a decree!" Prayer is a decree escaped out of the prison of obscurity, and come to life and liberty among men. Pray, brother, pray, for when God inspires you, your prayer is as potent as the decrees of God.

There is a second reason why the Church should continue in prayer, namely, that by her prayers *the world will most certainly be blessed.* In visiting the sick, I saw at the distance, down a long street, the bright light of a fire. In a moment or so the flames seemed to yield; but again it sprang up and lit the heavens, again it became dim, and dimmer still. As we walked along, we said, "They have got the fire under. The engines have been at work, how soon it is out!" I compare this to the Church's work upon the world. The world is as it were wrapped in flames of the fire of sin, and the Church of God must quench those flames. Whenever we meet together and are more earnest in prayer, angels might well see in the distance the flames dimmed and the fire giving way. Whenever we cease our exertions and become languid in our efforts, the flame gets the upper hand of us, and once more spirits from the far-off world can see the fiery mantle surrounding our globe. Hand up your buckets, sirs; every man to the pump; now strip to it every one of you, work while you have life and strength. Now each man to his knee, for it is on our knees that we overcome; each man to his station and to his work, and let us continue to pass from hand to hand the quenching water, till every spark shall be put out, and there shall be a new heaven and a new earth wherein dwelleth righteousness. To stop while but one part of the fabric is on fire, would be to condemn the whole; to pause until the last spark shall be extinct, would be to give up the world to the devouring element. Continue, then, in prayer, till the world be wholly saved, and Christ be universal King.

Thirdly, continue in prayer, because *souls shall be saved as the result of your entreaties.* Can you stand on the beach a moment, —you can scarcely see, but yet you may discern by the lights of lanterns sundry brave men launching the life-boat. It is out —they have taken their seats; helmsman and rowers, all strong hearts, determined to save their fellows or to perish. They have gotten far away now into the midst of the billows and we have lost sight of them, but in spirit we will take our stand in the midst of the boat. What a sea rolled in just then! If she were not built for such weather, she would surely have been overset. See that tremendous wave, and how the boat leaps like a sea-bird over its crest. See now again, it has plunged into a dreary furrow, and the wind, like some great plough, turns up the water on either side as though it were clods of mould. Surely the boat will find her grave, and be buried in the sheet of foam;—but no, she comes out of it, and the dripping men draw a long breath. But the mariners are discouraged, they have strained themselves bending to yonder oars, and they would turn back, for there is small hope of living in such a sea, and it is hardly possible that they will ever reach the wreck. But the brave captain cries out, "Now, my bold lads, for God's sake, send her on! A few more pulls of the oar and we shall be alongside; the poor fellows will be able to hold on a minute or two longer, now pull as for dear life." See how the boat leaps, see how she springs as though she were a living thing, a messenger of mercy intent to save. Again he says, "Once more, once again, and we will do it";—no, she has been dashed aside from the ship for a moment, that sea all but stove her in, but the helmsman turns her round, and the captain cries, "Now, my boys, once more"; and every man pulls with lusty sinews, and the poor shipwrecked ones are saved. Ay, it is just so with us now. Long have Christ's ministers, long have Christ's Church pulled with the Gospel life-boat, let us pull again. Every prayer is a fresh stroke of the oar, and all of you are oarsmen. Pull yet once more, and let us drive the boat ahead, and it may be it will be the last tremendous struggle that shall be required, for sinners shall be saved, and the multitude of the redeemed shall be accomplished. Not we, but grace shall do the work, yet it is ours to be workers for God.

But continue in prayer once more, because prayer is a *great weapon of attack against the error and wickedness of the world*. I see before me the strong bastions of the castle of Sin. I mark the host of men who have surrounded it. They have brought the battering-ram, they have dashed it many times against the gate; it has fallen with tremendous force against it, and you would have supposed that the timbers would be split asunder the first time. But they are staunch and strong; he who made them was a cunning architect, he who depends upon them for his protection is one who knew how to make the gate exceeding massive,—is one who knew the struggle full well which he would have to endure—Prince of Darkness as he is. If he knew of his defeat, yet well he knew how to guard against it if it were possible. But I see this ponderous battering-ram as it has been hurled with giant force again and again upon the gate, and has as often seemed to recoil before the massive bars. Many of the saints of God are ready to say, "Let us withdraw the instrument. Let us take away the besieging armament, we shall never be able to storm this castle, we shall never effect an entrance." Oh, be not craven, sirs, be not craven. The last time the battering-ram thundered in its course, I saw the timbers shake. The very gate did reel, and the posts did rock to and fro; see now they have moved the earth around their sockets. Hell is howling from within because it knows how soon its end must come. Now, Christian warriors, use your battering-rams once more, for the gates begin to shake, and the walls are tottering. They will reel, they will fall ere long,—one more blow, and yet another, and another, and another, and as Israel went up over the walls of Jericho of old, so shall we soon go up over the fallen ruins of the walls of the castle of Sin and Satan. The Church does not know how near her victory is, we do not believe how much God is doing, but let the Holy Spirit for once give us a little more faith, and in confidence that we are nearing the victory, we shall continue in prayer. Turn not back when we have all but overcome, continue still, even till the end shall be, and the voice shall be heard! "Hallelujah, it is done; the kingdoms of this world have become the kingdoms of our Lord and of his Christ."

The second exhortation is WATCH.

Watch, *for you will soon be drowsy if you watch not*. Joshua fought the Amalekites, and I never read that his hand was weary, though the battle occupied a very long day. Moses was on the mountain in prayer, and his hands grew heavy, because prayer is such spiritual work, and we are so un-spiritual that the tendency of prayer upon our nature will be to make us drowsy, unless we watch. It is ill-praying, when we are drowsy. It is ill for a Church that is not half-awake to be in supplication. All eyes must be opened; the judgment, the imagination, the hope, the memory, all must be in full vigour, or else we can scarcely hope that prayer shall be successful. I think I see the Church as I fear she is now. There she is upon her knees, with hands clasped; she mutters a few words; her head droops, for she is weary; again she pleads, and yet again her head is well nigh fallen on her bosom; she is a sleeping Church in prayer. Am I too severe in this my picture? I believe it is true; I think there are some members of the Church thoroughly awake, but they are few. Here, then, we see the value of the exhortation of the apostle—"Continue in prayer and *watch the same.*"

But watch for another reason: because *as soon as ever you begin to pray there will be enemies who will commence the attack.* The Church never was earnest yet without sooner or later discovering that the devil was in earnest too. The devil has had an easy time of it up till the last six or seven years for the Church has been going on her old-fashioned way, doing nothing at all. There was very little abuse of ministers; ministers were getting to be very respectable men, and very little abuse of any section of Christians—they were all getting to be very easy and loveable sort of people. But as sure as the Church, or any section of the Church, shall be right-down in earnest, they will be abused. Never think you are good for anything till the world finds fault with you. Never expect that the world will be friends with the Church. Indeed the world will be friendly enough with the Church, if the Church will not do her duty. Martin Luther used to say, "The world gives me a very bad character, but there is no love lost between us; I can give to it as bad a character as ever it gives to me." Either way we will gratefully accept the honour, and write it down as being a proof of our success.

But watch, O Church of Christ, watch; a struggle awaits thee as sure as ever thou art earnest in prayer. In riding along the south coast of England you may have noticed the old Martello towers in constant succession very near to each other. They are the result of an old scheme of protecting our coast from our ancient enemies. It was supposed that as soon as ever a French ship was seen in the distance the beacon would be fired at the Martello tower, and then, across old England, wherever her sons dwelt, there would flash the fiery signal news that the enemy was at hand, and every man would seize the weapon that was next to him to dash the invader from the shore. Now we need that the Church of Christ should be guarded with Martello towers of sacred watchers, who shall day and night look out for the attack of the enemy. For the enemy will come; if he come not when we are prayerless he will surely come when we are prayerful. If our motto be "Prayer", his watchword will be "Fierce attack." Watch, then, while ye continue in prayer.

But yet again; watch while ye pray *for propitious events which may help you in the answer to your prayer.* I have known sea captains, when they have got their ships loaded with coal, and they have wished to come up to London with their cargo, have been unable to get down the Tyne and out to sea; if they could have got to sea, they could make their passage. And I have once or twice known a wary captain, being well upon the watch, manage to sail out of the river just while there was a little change of the wind, and when his fellows have awakened in the morning, they have missed him from his berth, and he has stolen a march upon them. He watched and they did not, and having lost the wind, they have had to lie in port till he has emptied out his cargo and returned. Now the Church should watch while she prays, to see if she cannot fulfil her own prayers, look out for opportunities of doing good, and see if she cannot steal a march upon her enemies. God doth not always send the Spirit to blow with the same force. We cannot make the wind blow, but we can spread the sails; so, if we cannot command the Spirit of God, when the Spirit of God does come, we can observe his coming and avail ourselves of the glorious opportunity. Watch, then, while ye pray.

Watch, too, *for fresh arguments in prayer.* Heaven's gate is not to be stormed by one weapon but by many. Spare no arrows, Christian. Watch and see that none of the arms in thy armoury are rusty. Besiege the throne of God with a hundred hands, and look at the promise with a hundred eyes. You have a great work on hand for you have to move the arm that moves the world; watch, then, for every means of moving that arm. See to it that you ply every promise; that you use every argument; that you wrestle with all might. When you are wrestling with an antagonist, you must keep your eye on him; you must look to see what he means to do next, or where you can get the next grip at him; see where you can get a hold, or plant your foot, so that you can throw him down. So wrestle with the angel of mercy. Watch while you pray. You cannot wrestle with your eyes shut, nor can you prevail with God unless your own soul be in a watchful state.

One other remark; *watch for the answers to your prayers*. When you post a letter to a friend, requesting a favour, you watch for an answer. When you pray to God for a favour you do not expect him to hear you, some of you. If the Lord were to hear some of your prayers, you would be surprised. I do believe that if God should send to you what you have asked for, you would be quite astonished. Sometimes when I have met with a special answer to prayer and have told it, some have said—"Is it not wonderful!" Not at all; it would be wonderful if it were not so. God says, "Ask, and ye shall receive"; if I should ask and not receive, it would be wonderful. "Seek, and ye shall find"; if you seek and do not find, it is not only wonderful, but I think it is contradictory to God's Word. The Church has but to ask, and she shall receive; she has but to knock, and the door of mercy shall be opened. But we do not believe this. We fritter away God's promises, and clip the edge of them, and then we go to God in prayer, and we think that prayer is a very holy exercise, but we do not think that God really hears us. Too many professors believe it is their duty to pray, but really they are not so enthusiastic as to think that God actually listens, and sends them what they ask for. A man who should say that he knew that God heard his prayers is in some quarters looked upon as an enthusiast. And what is that but a proof that we do not believe this precious Book? For let the most unprejudiced man be a judge, if this Book does not teach that. "Whatsoever we ask in prayer, believing, we shall receive," then it does not teach anything at all; and if it be not true that prayer is a power which prevails with God, then shut this Book; it is not worthy of any confidence, for it does plainly say that which you say it does not mean. The fact is the answers to our prayers are always on the way while we are asking. Sometimes they come while we are yet speaking; sometimes they delay, because we have not prayed as we should. God keeps the mercy back at times, and puts it out at compound interest, because he means to pay it to us interest and all; whereas if we had it at once, we should miss the interest, which sometimes doubles and trebles the principal. We are never losers by his delays, but always gainers. We ought never to say, even though providence should tell us

so, that God forgets or is unmindful, we never ought to believe
that God has been deaf to our cries, or refused to answer our
petitions. A true believer pleading Christ's name and sacrifice,
and asking in faith, must and shall receive that which he asks of
God.

I am sure that the people of God universally could prove that
God does hear prayer. As certainly as ever when you write to
a friend you get your answer, more surely and certainly still if
you be pleading the name of Christ, God will hear you. But
oh! do open your eyes and look out for the blessing. Do watch
for it. Be not so simple as to sow the seed and never to look for
harvest; do not be planting and never looking for fruit. Give up
your prayers, or else expect them to be successful. When we
were little children we had a little plot of garden-ground, and
we put our seeds into it. I well recollect how the day after I had
put in my seed I went and scraped the soil away to see if it was
not growing, as I expected it would have been after a day or so
at the very longest, and I thought the time amazingly long
before the seed would be able to make its appearance above the
ground. "That is childish," you would say. I know it is, but I
wish you were childish too with regard to your prayers; that you
would, when you have put them in the ground, go and see
if they have sprung up; and if not at once—be not childish in
refusing to wait till the appointed time comes, always go back
and see if they have begun to sprout. If you believe in prayer
at all, do expect God to hear you. If you do not expect, you will
not have it. He will never allow you to think better of him
than he is; he will come up to the mark of your thoughts, and
according to your faith so shall it be done unto you.

The third point is, GIVE THANKS.

Prayer should be mingled with praise. I have heard that in
New England after the Puritans had settled there a long while,
they used to have very often a day of humiliation, fasting, and
prayer, till they had so many days of fasting, humiliation, and
prayer, that at last a good senator proposed that they should
change it for once, and have a day of thanksgiving. It is of little
use to be always fasting; we ought sometimes to give thanks for
mercies received. Why should we go to God as mournful beings,
who plead piteously with a hard master who loves not to give?

Go not before God with a rueful face, ye people of God, as

though he had never heard you before, and you were about to try a great experiment on one who was exceedingly deaf and did not like to give you mercies. God is as pleased to give you his blessing as ever you are to receive it. It is as much to *his* honour as it is to *your* comfort. He takes more pleasure in your prayers than you do in his answers. Come, therefore, boldly, come with thankfulness in your heart and upon your lip, and join the hymn of praise with the cry of prayer. Be thankful for what God has done. "Sing unto him, sing, sing psalms unto him; come into his presence with thanksgivings, and show thyself glad in him with psalms, for the Lord is God and a great King above all gods." So thank him for the past and pray to him for the future. Thank him, too, for the power to pray. Thank him for the privilege of taking the Church's wants before him. And do better still; thank him for the mercy which is to come. Great God I thank thee for the land of China, which shall come unto thee. I praise thee for India, which shall receive thee. I praise thee for Ethiopia, which shall stretch out her arms unto thee. Great God, today we bless thee for what thou wilt do. Thy promise is, in the estimation of our faith, as good as the performance itself. We extol and glorify thee. For thy right hand, O Lord! thy right hand, O Lord, hath dashed in pieces the enemy. Thou hast broken the bow and cut the spear in sunder; thou hast burned the chariot in the fire; thy right hand, O Lord, hath gotten thee the victory. Oh come let us sing unto the Lord, for he hath triumphed gloriously. Let us laud and extol him, for he is King for ever and ever! Say unto Zion, "Thy God reigneth." Behold, he cometh; he cometh to judge the world in righteousness and the people with equity. Rejoice before him, O ye hills, clap your hands, O ye cedars! Let the sea roar and the fulness thereof; the world, and all that dwell therein! Praise him, ye heavens; and ye heaven of heavens; ye spirits that stand before his throne, for he is God, and beside him there is no God. The whole earth praises thee, O God, and all thy creatures bless thee for ever and ever!

Thus with the censor of prayer and praise let us be like priests of God; and thou great High Priest, take thou our sacrifice and offer it before thy Father's face. Put God to the test! See if he do not open the windows of heaven upon you. Be you much in prayer and you shall be much blessed.

XIV

"A PEOPLE PREPARED FOR THE LORD"

"To make ready a people prepared for the Lord."—Luke
1 : 17.

JOHN was the herald of Christ; he was to prepare the way for
the coming King, but from this text it appears that he was
to do more than that. He was not only to make the road ready
for the Lord, but he was also "to make ready a people prepared
for the Lord." That was a great work, a task in which he would
require strength and wisdom greater than his own. He would
need that the Spirit of God, who was to be given without
measure to the coming One, should also be in a measure within
himself, if he should really "make ready a people prepared for
the Lord."

This is not at all a usual expression; at first sight, it hardly
looks to us like a Gospel expression. We sang,

Just as I am—and waiting not
To rid my soul of one dark blot,
To thee, whose blood can cleanse each spot,
O Lamb of God, I come.

We sang over and over again those words, "Just as I am,"
"Just as I am," and we are prone to protest against the idea
of being prepared for Christ; we preach constantly that no
preparation is needed, but that men are to come to Jesus just
as they are. Yet here is John the Baptist set apart "to make
ready a people prepared for the Lord."

The fact is, that to get men to come to Jesus just as they
are, is not an easy thing. To get them to give up the idea of
preparing to get them prepared to come without preparing
to get them ready to come just as they are, this is the hardest
part of our work, this is our greatest difficulty. If we came and

preached to men the necessity of preparation so many weeks of fasting during a long Lent, or through so many days of scourging and penitence, they would attend to us at once, for they would be willing enough to make any preparation of that kind; but, when we say to them, "Come just as you are now, with nothing in your hand to buy the mercy of God, with nothing wherewith to demand or to deserve it," men want a great deal of preparing before they will come to that point. Only the grace of God, working mightily through the Word, by the Spirit, will prepare men to come to Christ thus, prepared by being unprepared so far as any fitness of their own is concerned. The only fit state in which they can come is that of sinking themselves, abandoning all idea of helping Christ, and coming in all their natural impotence and guilt, and taking Christ to be their all in all.

Beloved friends, this is the true preparedness of heart for coming to Christ, the preparedness of coming to him just as you are; and it was John's business thus "to make ready a people prepared for the Lord." That is also my business at this time.

First, *John* made ready "a people prepared for the Lord" BY AROUSING THEIR ATTENTION.

The people were asleep; they had fallen into a condition of religious lethargy, when suddenly there stood in their midst a man clothed with camel's hair, and with a leathern girdle about his loins, a prophet, manifestly, by the boldness and truthfulness of his utterances. He spoke in such a way that the people in general heard of his speaking, and they advertised him by saying the one to the other, "That is a strange man who has begun to preach by the River Jordan, and whose meat is locusts and wild honey."

The whole style of the man set the people wondering and talking; and when they came to listen to him, he did not flatter them, he did not utter more commonplace truths to them, but with burning earnestness he drove straight at their hearts, and spoke like Elijah, the great prophet of fire, had done in the ages gone by. So *he set them thinking.* We have always hope of men when they once begin to think about religion and the things of God. See how the bulk of them hurry on with their eyes tightly shut, rushing fast and yet faster still down to destruction.

You cannot make them stop and think. There are thousands of men who would almost sooner be whipped than be made to think. The last thing to which they will ever come of themselves is thoughtfulness.

Let me appeal to some who are still unconverted. Did you ever give the affairs of your soul the benefit of an hour's serious consideration? You have your regular time for stock-taking, those of you who are in business; do you ever take stock of your spiritual estate? I know that you are not such fools as to neglect your ledgers, you cast up your accounts to see whereabouts you are financially; but do you cast up the account between God and your own soul, and look the matter fairly and squarely in the face? Oh, if we could but bring you to do this, we should feel that you were being prepared for coming to Christ just as you are, for no man will come to Christ while he is utterly careless and thoughtless! Faith is a matter of thought; it requires a mind aroused from slumber, a mind that has taken wing; and John the Baptist did good service for his Master when he startled men into that condition, and so made them consider their ways.

He did more than that, for, having first made them think, *he preached to them a Saviour.* He told them that One was coming with power to baptize them after a higher sort than his baptism. He cried, "Behold the Lamb of God, which taketh away the sin of the world," and this message infused into the people a measure of hope. The poor people said, "What shall we do?" for they had a hope that there was something to be gained. Even the tax-gatherers, despised as they were, began to look up, and think that there might be something even for them, so they said to John, "Master, what shall we do?" And the rough Roman soldiers thought, "There may be something for us," so they also asked, "And what shall we do?" John inspired the multitudes with hope.

It is a very blessed state of mind for a man to get in when he begins to hope that he may be saved. Then he will be prepared to come to Jesus, just as he is, when he feels that he is not shut up to despair. "Oh!" says the poor man, "I need not, after all be lost; I need not abide for ever under the wrath of God. There is an open door set before me, there is a way of mercy even for me." I wish it were possible that everybody whom

I am now addressing had that feeling; it would be part of the making ready of "a people prepared for the Lord" when thought had blossomed into hope.

But John led his hearers on further than that, for *they began to expect something as well as to hope for it.* They epected that the Christ would speedily come, and they expected some great blessings through the coming of the Messiah. And oh! when men, after hearing the gospel, have great expectations concerning God and his salvation, surely their expectations will not be long disappointed. I remember a man coming one day to see me, and he said that he wished to take a sitting in the Tabernacle. He had been hearing me for some time, and he wanted to take a seat; but he desired to be very honest with me, and not to take a seat except upon a right understanding. I asked, "What is the difficulty, my friend?" "Well," he replied, "the person who sat next to me on Sunday told me that, if I became a regular hearer here, you would expect me to be converted." "Well," I answered, "that is true, I shall expect it." "But," said he, "you do not mean that you will require it of me." "Oh, dear no!" I replied, "nothing of the sort; I do not expect you to convert yourself; but I hope and trust that you will be converted, that is what I mean. I shall expect that God, in his grace, will meet with you and save you." "Oh!" he said, "I hope that, too; only I mean that I could not guarantee it." "Ah!" I said, "I see that you have taken the word 'expect' in the wrong sense; but I think, dear friend, that if you come expecting to be converted, and I preach expecting that you will be converted, it is highly probable that it will soon take place." "Oh!" he exclaimed, "God grant it!" A very few weeks after our conversation, he came and told me that the expectation in which we had united had been fulfilled, and he trusted that he had found the Saviour. When people come really expecting a blessing, they will be sure to get it. I do believe that some folk go to hear ministers with the idea that there will be something to find fault with, and, of course, they find that it is so; and when people come to hear another preacher, with the hope and expectation that God will bless them, of course God does bless them. Their expectation is divinely fulfilled. I have always a bright hope that a man will lay hold on Christ when he begins to expect to be saved, for he feels then that the time has come for him to find eternal life.

John did more than this, for he cried, "Repent ye: for the kingdom of heaven is at hand." that is to say, *he put a pressure of presentness upon the people.* A brother, who is an eminent preacher, but who uses rather long words, was explaining to me the benefit of the preaching of Mr. Fullerton and Mr. Smith in his place of worship. He said, "I do not know exactly why these brethren were the means of the conversion of many in my place whom I had never reached, but I perceived that they had the power to precipitate decision." It sounded rather strange, but when I thought it over a little while, I rather liked the expression, "the power to precipitate decision." That is the power that leads men to make up their minds, and say "Yes," or "No," to feel that the decision has to be made at once, and that the putting of it off is impossible because it would be a kind of insanity. Now that is the meaning of what John said, "The kingdom of heaven is at hand! Repent ye! He is coming who wields the axe of the divine justice; bear fruit, or else be cut down. He is coming who uses the great winnowing fan; be the true wheat, or else be blown away." He put the truth so pointedly, and so earnestly, that he did by that means make ready "a people prepared for the Lord."

Now, secondly, John made the people ready for Christ BY AWAKENING THEIR CONSCIENCES.

His very first utterance, as I have reminded you, was, "Repent ye, for the kingdom of heaven is at hand." "Repent! Repent! Repent!" was John's continual cry. This awakened the consciences of his hearers concerning *their sin.* Preaching repentance meant, "You have sinned; change your mind in reference to that sin. You have sinned; quit the sin, mourn over it, ask forgiveness for it. Repent ye!" Whenever a man brings to the minds of others their sins, when he so does it that they begin to feel that they have sinned, then they are being prepared for the Lord, for no man will come to the Saviour unless he knows that he needs a Saviour; and no man will feel that he needs a Saviour until he feels that he is a sinner. Hence it is a real preparation of men for Christ to convince them of sin.

This John did; he brought their sin before them, and then *he showed them their need of cleansing,* for he stood by the River Jordan, not with a scallop shell, as some depict him, but he stood by the flowing stream, ready to immerse all those who repented. This was practically saying to them, "You need to be washed, you need to be cleansed; and I show you this truth as I baptize you with water unto repentance. As your bodies are washed with pure water, so must your souls be washed and made clean ere you can enter heaven." This was John's plain teaching by his action as well as by his words.

Then he went straight away to arousing their consciences by telling them of *their need of a change of life.* He said that it was no use for them to pretend to grieve over the past, and then continue to sin in the same fashion. "Bring forth fruits," said he, "meet for repentance," or, "answerable to amendment of life," as the margin has it. And he took pains to point out what the fruits must be. If they were men of greed, they must become generous, and give to their needy neighbours. If they had been unrighteous and exacting, they must become honest. If they had been domineering, and brutal, and murmuring, they must become contented and quiet and gentle.

He not only preached to the multitudes about repentance of sin in general, but *he pointed out the precise sin of each class of persons* that came to him, and urged them to perform the special duties which they had neglected. Now I believe, as I have often said, that there is no sewing with silk thread alone; you must have a needle as well. You need a sharp needle to go first to draw the thread through the material; so you must preach the law, you must denounce sin, and you must individualize, and condemn special sins; and you must be personal, and pointed, or else men will not feel in their consciences what you say to them. Conscience is very apt to get seared as with a hot iron, to lose sensitiveness, so as to be no use at all as a conscience. Some say that conscience is a spark of deity, a divine monitor; it is nothing of the sort, in many a man it is almost extinct, for it does not act at all. The preacher who would "make ready a people prepared for the Lord" must come out with his axe, and lay it to the root of the trees; he must be definite and distinct in indicating this sin and that sin, and crying to all men, "Repent of these sins. Give them up. Get clear from them. Be washed from them; or else, as

God lives, when the Christ himself comes, it will not be to save
you, but to blow you away with his winnowing fan as the chaff
is blown into the fire."

Thirdly, John had "to make ready a people prepared for
the Lord" BY POINTING OUT THE NATURE OF TRUE RELIGION.

He showed that *it did not depend upon external privileges.*
As soon as ever John began to preach, the men of Jewish race,
proud of their pedigree, pressed near; and John, with all the
courage that a servant of the Lord could have, said, "Begin
not to say within yourselves, We have Abraham to our father:
for I say unto you, That God is able of these stones to raise up
children unto Abraham." You see the drift of his preaching
do you not? He says, practically, "Men and women, there is
no virtue in your boasted privileges, there is no merit in your
religious descent. As for supposing yourselves to be the peculiar
people of God, you are not to be saved that way. Say not, We
have Abraham to our father." Oh, how many hug that idea,
"My father was a Christian." Others say, "Well, I live in a
Christian country." They suppose that there is something in
the very race from which they have sprung. Away with all
such notions, for whatever external privileges you may have
had, they are not sufficient to secure salvation for you.

Then came the Pharisees and the Sadducees; they were the
religious people of the time, the great observers of all outward propriety, but John taught them that *true religion is not
the same as official pretension.* He called them a "generation of
vipers." This was very disrespectful, and very shocking indeed
on his part; all the newspapers of the period, if there had been
any, would have cried him down for his want of charity, but
he wanted those who came to him to understand that true
religion was not the same as professing to be religious. It was
not making broad the borders of their garments, it was not
wearing a text of Scripture as a phylactery between their eyes,
it was not making long prayers at the corners of the streets,
that would save them; there must be a thorough change of
heart. So John spoke straight out; and this, I believe, is a
great way of preparing men for coming to Christ, when you
tell them, "It 'is not your early training, it is not your going
to church or chapel, it is not your infant sprinkling and your
confirmation, it is not even your adult baptism, nor your saying

prayers and reading the Bible, that will save you; but 'ye must be born again.' There must be an inward spiritual change, wrought by the Holy Spirit. You must believe in Jesus Christ, whom God has sent, and you must so believe in him as to be made new creatures in him, or else you cannot be saved." Now, when men realize that all this is true, it startles them out of their false refuges, and makes them ready to flee to the only true refuge, so that it is really the way of making ready "a people prepared for the Lord."

While John set forth this matter negatively, putting down all the wrong hopes of his hearers, he was exceedingly plain in telling them that the way of salvation would involve them in *the necessity of being right before God.* "There," said he, "the proof of a tree's life is its fruit, and the evidence of your new life will be your good works. 'Now also the axe is laid unto the root of the trees; therefore, every tree which bringeth not forth good fruit is hewn down, and cast into the fire.'" Unless our religion makes us holy, it has not done anything for us that is really worth doing. Unless we hate sin, and love righteousness, our religion is a sham and a lie. John stated that truth very plainly; and that is the way to drive men to Christ.

He told them also that the trial of a life would be by its weight as well as by its fruit. "Look," said he, "at the heap that lies on the threshing-floor. He that hath the fan in his hand begins to winnow it; that which is light and chaffy is blown away, that which has wheat in it remains on the floor. So," said he, "there must be weight about your religion— stability, reality, sincerity. There must be heart-work in it, it must be no pretence; it must be true from beginning to end, or else it shall no more avail you than a heap of chaff would avail the husbandman when it is blown into the fire."

Then John taught his hearers that Christ himself would be the great Trier of human hearts; not ministers or fellow-professors, but Christ himself. When men feel this to be true, then they begin to say to themselves, "There is more required than we at present possess. There is more demanded than we can ever manufacture of ourselves. Let us go to him that hath it, and ask him for it. Let us go to Christ, who hath grace to bestow upon the poor and needy."

Not the labours of my hands
Can fulfil thy law's demands:
Could my zeal no respite know,
Could my tears for ever flow,
All for sin could not atone
Thou must save and thou alone.

Now I shall close my discourse by noticing a fourth way in which John made ready "a people prepared for the Lord." He did it BY DECLARING THE GRACE AND POWER OF JESUS CHRIST.

If I were to preach to you merely to arouse your attention, to awaken your consciences to a sense of sin, or simply to show you the nature of true religion, yet you would not be prepared for Christ unless also you knew something about him, something about his suitableness and his power to save you. So, *John preached Jesus Christ as a mighty and glorious Saviour on whom the Spirit rested.* He says that, when he baptized our Lord, as Jesus came up out of the water, "I saw the Spirit descending from heaven like a dove, and it abode upon him. And I knew him not: but he that sent me to baptize with water, the same said unto me, Upon whom thou shalt see the Spirit descending, and remaining on him, the same is he which baptizeth with the Holy Ghost." John boldly preached, and told the people that the Spirit of God rested upon Jesus Christ, yea, abode upon him. Now, this would lead them to him, and this should lead you to him. If you want the grace of penitence, Christ has it to give you. If you want the grace of supplication, he has it to give you. If you want the grace of faith, he has it. If you want the grace of holiness, he has it. "It pleased the Father that in him should all fulness dwell," "and of his fulness have all we received, and grace for grace." John taught this to his hearers, and I teach it to you. If you are willing to have it, it is freely presented to you. He who makes you willing to receive is certainly willing to give. If he has emptied you, and prepared you to receive of his fulness, do not think that he will refuse you when you come to him for it. He hath said, "Him that cometh to me I will in no wise cast out." All thy requirements are fully met in him. The Spirit of God dwells in him as a fulness, and as an abiding fulness; therefore, do but believe in

him, and even that faith he will give thee, do but trust him,
and thou art saved, and fully supplied in him who can meet
all the necessities of thy case.

John also told his hearers that *the Christ whom he preached
was able to baptize them with the Holy Ghost.* "See," says he,
"I only plunge you in the flowing stream, I can do nothing
more for you than dip you in this River Jordan, on profession
of your repentance of sin; but this Saviour, this Christ of God,
can immerse you into the Spirit of God. He can give you of his
power to fill you; you can be baptized into the Holy Ghost by
him." Dost thou hear this? Jesus Christ can come and give
thee the Holy Spirit in such measure that thou shalt be
baptized into him

> *Plunged in the Godhead's deepest sea,*
> *And lost in his immensity.*

This will make thee to be really his, and make thee truly to
live unto him. The very fulness of grace, then, is with Christ,
and he is prepared to give it; and this should make men prepared to receive it. Did not the poor prodigal son say of the
provision in his father's house, "There is bread enough and to
spare"? It was partly that which made him go to his father's
house; and we may say of the Spirit who is in Christ, "There
is enough and to spare for every poor sinner who comes to
him;" therefore, come along with thee, be prepared at once
to come and receive the Saviour.

Lastly, John said in his preaching, "Behold the Lamb of
God, which taketh away the sin of the world." *He pointed out
Christ as the Sin-bearer,* bearing human guilt in his own person.
That is the master-key which lets men into the kingdom of
heaven. Oh! how I do delight to preach Christ as the Substitute
Christ as the atoning sacrifice; and when you have heard Christ
preached in that way, it makes you ready, "a people prepared
for the Lord." How can men come to Christ if they do not
know what Christ has done for them? If you do not understand
that he suffered in your stead, the Just for the unjust, to bring
you to God, how can you come to Christ? But when you have
learned that holy and blessed doctrine of Christ's propitiation
for human sin, why, then, methinks, you will leap at the very

sound of it, and say, "Yes, I will take this propitiation to be a sacrifice for me. Blessed Lamb of God,

> *My faith would lay her hand*
> *On that dear head of thine,*
> *While like a penitent I stand*
> *And there confess my sin.*

John's preaching Christ was the best way of making ready "a people prepared for the Lord," and there is no better way of preparing you to come to Jesus. Oh, that God would grant to some of you that "precipitation of decision" of which my learned friend spoke! Oh, that in some lives the turning-point might be reached now, the happy moment when they should decide for Christ! Lord, decide them! My friend, you have come to the cross-roads; peradventure, today, if you reject the Saviour, it will be your last rejection of him, and it will finally seal your doom; and I am sure, with no peradventure whatever, that if this day you look to Jesus, and trust to his finished work, you shall be saved, and saved for ever.

XV

WITHOUT CHRIST—NOTHING

"Without me ye can do nothing."—John 15: 5.

THIS is not the language of a man of ordinary mould. No saint, no prophet, no apostle would ever have addressed a company of faithful men, and have said to them, "without me ye can do nothing." Had Jesus Christ been, as some say, a good man, and nothing more, such language as this would have been unseemly and inconsistent. Among the virtues of a perfect man we must certainly reckon modesty, but this from a mere man would have been shamelessly immodest. It is impossible to conceive that Jesus of Nazareth, had he not been more than man, could ever have uttered the sentence, "Without me ye can do nothing." I hear in this sentence the voice of that Divine Person without whom was not anything made that was made. The majesty of the words reveals the Godhead of him that uttered them. The "I am" comes out in the personal word "me," and the claim of all power unveils the Omnipotent. These words mean Godhead or nothing. The spirit in which we listen to this language is that of adoration. Let us bow our heads in solemn worship, and so unite with the multitude before the throne who ascribe power and dominion and might to him that sitteth upon the throne and to the Lamb.

In this adoring state of mind we shall be the better prepared to enter into the innermost soul of the text. I am not going to preach upon the moral inability of the unregenerate, although in that doctrine I most firmly believe; for that truth did not come in our Lord's way when he uttered these words, neither did he allude to it. It is quite true that unregenerate men, being without Christ, can do no spiritual action whatever, and can do nothing which is acceptable in the sight of God; but our Lord was not speaking to unregenerate men at all, nor speaking about them. He was surrounded by his apostles, the eleven out of whom

Judas had been weeded, and it is to them as branches of the true vine that he says, "Without me ye can do nothing." The statement refers to such as are in the wine, and even to such as have been pruned, and have for a while been found abiding in the stem, which is Christ; even in such there is an utter incapacity for holy produce if separated from Christ.

We are not called upon just now to speak upon all forms of doing, as beyond us, but of that form of it which is intended in the text. There are certain forms of doing in which men excel who know little or nothing of Christ; but the text must be viewed in its own connection, and the truth is clear. Believers are here described under the figure of branches in the vine, and the doing alluded to must therefore be the bearing of fruit. I might render it, "Apart from me ye can produce nothing— make nothing, create nothing, bring forth nothing." The reference, therefore, is to that doing which may be set forth by the fruit of the vine branch, and therefore to those good works and graces of the Spirit which are expected from men who are spiritually united to Christ: it is of these that he says, "Without me ye can do nothing." Our text is only another form of the fourth verse: "As the branch cannot bear fruit of itself, except it abide in the vine; no more can ye except ye abide in me." I am therefore going to address myself to you who profess to know and love the Lord, and are anxious to glorify his name, and I have to remind you that union to Christ is essential; for only as you are one with him, and continue to be so, can you bring forth the fruits which prove you to be truly his.

Reading again this solemn sentence, "Without me ye can do nothing," it first of all excites in me AN ASPIRATION OF HOPE. There is something to be *done*, our religion is to have a grand practical outcome. I have been thinking of Christ as the vine, and of the myriads of branches in him, and my heart has hoped for great things. From such a root what a vintage must come! Being branches in him, what fruit we must produce! There can be nothing scanty or poverty-stricken in the fruitage of a vine so full of sap. Fruit of the best quality, fruit in the utmost abundance, fruit unrivalled, must be borne by such a vine. That word "*do*" has music in it. Yes, Jesus went about doing good, and, being in him, we shall do good. Everything about him is efficient, practical,—in a word, fruitbearing; and being joined to him much will yet be done by us. We have been saved by the almighty grace of God apart from all doings of our own, and now that we are saved we long to *do* something in return: we feel a high ambition to be of some use and service to our great Lord and Master. The text, even though there be a negative in it, yet raises in our soul the hope that ere we go hence and be no more we may even here on earth do something for Christ.

Beloved, there is the ambition and hope before us of doing something in the way of glorifying God by bringing forth *the fruits of holiness, peace, and love.* We would adorn the doctrine of God our Saviour in all things. By pureness, by knowledge, by longsuffering, by love unfeigned, by every good and holy work we would show forth the praises of our God. Apart from the Lord Jesus we know we cannot be holy; but joined unto him we overcome the world, the flesh, and the devil, and walk with garments unspotted from the world. The fruit of the Spirit is love, joy, peace, longsuffering, gentleness, goodness, faith, meekness, temperance, and all manner of holy conversation. For none of these things are we equal in and of ourselves, and yet by faith we say with Paul, "I can do all things through Christ which strengtheneth me." We may be adorned with plentiful clusters, we may cause the Saviour to have joy in us that our joy may be full: great possibilities are before us.

We aspire not only to produce fruit in ourselves, but to bear much *fruit in the conversion of others*, even as Paul desired concerning the Romans, that he might have fruit among them. In this matter we can do nothing whatever alone; but being united unto Christ we bring forth increase unto the Lord. Our Lord Jesus said, "The works that I do shall ye do also, and greater works than these shall ye do, because I go unto the Father." A hope springs up in our bosom that we may each one of us bring many souls to Jesus. Not because we have any power in ourselves, but because we are united to Jesus we joyfully hope to bring forth fruit in the way of leading others to the knowledge of the Gospel.

My soul takes fire of hope, and I say to myself, If it be so, all these branches, and all alive, how much *fruit of further blessing* will ripen for this poor world. Men shall be blessed in us because we are blessed in Christ. What must be the influence of ten thousand godly examples! What must be the influence upon our country of thousands of Christian men and women practically

advancing love, peace, justice, virtue, holiness! And if each one
is seeking to bring others to Christ what numerous conversions
there must be, and how largely must the church of God be
increased. Do you not know that if there were only ten thousand
real Christians in the world, yet if each one of these brought
one other to Christ every year it would not need twenty years to
accomplish the conversion of the entire population of the globe?
This is a simple sum in arithmetic which any schoolboy can work
out. I sit me down and dream right comfortably, according to the
promise, "Your young men shall see visions, and your old men
shall dream dreams." See these thousands of branches, pro-
ceeding from such a stem as Christ Jesus, and with such sap as
the Holy Ghost flowing through them; why, surely, this vine
must soon clothe the mountains with its verdure, and there shall
not remain a single barren rock unadorned with the blessed
foliage! Then shall the mountains drop sweet wine, and all the
hills shall melt. Not because of any natural fertility in the
branches, but because of their glorious root, and stem, and sap,
each one shall bear full clusters, and each fruitful bough shall
run over the wall. Beloved friends in Christ, have you not
strong desires to see some such consummation? Do you not
long to take a share in the high enterprise of winning the world
to Christ? Oh, ye that are young and full of spirits, do you not
long to press to the front of this great crusade? Our souls pine
to see the knowledge of the Lord covering the earth as the waters
cover the sea. It is glad tidings to us that, joined unto Christ,
we can do something in this great business, something upon
which the Lord will smile, something which shall redound to the
glory of his name. We are not condemned to inaction; we are
not denied the joy of service, the superior blessedness of giving
and of doing: the Lord hath chosen us and ordained us to go and
bring forth fruit, fruit that shall remain. This is the aspiration
which rises in our soul; the Lord grant that we may see it take
actual form in our lives.

But now, in the second place, there passes through my heart a
shudder, A SHUDDER OF FEAR. Albeit I glow and burn with strong
desire and rise upon the wing of a mighty ambition to do something great for Christ, yet I read the text, and a sudden trembling
takes hold upon me. "Without me"; it is possible, then, that
I may be without Christ, and so may be utterly incapacitated for

all good. Come, friends, I want you to feel, even though it cast a cold chill over you, that you may possibly be "without Christ". You profess to be in Christ; but are you so? The large majority of those to whom I speak are visible members of the visible church of Christ; but what if you should *not be so in him as to bring forth fruit?* Evidently there are branches which in a certain sense are in the vine, and yet bring forth no fruit! It is written, "Every branch in me that beareth not fruit he taketh away." Yes, you are a member, perhaps an elder, perhaps a deacon, possibly a minister, and so you are in the vine; but are you bringing forth the fruits of holiness? Are you consecrated? Are you endeavouring to bring others to Jesus Christ? Or is your profession a thing apart from a holy life, and devoid of all influence upon others? Does it give you a name among the people of God and nothing more? Say, is it a mere natural association with the church, or is it a living, supernatural union with Christ? Let the thought go through you and prostrate you before him who looks down from heaven upon you, and lifts his pierced hand, and cries, "Without me ye can do nothing." If you are without Christ, what is the use of carrying on that Bible Class, for you can do nothing? What is the use of my coming to this pulpit if I am without Christ? What is the use of your going down into the Sunday School this afternoon if, after all, you are without Christ? Unless we have the Lord Jesus ourselves we cannot take him to others. Unless within us we have the living water springing up unto eternal life, we cannot overflow so that out of our midst shall flow rivers of living water.

I will put the thought another way; what if you should be in Christ, and *not so in him as to abide in him?* It appears from our Lord's words that some branches in him are cast forth and are withered. "If a man abide not in me, he is cast forth as a branch, and is withered." Some who are called by his name, and reckoned among his disciples, whose names are heard whenever the muster-roll of the church is read, yet do not continue in him. What if it should happen that you are only in Christ on a Sunday, but in the world all the week! What if you are only in Christ at the communion table, or at the Prayer Meeting, or at certain periods of devotion? What if you are off and on with Christ! What if you play fast and loose with the Lord! What if you are an outside saint and an inside devil! And yet some persist in attempting to hold an intermittent communion with Christ. This will not do. We must be so in Christ as to be always in him, or else we are not living branches of the living vine, and we cannot produce fruit. If there were such a thing as a vine branch that was only occasionally joined to the stem, would you expect it to yield a cluster to the husbandman? So neither can you if you are off and on with Christ. You can do nothing if there be not constant union.

One year when I was travelling towards my usual winter resting-place I halted at Marseilles, and there was overtaken by great pain. In my room in the hotel I found it cold, and so I asked for a fire. I was sitting in a very desponding mood, when suddenly the tears came to my eyes, as if smitten with a great sorrow. I shall never forget the thoughts which stirred my heart. The porter came in to light the fire. He had in his hand a bundle of twigs. I called to him to let me look at it. He was about to push it into the stove as fuel with which to kindle the fire. As I took the bundle into my hand, I found it was made of vine branches that had been cut off now that the pruning time was come. Ah me, I thought, will this be my portion? Here I am, away from home, unable to bear fruit, as I love to do. Shall I end with this as my portion? Shall I be gathered for the fire? Those vine shoots were parts of a good vine, no doubt—branches that once looked fair and green; but now they were fuel for the flame. They had been cut off and cast off as useless things, and then men gathered them and tied them in bundles, and they were ignobly thrust into the fire. What a picture!

"Men gather them, and cast them into the fire, and they are burned." Shall this be the lot of any of us who have named the name of Christ? Well did I say a shudder may go through us as we listen to those words, "without me." Our end without Christ will be terrible indeed. First, no fruit; then no life; and at last no place among the saints, no existence in the church of God. Without Christ we do nothing, we are nothing, we are worse than nothing. Here is grave cause for heart-searching, and I leave the matter with you to that end.

Having come so far in our second head, under the third I behold A VISION OF TOTAL FAILURE. "Without me," says the text, "ye can do nothing"—ye can produce nothing. The visible Church of Christ has tried this experiment a great many times already, and always with the same result. Separated from Christ, his church can do nothing which she was formed to do. She is sent into the world upon a high enterprise, with noble aims before her, and grand forces at her disposal; but if she could cease from communion with Christ she would become wholly incapable.

Now what are the outward signs of any community being apart from Christ? Answer, first, It may be seen in *a ministry without Christ in its doctrine.* This we have seen ourselves. Woe worth the day that it is so! History tells us that not only in the Romish church and the Anglican church, but among the Non-conformist churches, Christ has been at times forgotten. Not only among Unitarians, but among Presbyterians, Methodists, Baptists, all round, Jesus has been dishonoured. Attempts have been made to do something without Christ as the truth to be preached. What folly it is! They preach up intellectualism, and hope that this will be the great power of God; but it is not. "Surely," say they, "novelties of thought and refinements of speech will attract and win! The preachers aspire to be leaders of thought; will they not command the multitude and charm the intelligent? Add music and architecture, and what is to hinder success?" Many a young minister has given up his whole mind to this—to try and be exceedingly refined and intellectual; and what has he done with these showy means? The sum total is expressed in the text—"Nothing": "Without me ye can do nothing." What emptiness this folly has created: when the pulpit is without Christ the pews are soon without people. I knew a chapel where an eminent divine was to be heard for years. A converted Jew coming to London to visit a friend, set out on Sunday morning to find a place of Christian worship, and he chanced to enter the chapel of this eminent divine. When he came back he said, that he feared he had made a mistake; he had turned into a building which he hoped was a Christian place of assembly; but as he had not heard the name of Jesus all the morning, he thought perhaps he had fallen in with some other religionists. I fear that many modern sermons might just as fairly have been delivered in a Mahometan mosque as in a Christian church. We have too many preachers of whom we might complain, "they have taken away my Lord, and I know not where they have laid him." Christianity without Christ is a strange thing indeed. A sermon without Christ as its beginning, middle, and end is a mistake in conception and a crime in execution. However grand the language it will be merely much-ado-about-nothing if Christ be not there.

Further, without acknowledging always *the absolute supremacy of Christ* we shall do nothing. Jesus is much complimented nowadays; but he is not submitted to as absolute Lord. I hear many pretty things about Christ from men who reject his Gospel. "Lives of Christ" we have in any quantity. Oh for one which would set him forth in his glory as God, as Head of the church and Lord of all. I should greatly like to see a "Life of Christ" written by one who knew him by communion with him and by reverently sitting at his feet. Most of the pretty things about Jesus which I read nowadays seem to have been written by persons who have seen him through a telescope at a great distance, and know him "according to Matthew," but not according to personal fellowship. Oh for a "Life of Christ" by Samuel Rutherford or George Herbert, or by some other sweet spirit to whom the everblessed One is as a familiar friend.

It is fortunate for Jesus that he commends himself to the "best thought" and ripest culture of the period; for, if he had not done so, these wise gentlemen would have exposed him as being behind the times. Of course they have every now and then to rectify certain of his dogmas, especially such as justification by faith, or atonement, or the doctrine of election—these are old-fashioned things, which belong to an older and less enlightened period, and therefore they adapt them by tearing out their real meaning. The doctrines of grace, according to the infallible critics of the period, are out of date—nobody believes them now, and so they settle off old-fashioned believers as nonexistent. Christ is rectified and squared, and his garment without seam is taken off, and he is dressed out in proper style, as by a West-End clothier; then he is introduced to us as a remarkable teacher, and we are advised to accept him as far as he goes.

For the present the wise ones tolerate Jesus; but there is no telling what is to come: the progress of this age is so astonishing that it is just possible we shall before long leave Christ and Christianity behind. Now, what will come of this foolish wisdom? Nothing but delusions, mischief, infidelity, anarchy, and all manner of imaginable and unimaginable ills. The fact

is, if you do not acknowledge Christ to be all, you have virtually
left him out, and are without him. We must preach the Gospel,
because Christ has revealed it. "Thus saith the Lord," is to be
our logic. We must preach the Gospel as ambassadors delivering
their message; that is to say, in the King's name, by an authority
not their own. We preach our doctrines, not because we consider that they are convenient and profitable, but because
Christ has commanded us to proclaim them. We believe the
doctrines of grace, because they are true and are the voice of
God. Age or no age has nothing to do with us. The world hates
Christ and must hate him: if it would boldly denounce Christ it
would be to us a more hopeful sign than its deceitful Judas kiss.
We keep simply to this, the Lord hath said it, and we care not
who approves or disapproves. Jesus is God and Head of the
Church, and we must do what he bids us, and say what he tells
us: if we fail in this, nothing of good will come of it. If the
church gets back to her loyalty, she shall see what her Lord will
do; but without Christ as absolute Lord, infallible Teacher, and
honoured King, all must be failure even to the end.

Go a little further: you may have sound doctrine, and yet do
nothing unless you have Christ *in your spirit*. I have known all
the doctrines of grace to be unmistakably preached, and yet
there have been no conversions; for this reason, that they were
not expected and scarcely desired. In former years many
orthodox preachers thought it to be their sole duty to comfort
and confirm the godly few who by dint of great perseverance
found out the holes and corners in which they prophesied. These
brethren spoke of sinners as of people whom God might possibly
gather in if he thought fit to do so; but they did not care much
whether he did so or not. As to weeping over sinners as Christ
wept over Jerusalem; as to venturing to invite them to Christ as
the Lord did when he stretched out his hands all the day long;
as to lamenting with Jeremiah over a perishing people, they had
no sympathy which such emotions and feared that they savoured
of Arminianism. Both preacher and congregation were cased
in a hard shell, and lived as if their own salvation was the sole
design of their existence. If anybody did grow zealous and seek
conversions, straightway they said he was indiscreet, or conceited. When a church falls into this condition it is, as to its
spirit, "without Christ." What comes of it? Some of you know

by your own observation what does come of it. The comfortable
corporation exists and grows for a little while, but it comes to
nothing in the long run; and so it must: there can be no fruitbearing where there is not the spirit of Christ as well as the
doctrine of Christ. Except the spirit of the Lord rests upon you,
causing you to agonize for the salvation of men even as Jesus
did, ye can do nothing.

But above all things we must have Christ with us in the power
of *his actual presence*. Do we always think of this—"Without
me ye can do nothing"? We are going out this afternoon to
teach the young; shall we be quite sure to take Christ with us?
or on the road shall we suddenly stop and say, "I am without
my Master, and I must not dare to go another step"? The
abiding consciousness of the love of Christ in our souls is the
essential element of our strength. We can no more convert a
sinner without Christ than we could light up new stars in the sky.
Power to change the human will, power to enlighten the intellect as to the things of God, and to influence the mind as to
repentance and faith, must come entirely from the Most High.
Do we feel that? or do we put our thoughts together for an
address, and say, "Now, that is a strong point, and that will
produce effect"; and do we rest there? If so, we can do nothing
at all. The power lies with the Master, not with the servant; the
might is in the hand, not in the weapon. We must have Christ
in these pews and in these aisles, and in this pulpit, and Christ
down in our Sunday School, and Christ at the street corner when
we stand up there to talk of him, and we must feel that he is
with us even at the end of the world, or we shall do nothing.

Now, fourthly, I hear A VOICE OF WISDOM, a still small voice
which speaks out of the text, and says to us who are in Christ,
let us acknowledge this. Down on your knees, bow your mouths
in the dust and say, "Lord, it is true: without thee we can do
nothing, nothing whatever that is good and acceptable in the
sight of God. We have not ability of ourselves to think anything
of ourselves, but our ability is of God." Now, do not speak thus,
as if you paid a compliment which orthodoxy requires you to
make; but from the deeps of your soul, smitten with an absolute
self-despair, own the truth unto God. "To will is present with
me, but how to perform that which I would I find not." Lord, I
am a good-for-nothing do-nothing, a fruitless, barren, dry,

rotten branch without thee, and this I feel in my inmost soul. Be not far from me, but quicken me by thy presence.

Next, *let us pray*. If without Christ we can do nothing, let us cry to him that we may never be without him. Let us with strong crying and tears entreat his abiding presence. He comes to those who seek him : let us never cease seeking. In conscious fellowship with him, let us plead that the fellowship should be unbroken evermore. Let us pray that we may be so knit and joined to Jesus that we may be one spirit with him, never to be separated from him again. Master and Lord, let the life floods of thy grace never cease to flow into us, for we know that we must be thus supplied or we can produce nothing. Let us have much more prayer than has been usual among us. Prayer is appointed to convey the blessings God ordains to give; let us constantly use the appointed means, and may the result be ever increasing from day to day.

Next, *let us personally cleave to Jesus*. Let us not attempt a life of separation; for that were to seek the living among the dead. Do not let us depart from him for a single minute. Would you like to be caught at any one second of your life in a condition in which you could do nothing? I must confess I should not like to be in that state—incapable of defence against my enemies, or of service for my Lord. If an awakened one should come before you under distress of mind, and you should feel quite incapable of doing any good to him, what a sad perplexity. Or if you did not *feel* incapable, and yet should really be so, and what if you should therefore talk on in a religious way, but know no power in it; would it not be a sad thing? May you never be in such a state that you would be a do-nothing, with opportunities afforded and yet without strength to utilize them! If you are divided from Christ you are divided from the possibility of doing good; cling, therefore, to the Saviour with your whole might, and let nothing take you off from him; no, not for an hour.

Heartily submit yourselves, also to the Lord's headship and leadership, and ask to do everything in his style and way. He will not be with you unless you accept him as your Master. There must be no quarrel about supremacy, but you must yield yourself up absolutely to him, to be, to do, or to suffer, according to his will. When it is wholly so he will be with you, and you shall

do everything that is required of you. Wonderful things will
the Lord perform through you when once he is your all in all.
Will we not have it so?

Once more; *joyfully believe in him.* Though without him
you can do nothing, yet with him all things are possible. Omnipotence is in that man who has Christ in him. Weakness itself
you may be, but you shall learn to glory in that weakness because
the power of Christ doth rest upon you if your union and communion with Christ are continually kept up. Oh for a grand
confidence in Christ! We have not believed in him yet up to the
measure of the hem of his garment; for even that faith made the
sick woman whole. Oh to believe up to the measure of his
infinite Deity! Oh for the splendour of the faith which measures
itself by the Christ in whom it trusts! May God bring us there,
then shall we bring forth much fruit to the glory of his name.

And now, lastly, while I was listening to my text as a child
puts a shell to its ear and listens till it hears the deep sea rolling
in its windings, I heard within my text A SONG OF CONTENT.
"Without me ye can do nothing." My heart said, "Lord, what is
there that I want to do without thee? There is no pain in this
thought to me. If I can do without thee I am sorry to possess
so dangerous a power. I am happy to be deprived of all strength
except that which comes from thee. It charms, it exhilarates,
and delights my soul to think that thou art my all. Thou hast
made me penniless as to all wealth of my own, that I might dip
my hand into thy treasury; thou hast taken all power away
from every sinew and muscle of mine, that I may rest on thy
bosom." "Without me ye can do nothing." Be it so. Are you
not all agreed? Do you wish to have it altered, any of you that
love his dear name? I am sure you do not; for suppose, dear
friends, we could do something without Christ, then he would
not have the glory of it. Who wishes that? There would be little
crowns for our poor little heads, for we should have done something without him; but now there is one great crown for that
dear head which once was girt with thorns; for all his saints put
together cannot do anything without him. The goodly fellowship of the apostles, the noble army of martyrs, and the triumphant host of the redeemed by blood, all put together, can do
nothing without Jesus. Let him be crowned with majesty who
worketh in us both to will and to do of his own good pleasure.

For our own sakes, for our Lord's sake, we are glad that it is so. All things are more ours by being his; and if our fruit is his rather than our own, it is none the less but all the more ours. Is not this rare music for a holy ear?

I feel so glad that without Christ we can do nothing because I fear that if the Church could do something without Christ she would try to live without him. If she could teach the School and bring the children to salvation without Christ, I am afraid Christ would never go into a Sunday School again. If we could preach successfully without Jesus, I suspect that the Lord Jesus Christ would seldom stand on high among the people again. If our Christian literature could bless men without Christ, I am afraid we should set the printing-press going, and never think about the crucified One in the matter. Yes, it is a blessed thing for the whole Church that she must have Christ everywhere.

"Without me ye can do nothing." As I listened to the song within these words I began to laugh: I wonder if you will laugh too? I laughed, because I recollected a story of a New England service when the pastor one afternoon was preaching in his own solemn way, and the good people were listening or sleeping, as their minds inclined. It was a substantial edifice wherein they assembled, fit to outlive an earthquake. All went on peacefully in the meeting-house that afternoon till suddenly a lunatic started up, denounced the minister, and declared that he would at once pull down the meeting-house about their ears. Taking hold of one of the pillars of the gallery, this newly-announced Samson repeated his threatening. Everybody rose; the women were ready to faint; the men began to rush to the door, and there was danger that the people would be trodden on as they rushed down the aisles. There was about to be a great tumult; no one could see the end of it; when suddenly one cool brother sitting near the pulpit produced a calm by a single sentence. "Let him try!" was the stern sarcasm which hushed the tempest. Even so today the enemy is about to disprove the Gospel and crush out the doctrines of grace. Are you distressed, alarmed, astounded? So far from that, my reply to the adversary's boast that he will pull down the pillars of our Zion is this only, LET HIM TRY!

XVI

MESSAGE FOR THE TIME PRESENT

"In that day it shall be said to Jerusalem, Fear thou not:
and to Zion, Let not thine hands be slack. The Lord thy God
in the midst of thee is mighty; he will save, he will rejoice over
thee with joy; he will rest in his love, he will joy over thee
with singing. I will gather them that are sorrowful for the
solemn assembly, who are of thee, to whom the reproach of
it was a burden."—Zeph. 3: 16–18.

HOLY Scripture is wonderfully full and abiding in its inner
sense. It is a springing well, whereat you may draw, and
draw again; for as you draw, it springs up for ever new and fresh.
It is a well of water springing up everlastingly. The fulfilment
of a divine promise is not the exhaustion of it. When a man
gives you a promise, and he keeps it, there is an end of the
promise; but it is not so with God. When he keeps his word to
the full, he has but begun; he is prepared to keep it, and keep
it, and keep it for ever and ever.

What would you say of a man who had wheat upon his barn
floor, and threshed it until he had beaten out the last golden
grain; but the next day he went and threshed again, and
brought back as much as the day before; and on the day after,
again taking his flail, he went to the same threshing, and again
brought back his measure as full as at the first, and so on for
all the days of the year? Would it not seem to you as a fairy
tale? It would certainly be a surprising miracle.

But what should we say if, throughout a long life, this miracle
could be prolonged? Yet we have continued to thresh the
promises ever since faith was given us, and we have carried
away our full portion every day. What shall we say of the
glorious fact that the saints in all generations, from the first
day until now, have done the same; and of that equal truth,
that as long as there is a needy soul upon earth, there will be
upon the threshing floor of the promises the same abundance
of the finest wheat as when the first man filled his measure and

returned rejoicing? I will not dwell upon the specific application of the text before us: I do not doubt that it was specially fulfilled as it was intended; and if there still remains some special piece of history to which this passage alludes, it will again be fulfilled in due time; but this I know, that those who have lived between whiles have found this promise true to them. Children of God have used these promises under all sorts of circumstances, and have derived the utmost comfort from them. Let our prayer then be that we may enjoy this marvellous portion of the sacred word, and take intense delight in it. As God rests in his love, so may we rest in it now; and as he joys over us with singing, so may we break forth into joyous psalms to the God of our salvation.

I am going to begin with the last verse of the text, and work my way upwards. The first head is, *a trying day for God's people*. They are sorrowful because a cloud is upon their solemn assembly, and the reproach thereof is a burden. Secondly, we will note *a glorious ground of consolation*. We read in the seventeenth verse, " The Lord thy God in the midst of thee is mighty; he will save, he will rejoice over thee with joy; he will rest in his love, he will joy with thee over singing." And, thirdly, here is *a brave conduct suggested thereby*: " In that day it shall be said to Jerusalem, Fear thou not: and to Zion, Let not thine hands be slack."

Beginning at the eighteenth verse, we notice A TRYING DAY FOR GOD'S PEOPLE. *The solemn assembly had fallen under reproach.* The solemn assemblies of Israel were her glory: her great days of festival and sacrifice were the gladness of the land. To the faithful their holy days were their holidays. But a reproach had fallen upon the solemn assembly, and I believe it is so now at this present moment. It is a sad affliction when in our solemn assemblies *the brilliance of the Gospel light is dimmed by error*. The clearness of the testimony is spoiled when doubtful voices are scattered among the people, and those who ought to preach the truth, the whole truth, and nothing but the truth, are telling out for doctrines the imaginations of men, and the inventions of the age. Instead of revelation, we have philosophy, falsely so-called; instead of divine infallibility, we have surmises and larger hopes. The Gospel of Jesus Christ, which is the same yesterday, today, and for ever, is

taught as the production of progress, a growth, a thing to be
amended and corrected year by year. It is an ill day, both for
the Church and the world, when the trumpet does not give a
certain sound; for who shall prepare himself for the battle?

If added to this we should see *creeping over the solemn assembly
of the Church a lifelessness, an indifference, and a lack of spiritual
power*, it is painful to a high degree. When the vitality of
religion is despised, and gatherings for prayer are neglected,
what are we coming to? The present period of Church history
is well portrayed by the Church of Laodicea, which was neither
cold nor hot, and therefore to be spewed out of Christ's mouth.
That Church gloried that she was rich and increased in goods,
and had need of nothing, while all the while her Lord was outside, knocking at the door, a door closed against him. That
passage is constantly applied to the unconverted, with whom it
has nothing to do: it had to do with a lukewarm Church, with a
Church that thought itself to be in an eminently prosperous
condition, while her living Lord, in the doctrine of his atoning
sacrifice, was denied an entrance. Oh, if he had found admission
—and he was eager to find it—she would soon have flung away
her imaginary wealth, and he would have given her gold
tried in the furnace, and white raiment with which she might
be clothed. Alas! she is content without her Lord, for she has
education, oratory, science, and a thousand other baubles.
Zion's solemn assembly is under a cloud, indeed, when the
teaching of Jesus and his apostles is of small account with her.

If in addition to this, *worldly conformity spreads in the church*,
so that the vain amusements of the world are shared in by the
saints, then is there reason enough for lamentation, even as
Jeremiah cried: "How is the gold become dim!" Her Nazarites,
who were purer than snow and whiter than milk, have become
blacker than a coal. "All our enemies have opened their
mouths against us." If no longer there is a clear distinction
between the Church and the world, but professed followers
of Jesus have joined hands with unbelievers, then may we
mourn indeed! Woe worth the day! An ill time has happened
to the Church and to the world also. We may expect great
judgments, for the Lord will surely be avenged on such a
people as this.

It appears from the text that *there were some to whom the*

reproach was a burden. They could not make sport of sin. True, there were many who said that the evil did not exist at all, and others who declared that it was not present in any great degree. Yes, and more hardened spirits declared that what was considered to be a reproach was really a thing to be boasted of, the very glory of the century. Thus they huffed the matter, and made the mourning of the conscientious to be a theme for jest. But there was a remnant to whom the reproach of it was a burden; these could not bear to see such a calamity. To these the Lord God will have respect, as he said by the prophet: "Go through the midst of the city, through the midst of Jerusalem, and set a mark upon the foreheads of the men that sigh and that cry for all the abominations that be done in the midst thereof." The many drank wine in bowls and anointed themselves with their chief ointments, but they were not grieved for the affliction of Joseph (Amos 6: 6); but these were pressed in spirit and bore the cross, counting the reproach of Christ greater riches than all the treasures of Egypt. God's people cannot bear that Christ's atoning sacrifice should be dishonoured; they cannot endure that his truth should be trodden as mire in the streets. To true believers prosperity means the Holy Ghost blessing the word to the conversion of sinners and the building up of saints; and if they do not see this, they hang their harps upon the willows. True lovers of Jesus fast when the Bridegroom is not with his Church: their glory is in his glory, and in nothing else. The wife of Phinehas, the son of Eli, cried out in her dying agony, "The glory has departed," and the reason that she gave was once because of the death of her husband and his father, but twice because "the ark of God is taken." For this she named her new-born child Ichabod—"The glory is departed from Israel, for the ark of God is taken." The bitterest pain of this godly woman was for the Church, and for the honour of our God. So it is with God's true people: they lay it much to heart that the truth is rejected.

This burdened spirit is a token of true love to God: those who love the Lord Jesus are wounded in his woundings, and vexed with the vexings of his Spirit. When Christ is dishonoured his disciples are dishonoured. Those who have a tender heart towards the Church can say with Paul: "Who is offended, and

I burn not?" The sins of the Church of God are the sorrows
of all living members of it. This also marks a healthy sensibility,
a vital spirituality. Those who are unspiritual care nothing
for truth or grace: they look to finances, and numbers, and
respectability. But men whose spirits are of God would sooner
see the faithful persecuted than see them desert the truth,
sooner see churches in the depths of poverty full of holy zeal
than rich churches dead in worldliness. Spiritual men care for
the Church even when she is in an evil case, and cast down
by her adversaries: "thy servants take pleasure in her stones,
and favour the dust thereof." The house of the Lord is to many
of us our own house, his family is our family. Unless the Lord
Jesus be extolled, and his Gospel conquer, we feel that our own
personal interests are blighted, and we ourselves are in disgrace. It is no small thing to us: it is our life.

Thus have I dwelt upon the fact that it is an ill day for
God's people when the solemn assembly is defiled: the reproach
thereof is a burden to those who are truly citizens of the New
Jerusalem, and because of this *they are seen to be sorrowful*.
The Lord here says, "I will gather them that are sorrowful
for the solemn assembly." They may well be sorrowful when
such a burden is laid on their hearts. Moreover, they see in a
hundred ways the ill effect of the evil which they deplore.
Many are lame and halting; this is hinted at in the promise
of the nineteenth verse: "I will save her that halteth." Pil-
grims on the road to Zion were made to limp on the road
because the prophets were "light and treacherous persons."
When the pure Gospel is not preached, God's people are robbed
of the strength which they need in their life-journey. If you
take away the bread, the children hunger. If you give the
flock poisonous pastures, or fields which are barren as the desert,
they pine and they become lame in their daily following of the
shepherd. The doctrinal soon affects the practical. I know
many of the people of God living in different parts of this
country to whom the Sabbath is very little of a day of
rest, for they hear no truth in which rest is to be found, but
they are worried and wearied with novelties which neither
glorify God nor benefit the souls of men. In many a place the
sheep look up and are not fed.

This causes much disquietude and breeds doubts and

questionings, and thus strength is turned to weakness, and the work of faith, the labour of love, and the patience of hope are all kept in a halting state. This is a grievous evil, and it is all around us. Then, alas! many are "driven out," of whom the nineteenth verse says, "I will gather her that was driven out." By false doctrine many are made to wander from the fold. Hopeful ones are made to stray from the path of life, and sinners are left in their natural distance from God. The truth which would convince men of sin is not preached, while other truths which would lead seekers into peace are beclouded, and souls are left in needless sorrow. When the doctrines of grace and the glorious atoning sacrifice are not set clearly before men's minds, so that they may feel their power, all sorts of evils follow. It is terrible to me that this dreadful blight should come upon our churches; for the hesitating are driven to destruction, the weak are staggered, and even the strong are perplexed. The false teachers of these days would, if it were possible, deceive the very elect. This makes our hearts very sorrowful. How can we help it?

Yet, all the time that the people of God are in this evil case, *they are not without hope;* for close upon all this comes the promise of the Lord to restore his wandering ones. We have the sense twice over: "I will get them praise and fame in every land where they have been put to shame." "I will make you a name and a praise among all people of the earth, when I turn back your captivity before your eyes, saith the Lord." The adversaries cannot silence the eternal testimony. They hanged our Lord himself upon a tree; they took down his body and buried it in a tomb in the rock; and they set their seal upon the stone which they rolled at the mouth of the sepulchre. Surely now there was an end of the Christ and his cause. Boast not, ye priests and Pharisees! Vain the watch, the stone, the seal! When the appointed time had come, the living Christ came forth. He could not be holden by the cords of death. How idle their dreams! "He that sitteth in the heavens shall laugh: the Lord doth have them in derision." Beloved, the reproach will yet be rolled away from the solemn assembly: the truth of God will yet again be proclaimed as with trumpet tongue, the Spirit of God will revive his Church, and converts as many as the sheaves of the harvest shall yet be gathered in.

How will the faithful rejoice! Those who were burdened and sorrowful shall then put on their garments of joy and beauty. Then shall the ransomed of the Lord return with songs and everlasting joy upon their heads. The conflict is not doubtful. The end of the battle is sure and certain. Methinks I even now hear the shout, "The Lord God omnipotent reigneth."

Secondly, let us think of something which shines like a star amid the darkness. The second verse of the text presents a GLORIOUS GROUND OF CONSOLATION. Here is a rich text indeed. This passage is like a great sea, while I am as a little child making pools in the sand which skirts its boundless flood. A series of discourses might well be founded on this seventeenth verse.

Our great consolation in the worst times lies in our God. The very name of our covenant God—"the Lord thy God"—is full of good cheer. That word, "the Lord," is really JEHOVAH, the self-existent One, the unchangeable One, the ever-living God, who cannot change or be moved from his everlasting purpose. Children of God, whatever you have not got, you have a God in whom you may greatly glory. Having God you have more than all things, for all things come of him; and if all things were blotted out, he could restore all things simply by his will. He speaketh, and it is done; he commandeth, and it stands fast. Blessed is the man that hath the God of Jacob for his trust, and whose hope Jehovah is. In the Lord Jehovah we have righteousness and strength; let us trust in him for ever. Let the times roll on, they cannot affect our God. Let troubles rush upon us like a tempest, but they shall not come nigh unto us now that he is our defence.

Jehovah, the God of his Church, is also the God of each individual member of it, and each one may therefore rejoice in him. Jehovah is as much your God, as if no other person in the universe could use that covenant expression. O believer, the Lord God is altogether and wholly your God! All his wisdom, all his foresight, all his power, all his immutability— all himself is yours. As for the Church of God, when she is in her lowest estate she is still established and endowed in the best possible sense—established by the divine decree, and endowed by the possession of God all-sufficient. The gates of hell shall not prevail against her. Let us exult in our possession.

Poor as we are, we are infinitely rich in having God; weak as we are, there is no limit to our strength, since the Almighty Jehovah is ours. "If God be for us, who can be against us? If God be ours, what more can we need? Lift up thy heart, thou sorrowful one, and be of good cheer. If God be thy God, thou hast all thou canst desire: wrapped up within his glorious name, we find all things for time and eternity, for earth and heaven. Therefore in the name of Jehovah we will set up our banners, and march onward to the battle. He is our God by his own purpose, covenant, and oath; and this day he is our God by our own choice of him, by our union with Christ Jesus, by our experience of his goodness, and by that spirit of adoption whereby we cry "Abba, Father."

To strengthen this consolation, we notice next, that *this God is in the midst of us.* He is not a long way off, to be sought with difficulty, if haply we may find him. Our God is "Jehovah in the midst of thee." Since that bright night in which a Babe was born at Bethlehem, and unto us a Son was given, we know God as "Emmanuel, God with us." God is in our nature, and therefore very near unto us. "The Word was made flesh, and dwelt among us." Though his bodily presence is gone, yet we have his spiritual presence with us evermore; for he saith, "Lo, I am with you alway." He walketh among the golden candlesticks. We have also the immediate presence of God, the Holy Spirit. He is in the midst of the Church to enlighten, convince, quicken, endow, comfort, and clothe with spiritual power. The Lord still works in the minds of men for the accomplishment of his purposes of grace. Let us think of this when we are going forth to Christian service; "The Lord of hosts is with us." When you call your class together in the Sabbath School, say to your Lord, "If thy presence go not with me, carry me not up hence." If we have God with us, we can bear to be deserted by men. What a word that is, "Where two or three are gathered together in my name, there am I in the midst of them!" Shall not the army shout when the King himself is in their ranks! Let God arise, let his enemies be scattered! When he is with us they that hate him must flee before him. Be it our concern so to love that we may never grieve away the Spirit of God. Beloved, there is such abundant consolation in the fact of the presence of God with us, that if we could only feel the power of it at this moment, we should enter into rest, and our heaven would begin below.

Let us go a step further, and note that our consolation is largely to be found in the fact that *this God in the midst of us is full of power to save.* "The Lord thy God in the midst of thee is mighty; he will save." That is to say, "Jehovah, thy God, is mighty to save." His arm is not shortened, he is still "a just God and a Saviour." Nor is he merely able to save, but he will display that ability; "he will save." Let us pray, then, that he *will* save; that he will save his own Church from luke-warmness and from deadly error; that He will save her from her worldliness and formalism; from unconverted ministers and ungodly members. Let us lift up our eyes and behold the power which is ready to save; and let us go on to pray that the Lord may save the unconverted by thousands and millions.

Oh, that we might see a great revival of religion. This is what we want before all things. This would smite the enemy upon the cheek-bone, and break the teeth of the adversary. If tens of thousands of souls were immediately saved by the sovereign grace of God, what a rebuke it would be to those who deny the faith! Oh, for times such as our fathers saw when first Whitefield and his helpers began to preach the life-giving word! When one sweet voice was heard clear and loud, all the birds of paradise began to sing in concert with him, and the morning of a glorious day was heralded. If we are importunate in prayer it must happen: "God shall bless us, and all the ends of the earth shall fear him." Let us not seek power of rhetoric, much less of wealth; but let us look for the power which saves.

This is the one thing I crave. Oh, that God would save souls! I say to myself, after being badgered and worried through the week by the men of modern thought: "I will go my way and preach Christ's Gospel, and win souls." One lifting up of Jesus Christ crucified is more to me than all the cavillings of the men who are wise above what is written. Converts are our unanswerable arguments. "Happy is the man," saith the Psalm, "that hath his quiver full of them: they shall speak with the enemies in the gate." Blessed is the man who has many spiritual children born to God under his ministry; for his converts are his defence. Beholding the man who was healed standing with

Peter and John, they could say nothing against them. If souls are saved by the Gospel, the Gospel is proved in the surest manner. Let us care more about conversions than about organizations. If souls are brought into union with Christ, we may let other unions go.

We go yet further, and we come to great deeps: behold *God's joy in his people.* "He will rejoice over thee with joy." Think of this! Jehovah, the living God, is described as brooding over his Church with pleasure. He looks upon souls redeemed by the blood of his dear Son, quickened by his Holy Spirit, and his heart is glad. Even the infinite heart of God is filled with an extraordinary joy at the sight of his chosen. His delight is in his Church, his Hephzibah. I can understand a minister rejoicing over a soul that he has brought to Christ; I can also understand believers rejoicing to see others saved from sin and hell; but what shall I say of the infinitely-happy and eternally-blessed God finding, as it were, a new joy in souls redeemed? This is another of those great wonders which cluster around the work of divine grace! "He will rejoice over thee with joy." Oh, you are trembling for the ark of the Lord; the Lord is not trembling, but rejoicing. Faulty as the Church is, the Lord rejoices in her. While we mourn, as well we may, yet we do not sorrow as those that are without hope; for God does not sorrow, his heart is glad, and he is said to rejoice with joy—a highly emphatic expression. The Lord taketh pleasure in them that fear him, imperfect though they be. He sees them as they are to be, and so he rejoices over them, even when they cannot rejoice in themselves. When your face is blurred with tears, your eyes red with weeping, and your heart heavy with sorrow for sin, the great Father is rejoicing over you. The prodigal son wept in his Father's bosom, but the Father rejoiced over his son. We are questioning, doubting, sorrowing, trembling; and all the while he who sees the end from the beginning knows what will come out of the present disquietude, and therefore rejoices. Let us rise in faith to share the joy of God. Let no man's heart fail him because of the taunts of the enemy. Rather let the chosen of God rouse themselves to courage, and participate in that joy of God which never ceaseth, even though the solemn assembly has become a reproach. Shall we not rejoice in him when he, in his boundless

condescension, deigns to rejoice in us? Whoever despairs for
the cause, he does not; wherefore let us be of good courage.

It is added, "*He will rest in his love.*" I do not know any
Scripture which is more full of wonderful meaning than this.
"He will rest in his love," as if our God had in his people found
satisfaction. He comes to an anchorage: he has reached his
desire. Jesus sees of the travail of his soul when his people are
won to him; he has been baptized with his baptism for his
Church, and he is no longer straitened, for his desire is fulfilled.
The Lord is content with his eternal choice, content with his
loving purposes, satisfied with the love which went forth from
everlasting. He is well pleased in Jesus—well pleased with all
the glorious purposes which are connected with his dear Son,
and with those who are in him. He has a calm content in the
people of his choice, as he sees them in Christ. This is a good
ground for our having a deep satisfaction of heart also. We
are not what we would be; but then we are not what we shall
be. We advance slowly; but then we advance surely. The end
is secured by omnipotent grace. It is right that we should be
discontented with ourselves, yet this holy restlessness should
not rob us of our perfect peace in Christ Jesus. If the Lord hath
rest in us, shall we not have rest in him? If he rests in his love,
cannot we rest in it? My heart is comforted as I plainly see
in these words love unchanging, love abiding, love eternal:
"he will rest in his love." Jehovah changes not. Our Lord
died for his Church, and so long as he lives he will remember his
own love, and what it cost him: "Who shall separate us from
the love of God which is in Christ Jesus our Lord?" "He will
rest in his love."

The love of God to us is undisturbed: "The peace of God,
which passeth all understanding," dwells with his love: he is
not disquieted about it, but peacefully loves, and is never
moved. The calm of God is wonderful to contemplate: his
infallible knowledge and infinite power put him beyond fear
or question. He sees no cause of alarm as to his redeemed,
nor as to the cause of truth and the reign of righteousness.
As to his true Church, he knows that she is right, or that he will
make her right. She is being transformed into the image of
Jesus, and he rests in the full assurance that the image will ere
long be complete. He can carry out his own purposes in his

own way and time. He can see the harvest as well as the sowing; therefore he doth "rest in his love." You have seen a mother wash her child, and as she washes its face the child perhaps is crying, for it does not for the present enjoy the cleansing operation. Does the mother share the child's grief? Does she also cry? Oh, no! she rejoices over her babe, and rests in her love, knowing that the light affliction of the little one will work its real good. Often our griefs are no deeper than the cry of a child because of the soap in its eyes. While the Church is being washed with tribulations and persecutions, God is resting in his love. You and I are wearying, but God is resting.

"He will rest in his love." The Hebrew of this line is, "He shall be silent in his love." His happiness in his love is so great, that he does not express it, but keeps a happy silence. His is a joy too deep for words. No language can express the joy of God in his love; and therefore he uses no words. Silence in this case is infinitely expressive. One of the old commentators says, "He is deaf and dumb in his love," as if he heard no voice of accusation against his chosen, and would not speak a word of upbraiding to her. Remember the silence of Jesus, and expound this text thereby.

Sometimes also the Lord does not speak to his people: we cannot get a cheering word from him; and then we sigh for a promise, and long for a visit of his love; but if he be thus silent, let us know that he is only silent in his love. It is not the silence of wrath, but of love. His love is not changed, even though he does not comfort us.

> *His thoughts are high, his love is wise,*
> *His wounds a cure intend;*
> *And though he does not always smile,*
> *He loves unto the end.*

When he does not answer our prayers with his hand, he yet hears them with his heart. Denials are only another form of the same love which grants our petitions. He loves us, and sometimes shows that love better by not giving us what we ask than he could do if he spoke the sweetest promise which the ear has ever heard. I prize this sentence: "He will rest in his love."

My God, thou art perfectly content with thy Church after all, because thou knowest what she is to be. Thou seest how fair she will be when she comes forth from the washing, having put on her beautiful garments. Lo, the sun goes down, and we mortals dread the endless darkness; but thou, great God, seest the morning, and thou knowest that in the hours of darkness dews will fall which shall refresh thy garden. Ours is the measure of an hour, and thine the judgment of eternity, therefore we will correct our short-sighted judgment by thine infallible knowledge, and rest with thee.

The last word is, however, the most wonderful of all: *"He will joy over thee with singing."* Think of the great Jehovah singing! Can you imagine it? Is it possible to conceive of the Deity breaking into a song: Father, Son and Holy Ghost together singing over the redeemed? God is so happy in the love which he bears to his people that he breaks the eternal silence, and sun and moon and stars with astonishment hear God chanting a hymn of joy. Among Orientals a certain song is sung by the bridegroom when he receives his bride: it is intended to declare his joy in her, and in the fact that his marriage has come. Here, by the pen of inspiration, the God of love is pictured as married to his Church, and so rejoicing in her that he rejoices over her with singing.

If God sings, shall not we sing? He did not sing when he made the world. No; he looked upon it, and simply said that it was good. The angels sang, the sons of God shouted for joy: creation was very wonderful to them, but it was not much to God, who could have made thousands of worlds by his mere will. Creation could not make him sing; and I do not even know that Providence ever brought a note of joy from him, for he could arrange a thousand kingdoms of providence with ease. But when it came to redemption, that cost him dear. Here he spent eternal thought and drew up a covenant with infinite wisdom. Here he gave his Only-begotten Son and put him to grief to ransom his beloved ones. When all was done, and the Lord saw what became of it in the salvation of his redeemed, then he rejoiced after a divine manner. What must the joy be which recompenses Gethsemane and Calvary! The Lord God receives an accession to the infinity of his joy in the thought of his redeemed people. "He shall rejoice over thee with singing." I tremble while I speak of such themes, lest I should say a word that should dishonour the matchless mystery; but still we are glad to note what is written, and we are bound to take comfort from it. Let us have sympathy with the joy of the Lord, for this will be our strength.

I close with a brief word upon THE BRAVE CONDUCT SUGGESTED THEREBY. Let us not sorrow under the burdens which we bear, but rejoice in God, the great Burden-bearer, upon whom this day we roll our load. Here it is—"In that day it shall be said to Jerusalem, Fear thou not; and to Zion, Let not thine hands be slack."

There are three things for God's people to do. The first is, to *be happy*. Read verse fourteen—"Sing, O daughter of Zion; shout, O Israel; be glad and rejoice with all thy heart, O daughter of Jerusalem." Any man can sing when his cup is full of delights; the believer alone has songs when waters of a bitter cup are wrung out to him. Any sparrow can chirp in the daylight; it is only the nightingale that can sing in the dark. Children of God, whenever the enemies seem to prevail over you, whenever the serried ranks of the foe appear sure of victory, then begin to sing. Your victory will come with your song. It is a very puzzling thing to the devil to hear saints sing when he sets his foot on them. He cannot make it out: the more he oppresses them, the more they rejoice. Let us resolve to be all the merrier when the enemy dreams that we are utterly routed. The more opposition, the more we will rejoice in the Lord; the more discouragement, the more confidence. Splendid was the courage of Alexander when they told him that there were hundreds of thousands of Persians. "Yet," he said, "one butcher fears not myriads of sheep." "Ah!" said another, "when the Persians draw their bows, their arrows are so numerous that they darken the sun." "It will be fine to fight in the shade," cried the hero.

O friends, we know whom we have believed, and we are sure of triumph! Let us not think for a single second, if the odds against us are ten thousand to one, that this is a hardship; rather let us wish that they were a million to one, that the glory of the Lord might be all the greater in the conquest which is sure.

When Athanasius was told that everybody was denying the Deity of Christ, then he said, "I, Athanasius, against the

world": *Athanasius contra mundum* became a proverbial
expression. It is a splendid thing to be quite alone in the warfare of the Lord. Suppose we had half-a-dozen with us. Six
men are not much increase to strength, and possibly they may
be a cause of weakness, by needing to be looked after. If you
are quite alone, so much the better: there is the more room for
God. When desertions have cleaned the place out, and left
you no friend, now every corner can be filled with Deity,
"for great is the Holy One of Israel in the midst of thee."

The next duty is *fearlessness*: "Fear thou not." What! not
a little? No, "Fear thou not." But surely I may show some
measure of trembling? No, "Fear thou not." Tie that knot
tight about the throat of unbelief. "Fear thou not": neither this
day, nor any day of thy life. When fear comes in, drive it
away; give it no space. If God rests in his love, and if God
sings, what canst thou have to do with fear? Have you never
known passengers on board ship, when the weather was rough,
comforted by the calm behaviour of the captain? One simple-
minded soul said to his friend, "I am sure there is no cause for
fear, for I heard the captain whistling." Surely, if the captain
is at ease, and with him is all the responsibility, the passenger
may be still more at peace. If the Lord Jesus at the helm is
singing, let us not be fearing. Let us have done with every
timorous accent. O rest in the Lord, and wait patiently for
him. "Your God will come with vengeance, even God with a
recompense; he will come and save you."

Lastly, let us *be zealous*: "Let not thine hands be slack."
Now is the time when every Christian should do more for God
than ever. Let us plan great things for God, and let us expect
great things from God. "Let not thine hands be slack." Now
is the hour for redoubled prayers and labours. Since the
adversaries are busy, let us be busy also. If they think they
shall make a full end of us, let us resolve to make a full end
of their falsehoods and delusions. I think every Christian man
should answer the challenge of the adversaries of Christ by
working double tides, by giving more of his substance to the
cause of God, by living more for the glory of God, by being more
exact in his obedience, more earnest in his efforts, and more
importunate in his prayers. "Let not thine hands be slack."
in any one part of holy service.

XVII

OUR URGENT NEED OF THE HOLY SPIRIT

"Through the power of the Holy Ghost."—Rom. 15: 13.
"By the power of the Spirit of God."—Rom. 15: 19.

I DESIRE to draw your attention at this time to the great necessity which exists for the continual manifestation of the power of the Holy Spirit in the Church of God if by her means the multitudes are to be gathered to the Lord Jesus. I did not know how I could much better do so than by first showing that the Spirit of God is necessary to the Church of God for its own internal growth in grace. Hence my text in the thirteenth verse, "Now the God of hope fill you with all joy and peace in believing, that ye may abound in hope, through the power of the Holy Ghost," where it is evident that the apostle attributes the power to be filled with joy and peace in believing, and the power to abound in hope, to the Holy Ghost. But, then, I wanted also to show you that the power of the Church outside, that with which she is to be aggressive and work upon the world for the gathering out of God's elect from among men, is also this same energy of the Holy Spirit. Hence I have taken the nineteenth verse, for the apostle there says that God had through him made "the Gentiles obedient by word and deed, through mighty signs and wonders, by the power of the Spirit of God." So you see that first of all to keep the Church happy and holy within herself there must be a manifestation of the power of the Holy Spirit, and secondly, that the Church may invade the territories of the enemy and may conquer the world for Christ she must be clothed with the self-same sacred energy. We may then go further and say that the power of the Church for external work will be proportionate to the power which dwells within herself. Gauge the energy of the Holy Spirit in the hearts of believers, and you may fairly calculate their influence upon unbelievers. Only let the Church be illuminated by the Holy Spirit and she will reflect the light and become to onlookers "fair as the moon, clear as the sun, and terrible as an army with banners."

Let us by two illustrations show that the work outward must always depend upon the force inward. On a cold winter's day when the snow has fallen and lies deep upon the ground you go through a village. There is a row of cottages, and you will notice that from one of the roofs the snow has nearly disappeared, while another cottage still bears a coating of snow. You do not stay to make enquiries as to the reason for the difference, for you know very well what is the cause. There is a fire burning inside the one cottage and the warmth glows through its roof, and so the snow speedily melts: in the other there is no tenant; it is a house to let, no fire burns on its hearth and no warm smoke ascends the chimney, and therefore there lies the snow. Just as the warmth is within, so the melting will be without. I look at a number of Churches, and where I see worldliness and formalism lying thick upon them, I am absolutely certain that there is not the warmth of Christian life within; but where the hearts of believers are warm with divine love through the Spirit of God, we are sure to see evils vanish, and beneficial consequences following therefrom.

Take another illustration. If you lived in Egypt, you would notice, once in the year, the Nile rising; and you would watch its increase with anxiety, because the extent of the overflow of the Nile is very much the measure of the fertility of Egypt. Now the rising of the Nile must depend upon those far-off lakes in the centre of Africa—whether they shall be well filled with the melting of the snows or no. If there be a scanty supply in the higher reservoirs, there cannot be much overflow in the Nile in its after-course through Egypt. Let us translate the figure, and say that, if the upper lakes of fellowship with God in the Christian Church are not well filled—if the soul's spiritual strength be not sustained by private prayer and communion with God—the Nile of practical Christian service will never rise to the flood.

The one thing I want to say is this: you cannot get out of the Church what is not in it. The reservoir itself must be filled before it can pour forth a stream. We must ourselves drink of the living water till we are full, and then out of the midst of us shall flow rivers of living water; but not till then. Out of an empty basket you cannot distribute loaves and fishes, however hungry the crowd may be. Out of the fulness of the heart the mouth speaketh, when it speaks to edification at all. So that the first thing is to look well to home affairs, and pray that God would bless *us* and cause his face to shine upon *us*, that his way may be known upon earth, and his saving health among all people.

> *To bless thy chosen race,*
> *In mercy, Lord, incline,*
> *And cause the brightness of thy face*
> *On all thy saints to shine.*
>
> *That so thy wondrous way*
> *May through the world be known;*
> *Whilst distant lands their tribute pay,*
> *And thy salvation own.*

In trying to speak of the great necessity of the Church, namely, her being moved vigorously by the power of the Holy Spirit, I earnestly pray that we may enter upon this subject with the deepest conceivable reverence. Let us adore while we are meditating; let us feel the condescension of this blessed Person of the Godhead in deigning to dwell in his people and to work in the human heart. Let us remember that this divine person is very sensitive. He is a jealous God. We read of his being grieved and vexed, and therefore let us ask his forgiveness of the many provocations which he must have received from our hands. With lowliest awe let us bow before him, remembering that, if there be a sin which is unpardonable, it has a reference to himself—the sin against the Holy Ghost, which shall never be forgiven, neither in this world nor in that which is to come. In reference to the Holy Ghost we stand on very tender ground indeed; and if ever we should veil our faces and rejoice with trembling, it is while we speak of the Spirit, and of those mysterious works with which he blesses us. In that lowly spirit, and under the divine overshadowing follow me while I set before you seven works of the Holy Spirit which are most necessary to the Church for its own good, and equally needful to her in her office of missionary from Christ to the outside world.

To begin, then, the power of the Holy Ghost is manifested in the QUICKENING of souls to spiritual life. All the spiritual life which exists in this world is the creation of the Holy Spirit, oy whom the Lord Jesus quickeneth whomsoever he will. You and I had not life enough to know our death till he visited us, we had not light enough to perceive that we were in darkness, nor sense enough to feel our misery: we were so utterly abandoned to our own folly that, though we were naked and poor, and miserable, we dreamed that we were rich, and increased in goods. We were under sentence of death as condemned criminals, and yet we talked about merit and reward; yea, we were dead, and yet we boasted that we were alive—counting our very death to be our life. The Spirit of God in infinite mercy came to us with his mysterious power, and made us live. The first token of life was a consciousness of our being in the realm of death, and an agony to escape from it; we began to perceive our insensibility, and, if I may be pardoned such an expression, we saw our blindness. Every growth of spiritual life, from the first tender shoot until now, has also been the work of the Holy Spirit. As the green blade was his production, so is the ripening corn. The increase of life, as much as life at the beginning, must still come by the operation of the Spirit of God, who raised up Christ from the dead. You will never have more life except as the Holy Ghost bestows it upon you; yea, you will not even know that you want more, nor groan after more, except as he worketh in you to desire and to agonise, according to his own good pleasure. See, then, our absolute dependence upon the Holy Spirit; for if he were gone we should relapse into spiritual death, and the Church would become a charnel-house.

The Holy Spirit is absolutely needful to make everything that we do to be alive. We are sowers, but if we take dead seed in our seed-basket there will never be a harvest. The preacher must preach living truth in a living manner if he expects to obtain a hundred-fold harvest. How much there is of Church work which is nothing better than the movement of a galvanized corpse. How much of religion is done as if it were performed by an automaton, or ground off by machinery. Now-a-days men care little about heart and soul, they only look at outward performances. Men can give mechanically, and come to the communion table mechanically: yes, and we ourselves shall do so unless the Spirit of God be with us. Most hearers know what it is to hear a live sermon which quivers all over with fulness of energy; you also know what it is to sing a hymn in a lively manner, and you know what it is to unite in a live prayer meeting; but, ah, if the Spirit of God be absent, all that the Church does will be lifeless, the rustle of leaves above a tomb.

As the Spirit of God is a quickener to make us alive and our work alive, so must he specially be with us to make those alive with whom we have to deal for Jesus. Imagine a dead preacher preaching a dead sermon to dead sinners: what can possibly come of it? Here is a beautiful essay which has been admirably elaborated, and it is coldly read to the cold-hearted sinner. It smells of the midnight oil, but it has no heavenly unction, no divine power resting upon it, nor, perhaps, is that power even looked for. What good can come of such a production? As well may you try to calm the tempest with poetry or stay the hurricane with rhetoric as to bless a soul by mere learning and eloquence. It is only as the Spirit of God shall come upon God's servant and shall make the word which he preaches to drop as a living seed into the heart that any result can follow his ministry; and it is only as the Spirit of God shall then follow that seed and keep it alive in the soul of the listener that we can expect those who profess to be converted to take root and grow to maturity of grace, and become our sheaves at the last.

We are utterly dependent here, and for my part I rejoice in this absolute dependence. If I could have a stock of power to save souls which would be all my own apart from the Spirit of God, I cannot suppose a greater temptation to pride and to living at a distance from God. It is well to be weak in self, and better still to be nothing: to be simply the pen in the hand of the Spirit of God, unable to write a single letter upon the tablets of the human heart except as the hand of the Holy Spirit shall use us for that purpose. That is really our position, and we ought practically to take it up; and doing so we shall continually cry to the Spirit of God to quicken us in all things, and quicken all that we do, and quicken the word as it drops into the sinner's ear. I am quite certain that a Church which is devoid of life cannot be the means of life-giving to the dead sinners around it. No. Everything acts after its kind, and we must have a living Church for living work. Oh that God would quicken every member of this Church! "What," say you, "do you think some of us are not alive unto God?" There are some of you concerning whom I am certain, as far as one can judge of another, that you have life, for we can see it in all that you do; but there are some others of you concerning whose spiritual life one has to exercise a good deal of faith and a great deal more charity, for we do not perceive in you much activity in God's cause, nor care for the souls of others, nor zeal for the divine glory. If we do not see any fruits, what can we do but earnestly pray that you may not turn out to be barren trees?

Next it is one of the peculiar offices of the Holy Spirit to ENLIGHTEN his people. He has done so by giving us his Word, which he has inspired; but the Book, inspired though it be, is never spiritually understood by any man apart from the personal teaching of its great Author. You may read it as much as you will, and never discover the inner and vital sense unless your soul shall be led into it by the Holy Ghost himself. The Spirit of God must come and make the letter of truth alive to you, transfer it to your heart, set it on fire and make it burn within you, or else its divine force and majesty will be hid from your eyes. No man knows the things of God save he to whom the Spirit of God has revealed them. We may use language as plain as a pikestaff, but the man who has no spiritual understanding is a blind man, and the clearest light will not enable him to see. Ye must be taught of the Lord, or you will die in ignorance. Now, suppose that in a Church there should be many who have never been thus instructed, can you not see that evil must and will come of it? Error is sure to arise where truth is not experimentally known. Half of the heresy in the Church of God is not wilful error, but error which springs of not knowing the truth, not searching the Scriptures with a teachable heart, not submitting the mind to the light of the Holy Ghost. We should, as a rule, treat heresy rather as ignorance to be enlightened than as crime to be condemned; save, alas, that sometimes it becomes wilful perversity, when the mind is greedy after novelty, or puffed up with self-confidence: then other treatment may become painfully necessary. Beloved, if the Spirit of God will but enlighten the

Church thoroughly there will be an end of divisions. Schisms are generally occasioned by ignorance, and the proud spirit which will not brook correction. On the other hand, real, lasting, practical unity will exist in proportion to the unity of men's minds in the truth of God. Hence the necessity for the Spirit of God to conduct us into the whole truth. If you think you know a doctrine, ask the Lord to make sure that you know it, for much that we think we know turns out to be unknown when times of trial put us to the test. Nothing do we really know unless it be burnt into our souls as with a hot iron by an experience which only the Spirit of God can give.

I think you will now see that, the Spirit of God being thus necessary, for our instruction, we pre-eminently find in this gracious operation our strength for the instruction of others; for how shall those teach who have never been taught? How shall men declare a message which they have never learned? "Son of man, eat this roll"; for until thou hast eaten it thyself thy lips can never tell it out to others. "The husbandman that laboureth must first be a partaker of the fruits." It is the law of Christ's vineyard that none shall work therein till first of all they know the flavour of the fruits which grow in the sacred enclosure. Thou must know Christ, and grace, and love, and truth thyself before thou canst even be an instructor of babes for Christ.

When we come to deal with others, earnestly longing to instruct them for Jesus, we perceive even more clearly our need of the Spirit of God. You think you will put the Gospel so clearly that they *must* see it; but their blind eyes overcome you. Ah! you think you will put it so zealously that they *must* feel it; but their clay-cold hearts defeat you. You may think you are going to win souls by your pleadings, but you might as well stand on the top of a mountain and whistle to the wind, unless the Holy Spirit be with you. After all your talking, your hearers will, perhaps, have caught *your* idea, but the mind of the Spirit, the real soul of the Gospel, you cannot impart to them; this remains, like creation itself, a work which only God can accomplish. Daily, then, let us pray for the power of the Spirit as the Illuminator. Come, O blessed light of God! thou alone canst break our personal darkness, and only when thou hast enlightened us can we lead others in thy light.

Thirdly, one work of the Spirit of God is to create in believers the spirit of ADOPTION. "Because ye are sons, God hath sent forth the Spirit of his Son into your hearts, whereby ye cry, Abba, Father!" "For ye have not received the spirit of bondage again to fear, but ye have received the Spirit of adoption, whereby we cry, Abba, Father!" We are regenerated by the Holy Spirit, and so receive the nature of children; and that nature, which is given by him, he continually prompts, and excites, and develops, and matures; so that we receive day by day more and more of the child-like spirit. Now, beloved, this may not seem to you to be of very great importance at first sight; but it is so; for the Church is never happy except as all her members walk as dear children towards God. Sometimes the spirit of slaves creeps over us: we begin to talk of the service of God as though it were heavy and burdensome, and are discontented if we do not receive present wages and visible success, just as servants do when they are not suited; but the spirit of adoption works for love, without any hope of reward, and it is satisfied with the sweet fact of being in the Father's house, and doing the Father's will. This spirit gives peace, rest, joy, boldness, and holy familiarity with God. A man who never received the spirit of a child towards God does not know the bliss of the Christian life; he misses its flower, its savour, its excellence, and I should not wonder if the service of Christ should be a weariness to him because he has never yet got to the sweet things, and does not enjoy the green pastures, wherein the Good Shepherd makes his sheep to feed and to lie down. But when the Spirit of God makes us feel that we are sons, and we live in the house of God to go no more out for ever, then the service of God is sweet and easy, and we accept the delay of apparent success as a part of the trial we are called to bear.

Now, mark you, this will have a great effect upon the outside world. Bring me a Church made up of children of God, a company of men and women whose faces shine with their heavenly Father's smile, who are accustomed to take their cares and cast them on their Father as children should, who know they are accepted and beloved, and are perfectly content with the great Father's will; put them down in the midst of a company of ungodly ones, and I will warrant you they will begin to envy them their peace and joy. Thus happy saints become most efficient operators upon the minds of the unsaved.

Fourthly, the Holy Spirit is especially called the Spirit of HOLINESS. He never suggested sin nor approved of it, nor has he ever done otherwise than grieve over it: but holiness is the Spirit's delight. The Church of God wears upon her brow the words, "Holiness to the Lord." Only in proportion as she is holy may she claim to be the Church of God at all. An unholy Church! Surely this cannot be her of whom we read, "Christ also loved the church, and gave himself for it; that he might sanctify and cleanse it with the washing of water by the word, that he might present it to himself a glorious church, not having spot, or wrinkle, or any such thing." Holiness is not mere morality, not the outward keeping of divine precepts out of a hard sense of duty, while those commandments in themselves are not delightful to us. Holiness is the entirety of our manhood fully consecrated to the Lord and moulded to his will. This is the thing which the Church of God must have, but it can never have it apart from the Sanctifier, for there is not a grain of holiness beneath the sky but what is of the operation of the Holy Ghost.

After all, the acts of the Church preach more to the world than the words of the Church. Put an anointed man to preach the gospel in the midst of a really godly people and his testimony will be marvellously supported by the Church with which he labours; but place the most faithful minister over an ungodly Church, and he has such a weight upon him that he must first clear himself of it, or he cannot succeed. He may preach his heart out, he may pray till his knees are weary, but conversions will be sorely hindered, if indeed they occur at all. There is no likelihood of victory to Israel while Achan's curse is on the camp. An unholy Church makes Christ to say that he cannot do many mighty works there because of its iniquity.

Do you not see in this point our need of the Spirit of God? And when you get to grappling terms with sinners, and have to talk to them about the necessity of holiness, and a renewed heart, and a godly life coming out of that renewed heart, do you expect ungodly men to be charmed with what you say? What cares the unregenerate mind for righteousness? Was a carnal man ever eager after holiness? Such a thing was never seen. As well expect the devil to be in love with God as an unredeemed heart to be in love with holiness. But yet the sinner must love that which is pure and right, or he cannot enter heaven. *You* cannot make him do so. Who can do it but that Holy Ghost who has made you to love what once you also despised? Go not out, therefore, to battle with sin until you have taken weapons out of the armoury of the Eternal Spirit.

Fifthly, the Church needs much PRAYER, and the Holy Spirit is the Spirit of grace and of supplications. The strength of a Church may pretty accurately be gauged by her prayer-fulness. We cannot expect God to put forth his power unless we entreat him so to do. Our great High Priest will put into his censer no incense but that which the Spirit has compounded. Prayer is the creation of the Holy Ghost. We cannot do without prayer, and we cannot pray without the Holy Spirit; and hence our dependence on him.

Furthermore, when we come to deal with sinners, we know that they must pray. "Behold he prayeth" is one of the earliest signs of the new birth. But can *we* make the sinner pray? Can any persuasion of ours lead him to his knees to breathe the penitential sigh and look to Christ for mercy? If you have attempted the conversion of a soul in your own strength you know you have failed; and so you would have failed if you had attempted the creation of one single acceptable prayer in the heart of even a little child. Oh then, let us cry to our heavenly Father to give the Holy Spirit to us; let us ask him to be in us more and more mightily as the spirit of prayer, making inter-cession in us with groanings that cannot be uttered, that the Church may not miss the divine blessing for lack of asking for it. I do verily believe this to be her present weakness, and one great cause why the kingdom of Christ does not more mightily spread: prayer is too much restrained, and hence the blessing is kept back; and it will always be restrained unless the Holy Ghost shall stimulate the desires of his people. O blessed Spirit, we pray thee make us pray, for Jesus' sake.

Sixthly, the Spirit of God is in a very remarkable manner the giver of FELLOWSHIP. So often as we pronounce the apostolic benediction we pray that we may receive the communion of the Holy Ghost. The Holy Ghost enables us to have communion with spiritual things. He alone can take the key and open up the secret mystery, that we may know the things which be of God. He gives us fellowship with God himself: through Jesus Christ by the Spirit we have access to the Father. Our fellowship is with the Father and with his Son Jesus Christ, but it is the Spirit of God who brings us into communion with the Most High. So, too, our fellowship with one another, so far as it is Christian fellowship, is always produced by the Spirit of God. If we have continued together in peace and love these many years, I cannot attribute it to our constitutional good tempers, nor to wise management, nor to any natural causes, but to the love into which the Spirit has baptized us, so that rebellious nature has been still. If a dozen Christian people live together for twelve months in true spiritual union and unbroken affection, trace it to the love of the Spirit; and if a dozen hundred, or four times that number, shall be able to persevere in united service, and find themselves loving each other better after many years than they did at the first, let it be regarded as a blessing from the Comforter, for which he is to be devoutly adored. Fellowship can only come to us by the Spirit, but a Church without fellowship would be a disorderly mob, a kingdom divided against itself, and consequently it could not prosper. You need fellowship for mutual strength, guidance, help, and encouragement, and without it your Church is a mere human society. Let us daily cry to him to work in us brotherly love, and all the sweet graces which make us one with Christ, that we all may be one even as the Father is one with the Son, that the world may know that God hath indeed sent Jesus, and that we are his people.

Seventhly, we need the Holy Spirit in that renowned office which is described by our Lord as THE PARACLETE, or Comforter. The word bears another rendering, which our translators have given to it in that passage where we read, "If any man sin we have an advocate (or Paraclete) with the Father." The Holy Spirit is both Comforter and Advocate.

The Holy Spirit at this present moment is our friend and *Comforter*, sustaining the sinking spirits of believers, applying the precious promises, revealing the love of Jesus Christ to the heart. Many a heart would break if the Spirit of God had not comforted it. Many of God's dear children would have utterly

died by the way if he had not bestowed upon them his divine
consolations to cheer their pilgrimage. That is his work, and
a very necessary work, for if believers become unhappy they
become weak for many points of service. I am certain that the
joy of the Lord is our strength, for I have proved it so, and
proved also the opposite truth. There are on earth certain
Christians who inculcate gloom as a Christian's proper state,
I will not judge them, but this I will say, that in evangelistic
work they do nothing, and I do not wonder. Till snow in
harvest ripens wheat, till darkness makes flowers blossom, till
the salt sea yields clusters bursting with new wine, you will
never find an unhappy religion promotive of the growth of the
kingdom of Christ. You must have joy in the Lord, if you are
to be strong *in* the Lord, and strong *for* the Lord. Now, as the
Comforter alone can bear you up amid the floods of tribulation
which you are sure to meet with, you see your great need of
his consoling presence.

We have said that the Spirit of God is the *Advocate* of the
Church—not with God, for there Christ is our sole Advocate—
but with man. What is the grandest plea that the Church has
against the world? I answer, the indwelling of the Holy Ghost,
the standing miracle of the Church. External evidences are
very excellent. You young men who are worried by sceptics
will do well to study those valuable works which learned and
devout men have with much labour produced for us, but,
mark you, all the evidences of the truth of Christianity which
can be gathered from analogy, from history, and from external
facts, are nothing whatever compared with the operations of
the Spirit of God. These are the arguments which convince.

A man says to me, "I do not believe in sin, in righteousness,
or in judgment." Well, the Holy Ghost can soon convince him.
If he asks me for signs and evidences of the truth of the Gospel,
I reply, "Seest thou this woman; she was a great sinner in the
very worst sense, and led others into sin, but now you cannot
find more sweetness and light anywhere than in her. Hearest
thou this profane swearer, persecutor, and blasphemer? He is
speaking with purity, truth, and humbleness of mind. Observe
yon man, who was aforetime a miser, and see how he consecrates
his substance. Notice that envious, malicious spirit, and see how
it becomes gentle, forgiving, and amiable through conversion.

How do you account for these great changes? They are happening here every day, how come they to pass? Is that a lie which produces truth, honesty, and love? Does not every tree bear fruit after its kind? What then must that grace be which produces such blessed transformations? The wonderful phenomena of ravens turned to doves, and lions into lambs, the marvellous transformations of moral character which the minister of Christ rejoices to see wrought by the Gospel, these are our witnesses, and they are unanswerable. Peter and John have gone up to the temple, and they have healed a lame man; they are soon seized and brought before the Sanhedrim. This is the charge against them—"You have been preaching in the name of Jesus, and this Jesus is an impostor." What do Peter and John say? They need say nothing, for there stands the man that was healed; he has brought his crutch with him, and he waves it in triumph, and he runs and leaps. He was their volume of evidences, their apology, and proof. "When they saw the man that was healed standing with Peter and John, they could say nothing against them."

If we have the Spirit of God amongst us, and conversions are constantly being wrought, the Holy Spirit is thus fulfilling his advocacy, and refuting all accusers. If the Spirit works in your own mind, it will always be to you the best evidence of the Gospel. I meet sometimes one piece of infidelity, and then another; for there are new doubts and fresh infidelities spawned every hour, and unstable men expect us to read all the books they choose to produce. But the effect produced on our mind is less and less. This is our answer. It is of no use your trying to stagger us, for we are already familiar with everything you suggest; our own native unbelief has outstripped you. We have had doubts of a kind which even you would not dare to utter if you knew them; for there is enough infidelity and devilry in our own nature to make us no strangers to Satan's devices. We have fought most of your suggested battles over and over again in the secret chamber of our meditation and have conquered. For *we have been in personal contact with God*. You sneer, but there is no argument in sneering. We are as honest as you are, and our witness is as good as yours in any court of law; and we solemnly declare that we have felt the power of the Holy Spirit over our soul as much as ever old

ocean has felt the force of the north wind: we have been stirred
to agony under a sense of sin, and we have been lifted to
ecstasy of delight by faith in the righteousness of Christ. We
find that in the little world within our soul the Lord Jesus
manifests himself so that we know him. There is a potency
about the doctrines we have learned which could not belong to
lies, for the truths which we believe we have tested in actual
experience. Tell us there is no such thing as light? We do not
know how we can prove its existence to you, for you are probably blind, but *we* can see. That is enough argument for us,
and our witness is true. Tell us there is no spiritual life! We
feel it in our inmost souls. These are the answers with which
the Spirit of God furnishes us, and they are a part of his
advocacy.

See, again, how entirely dependent we are on the Spirit of
God for meeting all the various forms of unbelief which arise
around us; you may have your societies for collecting evidence,
and you may enlist all your bishops and doctors of divinity
and professors of apologetics, and they may write rolls of
evidence long enough to girdle the globe, but the only person
who can savingly convince the world is the Advocate whom the
Father has sent in the name of Jesus. When he reveals a man's
sin, and the sure result of it, the unbeliever takes to his knees.
When he takes away the scales and sets forth the crucified
Redeemer, and the merit of the precious blood, all carnal
reasonings are nailed to the Cross. One blow of real conviction
of sin will stagger the most obstinate unbeliever, and afterwards, if his unbelief return, the Holy Ghost's consolations will
soon comfort it out of him. Therefore, as at the first so say I
at the last, all this dependeth upon the Holy Ghost, and upon
him let us wait in the name of Jesus, beseeching him to manifest
his power among us.

XVIII

DRESSING IN THE MORNING

"And that, knowing the time, that now it is high time to awake out of sleep: for now is our salvation nearer than when we believed. The night is far spent, the day is at hand: let us therefore cast off the works of darkness, and let us put on the armour of light. Let us walk honestly, as in the day; not in rioting and drunkenness, not in chambering and wantonness, not in strife and envying. But put ye on the Lord Jesus Christ, and make not provision for the flesh, to fulfil the lusts thereof."—Rom. 13: 11-14.

THIS passage is a piece of holy teaching set forth under the parable of rising in the morning and preparing for the work of the day. May the Holy Spirit help me to place it before you in a clear light.

It is a great mistake in a man's life when he does not know the times in which he lives, and how to act in them; and when he does not know the time as to the day of his own life, so as to apply his heart unto wisdom. The apostle speaks of His Roman brethren as "*knowing the time*." What, then, is the time of day with the Christian? It is no longer the dead of the night with us; but "the night is far spent, the day is at hand." A little while ago the dense darkness of ignorance was about us; but the Gospel has made us light in the Lord. We lay asleep in the gloom of sin; like a thick cloud it enveloped all our powers; but God hath brought us out of darkness into his marvellous light. Some of us were plunged in despair, a night without a moon, without a star; we were without hope, and feared that our future would be the "blackness of darkness for ever." That hopeless gloom is over, and we have light and joy in Christ Jesus.

The day-star is shining upon us, the light that lighteneth the Gentiles cheers our path, and we look for a perfect day. It is not as yet full day with us. Cloudless brightness is still a thing of desire and expectation. The sun has risen, but it is not noon as yet. For that we look when we shall see the Well-beloved in his kingdom, and wake up in his likeness. "The day is at hand," says the apostle, and that is a word of good cheer.

What, then, is "the time" which Paul would have us know? It is the early morning, it is the dawning of the eternal day. The sun has scattered the thick darkness of nature's night; we are enjoying his first golden beams: the time of the singing of birds has come, the time of the dew of grace, and of the fresh breath of the Spirit. It is not full day yet; but, still, the night has gone, and the perfect day of our salvation, when body and soul too shall be delivered from every taint and trace of the work of Satan, is "nearer than when we believed." The light and heat of day are strengthening; the darkness and chill of night are vanishing; we are getting further off from the power of ignorance, sin, and despair; we are getting more and more under the influence of knowledge, holiness, and hope. The apostle would have us know of a surety that the true light now shineth, even that which will grow brighter and brighter into the perfect day. Joy be to our souls, the Sun of righteousness hath risen upon us with healing beneath his wings.

Of what value is the knowledge of the time of day? It lies here. Certain duties arise out of the hour. "Man goeth forth unto his work and to his labour until the evening." From morning to evening, and from evening to morning again, there is a round of duty to be fulfilled, and each work is comeliest if attended to in its own season. When the shadows of evening fall the time has come for going home, where domestic joys await us at the hearth. It would not be right for the labouring man to go home in the morning, nor seemly for him to be going out at night. Each duty has its own time of day, and therefore the apostle would have us know the hour and be assured that it is high time to awake out of sleep. He urges us to the duties which attend the hour of rising, the hour to which we have now come.

First, LISTEN TO THE MORNING CALL.

I have shown you that the hour of the day is that in which men should rise and begin their daily service; and its first seasonable duty is to *awake*—"It is high time to awake out of sleep." When day begins sleep should end. The bugle sounds in the camp, "Awake! Awake!" But are not all Christians awake? Yes, from the sleep of death, but not from other kinds of sleep. Many need rough shaking and loud calling before they will be thoroughly awakened. You should rise from the sleep of inaction. Do not let your religion consist in receiving all and doing nothing. Work while it is called today, and as you wish to be faithful servants of your gracious Lord. Up, gird up your loins and yield your bodies a living sacrifice, holy, acceptable unto God.

Leave also all lethargy behind you. At night a man may yawn and stretch himself as he likes; but when the morning comes, good sir, have done with yawning, and display energy. Look about you and be brisk for the day will be none too long. Does not the song of the birds and the glitter of the dew bid you shake off your slumber and have done with listlessness? Oh, I hate to see some professing Christian people go about the Lord's work in such a languid way, as if it did not matter how their Lord was served. Ah me! If God was obeyed with half the activity with which the devil is served we should soon see a change in church life. Men are wide awake enough when they are serving themselves. Jingle a guinea seven miles off and they will hear it; but if service is to be done for Christ you must put the clarion to your mouth and blow a blast as loud as the judgment summons before you can wake up to hearty enthusiasm. It is high time that we woke out of half-heartedness.

Moreover, it is time to have done with dreaming. That is proper for the night, but not for the morning. An ungodly man's pursuits are mere dreams; he hunteth after shadows, he feedeth upon ashes; his weightiest business is a mere vision, a thing of nought. You who are not of the night, must not dote on the world's shadows, but look for heavenly substance. Live for eternal realities. Have done with day dreams as well as night dreams and come to stern matters of eternal fact. Trifle no longer; the time past may suffice you for that. Be earnest! Be all awake, put forth all your powers, arouse all your faculties. It is high time to awake out of sleep.

When awake, what is the next duty? Is it not to *cast off your night clothes?* Our text saith, "Let us therefore cast off the works of darkness." The man who is just awakened, and finds that it is morning light, must first of all put off the garments which covered him during the night. He quits his bed,

and in so doing shakes off his bed clothes and leaves them.
Your friends do not come downstairs wrapped in the sheets
which wrapped them at night; we should suppose they were
seeking their graves if they did so. The coverlet of night is not
our covering by day. There must be a putting off in the morning before there can be a putting on; there is a measure of
undressing before we commence to dress. Simply and homely
as the figure is, it conveys a lesson which I pray you to remember. Sins and follies are to be cast off when we put on the
garments of light. I have known a man profess to be converted,
but he has merely put religion over his old character. He has
been a passionate man with bad companions, and all he has
done is to carry his bad temper into a church-meeting. He
has been accustomed to drink more wine than is good for him,
and all the change is that he drinks it in respectable company
or in secret. He has taken up the saint without casting off the
sinner. The rags of his lust are rotting under the raiment of
his profession. This will never do; Christ has not come to save
you *in* your sins but *from* your sins. Anger and drunkenness
and such like, must be got rid of; Christ never came that you
might christen your anger by the name of warmth, and your
drunkenness with the name of liberty. I have heard of persons
living unclean lives who have heard that faith in Jesus Christ
would save them, who have misunderstood this doctrine so
grievously that they have thought of believing in Christ, and
continuing in their evil ways. The rags of sin must come off
if we put on the robe of Christ. There must be a taking away
of the love of sin, there must be a renouncing of the practices
and habits of sin, or else a man cannot be a Christian. It will
be an idle attempt to try and wear religion as a sort of celestial
overall over the top of old sins. The vision of Zechariah teaches
us the way of the Lord: when he saw Joshua clothed with
filthy garments, the Lord did not put upon him a goodly
vesture over these; but he first said, "Take away the filthy
garments from him," and then he added, "Behold I have
caused thine iniquity to pass from thee, and I will clothe thee
with change of raiment." You must be cleansed in the blood
of Jesus before you can be clothed in the white linen which
is the righteousness of the saints. See to it that, being awakened
out of your sleep, ye put off all the garments of the night.

So far we have described our getting up: now *we must put on our morning dress*. The believer should at once look to his toilet and array himself for the day: "Let us put on the armour of light." "What," says one, "armour? Why, I thought my danger was over. The darkness has departed, and I am no longer afraid of thieves and robbers, for the daylight has come. Why then, should I put on armour?" Is it not instructive that no sooner do we awake than we have to put on "the whole armour of God"? Does it not warn us that a day of battle is coming? You may as well expect a conflict, for it is sure to come, and it will be wise to put on your harness for the fight. Dress according to what you will meet with during the day. You are not at home yet; the land of peace is yet beyond you. Young converts think that they have got to heaven, or very near it; but it is not so: you *will* get there one day; but the time is not yet. You are in an enemy country: put on the armour of light. Perhaps before you get down to breakfast an arrow will be shot at you by the great enemy; or you may come downstairs after your morning prayer feeling as safe as if you were among the angels, and yet you will not get through the first meal in the day without an assault from the arch-enemy, or an outburst of your own corruptions, or an attack from the world. Your foes may be found in your own household, and they may wound you at your own table. Before you leave your bedchamber you had better put on girdle, helmet, breast-plate, shield—you had better take the complete panoply. A Christian is never safe unless he is protected from head to foot by grace, for in such a world as this you know not behind what bush the assassin may be lurking, or from what corner the fatal bolt may fly. Go forth as a mailed knight to the war, for the battle rages on all sides, and you need the armour of righteousness on the right hand and on the left.

The Greek word, however, may be understood to signify not only armour, but such garments as are fitted and suitable for the day's work. These should be put on at once, and our soul should be dressed for service. Pray God to clothe you in such style that you may be ready for whatever comes. You are not a gentleman on the parade, but a workman in his workday clothes. Some people are too fine to do real service for the Lord. When the Duke of Wellington asked one of our soldiers how he would like to be dressed if he had to fight the battle of Waterloo again, he answered that he should like to be in his shirt sleeves. How I wish that Christians would get into their shirt sleeves, as if they meant work for Jesus. I like to see the carpenter with his apron on bending down to his work, and not sitting on the bench swinging his legs all day. Alas, that some Christians should be usually seen in this latter posture! It is morning with you, and I beseech you, by the mercies of God, array yourselves to do your Lord's bidding. What said God to Jeremiah? "Gird up thy loins and arise." Brace your soul to action: there is work for you to do today which angels might well envy you. Go forth like a man ready for work. The Lord would have us live with our loins girt about, our lamps trimmed and our lights burning, because we have come to an hour when idleness and inaction are out of place, and earnest, watchful diligence is required of us. For our Father worketh hitherto, and Jesus works.

Now you are dressed, what next? *It remains that we walk forth and behave as in the light.* The directions are explicit— "Let us walk honestly, as in the day," which means, let our demeanour be such as becomes daylight. How should a child of light conduct himself?

The word translated "honestly," may mean decently—with decorum and dignity. In the middle of the night, if you have to go about the house, you are not particular as to how you are dressed; there is no person to see you, and so you will slip from one room to another in dishabille; but when you rise in the morning, and come down to your day's work, you choose to be somewhat neat. You do not go out to your business slip-shod and half-dressed. Let it be so with you spiritually: holiness is the highest decency, the most becoming apparel. You live in the daylight, therefore walk as one who is "compassed about with so great a cloud of witnesses." Yet more, walk as one who has the eye of God upon him, which is infinitely more. "Thou, God, seest me." King of kings, should I rush into thy court in dishabille? The soul's toilet should be a matter of great care. "Be ye clean," saith God. He will not walk with us unless we keep our garments unspotted from the world: he would have us observe that dignity of spirit and conduct which are becoming in the temple of God.

"Walk honestly," says our translation, because that is the right thing for daylight. The thief breaks through and steals beneath the cover of the darkness; but a child of light must be upright and just. I earnestly beg all professing Christians to be honest in heart, and then they will be honest in word and deed. You ask me, "Do you mean that we should pay our debts?" Of course, I mean all that, but I mean far more: be honest when you speak to others and of others. Do not say of any man behind his back that which you would not utter to his face. Do not carry a mask about with you, it is a horrible instrument of torture to an honest man. Say what you mean, and mean what you say. Walk honestly; let all your actions be such as will bear the light. A man that stands under a powerful electric light bearing right down on him, could feel uncomfortable with everybody looking at him; at any rate, he would be careful what he did. Behold, the light of eternity is shining full upon your soul, God himself sees you, you stand in the blaze of the eternal day. O Christian man, act with transparent honesty; have nothing to conceal: come to the light, that your deeds may be made manifest that they are wrought in God. Be clothed with light, and walk in the light as God is in the light.

Our position in the light of the morning demands of us one more point of behaviour: *we must renounce the deeds of darkness.* If we have been truly awakened, and have put on the garments of light, it behoves us to have done with the things that belong to the night. I will not dwell upon them at any great length; but I may not pass them over, since the apostle thought it necessary to mention three pairs of evils with which we must have done. He mentions them because even in Christian assemblies it is necessary to denounce these things. People exclaim against the preacher if he speak plainly home about the vices of the times. "Really, it is shocking," says one, "I do not like to hear such indelicate things referred to." No, no, ladies and gentlemen who do such things cannot bear to hear of them by way of rebuke. I have noticed that none are more fantastically nice than the morally nasty; none are so ready to find fault when a spade is called a spade as those whose morals most want digging. They will commit the vice themselves, but they cannot bear to hear it mentioned—it shocks their marvellously delicate minds. The apostle Paul felt none of the noxious

daintiness which touches sin with a delicate hand; he speaks
out plainly, and he says that all Christian people, first, must
have done with *sensuality*, which he describes as "rioting and
drunkenness." If a drinking bout is held it is usually at night.
Banquets generally begin in the evening; if they become
scenes of gluttony and drunkenness they advance far into the
night; but the sun rebukes such orgies, and men usually give
heed to the warning: "they that be drunken are drunken in
the night." Christian men have done with night, and ought
to have done with all excess in meat and drink. Alas, there are
some who spend more over a single dinner for a few than would
keep families of poor people a month. Gluttony is seldom
mentioned as a possible fault, and yet I fear it is far from being
an obsolete vice among professed followers of Jesus. "Drunkenness," well I need not say how shameful it is in any man;
but he that professes to be a Christian man, how temperate,
how abstinent should he be; for intoxication is a soul-destroying
sin, and no drunkard can enter the kingdom of God. These are
night vices; let the children of night have them if they will:
as for us, we desire to be filled with the Spirit and fed upon the
bread of heaven, for we are the children of the day.

Then Paul denounces *impurity* by saying, "not in chambering
and wantonness." It is an awful thing when a man calls himself
by the name of Christian, and yet can be foul in language,
unchaste in conversation, lascivious in spirit, wicked in life.
If any man indulges in fornication and adultery, and yet calls
himself a Christian, he will surely come under the curse of God.
We speak of such persons weeping, for they are the enemies of
the cross of Christ. Oh that you who are young might be kept
from anything like looseness or effeminacy. Avoid glances,
words, and thoughts which tend that way. Do not go near the
borders of that sin; for men and women sin not grossly all at
once, they slide by degrees, as the vessel slides from the stocks
into the sea at the time of its launching. It moves very little at
the first; but by-and-by it gathers impetus, and glides rapidly
into the deep. O you who have reached the morning light,
abhor these things, and hate even the garment spotted by the
flesh.

The next night deed is *passion;* passion taking the two
shapes of "strife and envying." Brawls are for the night.

Fierce assaults disturb us in our sleep, but they are not usual in the day. So Christian men, being of the day, are not to strive. It is a great pity when strife comes into a family, when brother is divided from brother and father from son, and when relatives cannot speak well of one another. These bitter things are for the night: you have reached the daylight, and must have done with them! Envy is a thing of darkness and shame. Sinners do not like good men because their excellence rebukes them, and hence they endeavour to mar their reputation. This evil is not of the day: leave it, scorn it, dread it, abhor it. God deliver you from it! Away, then, from all deeds of darkness, and seek only that which may be set in the face of the sun and cause no man to blush.

Now, I have preached so long upon things required of you that you are beginning to say, "Ah me, how much there is for us to do! How shall we ever accomplish it? We have to wake to put off our night garments, to dress in suitable attire, to behave ourselves as children of light, and to avoid the deeds of darkness. Alas, what shall we do?" Now listen, ye anxious ones; here is something sweet and blessed for you: you shall be inclined and helped to obey in all things; therefore hearken diligently and hear, that your souls may live. I preach to you THE MORNING GOSPEL. Here it is—"Put ye on the Lord Jesus Christ."

The verse has been rendered very famous in church history, since the chief among the fathers, the mighty teacher Augustine, found the light through reading this verse. He had been leading an ungodly and more or less dissipated life when he began in a measure to think upon his condition, and he thought he heard a voice saying to him. "Tolle, lege. Tolle, lege!" "Take up and read." So, taking up the New Testament which lay near, he began to read it, and, as God would have it, he opened upon this very place, and he read: "Let us walk honestly, as in the day; not in rioting and drunkenness, not in chambering and wantonness, not in strife and envying. But put ye on the Lord Jesus Christ." Here are his words, which I will read to you: "I would read no further, for I needed not; for when I had read to the end of this sentence all the darkness of doubtfulness vanished away, as if some clear light of security were poured into my heart. It was as if it had been said, 'O man, acknowledge thy misery, thou art naked; cover thy filthiness: *put upon thee Jesus Christ!'* And forthwith I felt a fire within me. My heart was lightened, the scales fell from mine eyes—I was able to see!" How earnestly do I desire that these words may strike some of you in the same powerful manner. Does any-one here desire to put off his old garments of sin and to dress in robes of holiness? And does he mourn over an empty ward-robe? See, here is a robe for him—"Put ye on the Lord Jesus Christ." Did I hear one cry, "You told us to put on armour, but we have neither shield nor breastplate; how can we put on the armour of light?" Here is the panoply—"Put ye on the Lord Jesus Christ." Does the man cry, "I am afraid to go into the world undressed, and I dare not put on the old garments of darkness; but what can I do?" Here it is; here is the death of sin and life of holiness—"Put ye on the Lord Jesus Christ." Oh, blessed, charming word, I wish I had the power fully to set forth its meaning before you.

For, first, in the Lord Jesus Christ, there is *covering for your nakedness.* The garment covers the man; he is hidden, and his garments are seen. Come then, poor sinner, and take by faith the Lord Jesus Christ to be a covering for your soul. You are naked, but he will be your robe of righteousness. There is in the Lord Jesus a complete and suitable apparel for thy soul, by which every blemish and defilement shall be put out of sight, according to the word, "Blessed is he whose transgression is forgiven, and whose sin is covered." In Christ Jesus there is merit to cover our demerit, purity to cover our impurity, obedience to cover our disobedience, beauty to cover our deformity, perfection to cover our imperfection, acceptance to cover our provocation. We are comely with the comeliness which the Lord Jesus puts upon us. He is seen, and we are hidden, or only seen in him so as to be accepted in the Beloved. We have nothing to do but to enter into Christ by faith; for, virtually, that is what a man has to do with his garments: he gets into them, and so he who puts on Christ is in Christ, Christ is over him and round about him.

"Put ye on the Lord Jesus Christ." Was there ever a sweeter message? You, poor soul, just awakened out of sleep, and startled into saying, "What must I do to be saved?" Here is Jesus set before you; he is perfect in righteousness, matchless in holiness, unrivalled in beauty, and you may put him on and stand clothed in that righteousness and beauty. I hear you say, "I see him, but how is he to be mine?" He is yours by God's free gift: put him on! You have not to improve upon him, or add to him, or embellish him, but to take him as you take your coat, and put him on. There he is, he is a robe that delights to be worn. Myriads of souls have tried this garment, and it has been exactly suitable to every one out of all who have put it on. This is all you have to do, to put it on, and that the Holy Spirit will help you to do. You have not to make the garment, to decorate the garment, or in any way to add to it or to alter it, but only to put it on.

This is a most vivid picture of what faith does. She puts Christ about her, and he covers all. Faith does not say, "I must clothe myself and then put on Christ." No, no! its cry is, "Because I am naked I cover myself with Christ." The soul saith, "I have nothing of my own that God can look upon with complacency, but I will put on Christ, for I know in him God is well pleased." The sufferings of Jesus will be set to my account, his merits shall avail for me, and his righteousness shall be my righteousness. Oh it is a blessed, blessed word. Put on the Lord Jesus Christ, and sing, "He hath clothed me with the garments of salvation, he hath covered me with the robe of righteousness."

"Ay," saith one, "I need more than just to be covered, I must have *a garment provided for my necessity*; suitable for my every-day work." My text points you to a full supply: "Put ye on the Lord Jesus Christ" as the most suitable dress for a saint at work, as well as for a sinner desiring justification before God.

As we have already said, a first necessity is to awake, and truly none can lie and dream after they have once beheld his glorious robe; they are eager to obtain it. Our next necessity is to cast off the old garments of the night, and nothing helps us more than to put on Christ. Only look at this robe of righteousness as yours, and you will loathe the filthy rags of sin at once. When a man perceives the perfection of the righteousness of Christ, which is freely given to him of God, he abhors his sin, he loves his God, and pines to be like him in holiness. There is no breeder of repentance like simple faith in Jesus Christ. Unbelieving philosophers tell us that if we preach salvation by faith in Christ alone people will take

licence to sin; but in this they err from want of observation.
Now speak your own experience, Christian man: did you ever
feel yourself moved to sin by the assurance of being justified
by Christ's righteousness? Never was there such a case in this
world. A man may hear about it and turn it into an excuse
for sin, but he cannot in his heart believe it and do so. I know
that when I most clearly see that I am saved by Christ alone
it is then that I most of all pine to be holy. I never follow after
personal righteousness so eagerly as when I know that my
righteousness comes wholly from the Lord. The grandest
motive power for the death of sin is the death of Christ; and
nothing makes us so eager to die *unto* sin as Christ's death *for*
sin. Off goes the filthy raiment at the sight of the glorious,
spotless righteousness which is freely presented to every needy
sinner in Christ Jesus.

Ay, and it is not only repentance that is thus wrought by
Christ, but all the power to be holy, to be gracious, to be forgiving, to be heroic, to be enthusiastic in the service of God, all
comes through Christ when we are in him. If you desire to be
holy in life the short path to it is to have done with your own
righteousness and put on Christ. If the man who has been a
drunkard resolves to be sober let him put on Christ, and in Jesus
he will deny himself. If the man who has been unchaste would
fain be pure in life and heart, let him put on the Lord Jesus
Christ, and make no provision for the flesh to fulfil the lusts
thereof. There is such a matchless power about a simple faith
in Christ, when it puts on Christ to be our righteousness, that
it leads the believer to such a walk as is decorous, dignified,
honourable, holy. The man is moved to walk worthy of the
noble garment in which he is arrayed, and his whole life rises
out of the common level into the excellence of grace.

The text says, "Put ye on the Lord Jesus Christ." What
made him use the three names there? Because he meant to
point out the three senses in which we clothe ourselves from
head to foot with Christ. "Put ye on the Lord," become his
servant, wear his livery, let him be your Rabbi, your Master,
your King, your Lord. Put ye on "Jesus" the Saviour, acknowledge yourself as a saved one, saved by him whose name is called
Jesus "for he shall save his people from their sins." Put ye
no "Christ,"—that is the Anointed: take an anointing from

God the Holy Spirit through Jesus Christ to whom he is given without measure. As Christ is anointed to be prophet, priest, and king, put him on in all these three offices and rejoice to do so. "Put ye on the Lord Jesus Christ." Do not put on Jesus only as your Saviour, put him on as your Commander. Do not only put him on as your Master and Saviour, but as your Christ, anointed for you. Take a whole Christ to yourself that you may be wholly in him, and so may be spiritual, gracious, holy. Henceforth may those around you see nothing of you, but much of your Lord. May your outward character be so Christ-like that men may see Christ displayed upon you, as a new garment is displayed by the act of wearing it. May the spirit of glory out of Christ rest upon you. May you be clothed with power. Our Lord said to his disciples "Tarry at Jerusalem until ye are endued with power from on high"—the word signifies "clothed." If we are clothed with Christ we shall be clothed with power from on high; even as he has said "the works that I do shall ye do also." Therefore put ye on the Lord Jesus Christ.

"Yes," but I hear another say, "I want not only raiment to cover my nakedness and supply my necessity, but I want *apparel for my dignity*. You told us that we were to walk abroad in a worthy and honourable manner." Ah, and so you will if you put on Christ. Oh what a bright creature in the sight of God is the man who has put on Christ. God himself asks no purer or more acceptable array. If you put on Christ, so that you become like to Christ, your walk and conversion will be bright and lustrous before the eyes of those about you. They, perhaps, will not like it, they may even hate you for it, but they will not be able to do otherwise than own your excellence. He who lives in Christ lives a charming life, which, by its love-liness, commands the homage of onlookers. "Put ye on the Lord Jesus Christ."

"Ay," says another, "but you have forgotten part of your sermon. You said that now we were awake we were to put on armour." I have not forgotten, for Christ is *armour for our defence*, therefore put on the Lord Jesus Christ. Here is a coat of mail for you. The man that does as Christ would do, and thinks as Christ would think, and lives as Christ would live, and makes Christ to be all in all to him, and thus armours himself with Christ, is thereby made impervious to the shafts of the enemy, and amid the darts of temptation or the arrows of slander he may abide unharmed. The Lord is our defence, and the Holy One of Israel is our King.

"Ay," saith one, "but you told us that the day when it was once up would never again darken into night, but brighten into a perfect day." It is even so, and here is *raiment provided for our expectancy*. We may expect to meet with years of mingled conflict, service, and suffering. "Put ye on the Lord Jesus Christ" and you will be prepared for all weathers, fair or foul, and for all conditions and requirements. This garment will never wax old: it will last you all the desert through, and, what is more, it is suitable for Canaan, and you shall keep it on for ever and ever. We need a dress that we can wear in all the events which will happen in the awful future, the endless future. It is on this account that I press home the words of my text— "Put ye on the Lord Jesus Christ." Our Lord is a fit robe for life and death, for time and for eternity. I expect to battle till I die; here is my armour, the integrity and uprightness which I learn of Christ will preserve me. I expect in death to rise out of this lower life into a higher one; and when I reach that higher life, that glory life, I shall require a dress, and I shall find it in my Lord. I cannot have a better garment than the Lord himself and there is a wedding coming on! Every believer expects to be married to his Lord. Then, dear friend, you must certainly have a wedding dress. How can you go in unto the marriage feast, not having on a wedding garment? but here you have it: "Put ye on the Lord Jesus Christ." When the King comes in to see his guests, and he sees Jesus Christ covering them all, he will be well pleased. He will see his dear Son reflected in them all, and from them all, and his delight shall be in them, even as it is in his Son. If you put on the Lord Jesus Christ you will be fit for the inspection of the King, fit for all the royalties and pomps of the eternal marriage, fit to stand in the coronation of Christ himself as one of the many brethren of the crowned Firstborn. May the Lord Jesus now be made unto you wisdom, righteousness, sanctification, and redemption.

XIX

THE SOUND IN THE MULBERRY TREES

"When thou hearest the sound of a going in the tops of the
mulberry trees, that then thou shalt bestir thyself: for then
shall the Lord go out before thee, to smite the host of the
Philistines."—2 Sam. 5: 24.

DAVID had just fought the Philistines in this very valley, and
gained a signal victory; so that he said, "the Lord hath
broken forth upon mine enemies before me as the breach of
waters." The Philistines had come up in great hosts, and had
brought their gods with them, that like Israel, when the ark of the
Lord was brought into their midst, they might feel quite sure of
victory. However, by the help of God David easily put them to
rout, burned their images in the fire, and obtained a glorious
victory over them. Note, however, that when they came a
second time against David, David did not go up to fight them,
without enquiring of the Lord. Once he had been victorious;
he might have said, as many of us have said, in fact, in other
cases—"I shall be victorious again; I may rest quite sure that
if I have triumphed once I shall triumph yet again. Wherefore
should I go and seek at the Lord's hands?"

Not so, now, David. He had gained one victory by the strength
of the Lord; he would not venture upon another, until he had
ensured the same. He went and asked the sacred oracle, "Shall
I go up against them?" and when he was informed that he was
not immediately to march against them, but to encamp so as to
surprise them at the mulberry trees, he did not demur a single
moment to the mandate of God; and when he was bidden to
wait until he should hear the sound in the tops of the mulberry
trees before he went to fight, he was not in an ill haste to rush
to battle at once, but he tarried until the mulberry trees began
to sing at the top by reason of the wind that rushed along the
leaves. He would wait until God's sign was given; he said, "I
will not lift my spear nor my hand till God hath bidden me do

it, lest I should go to war at my own charges, and lose all I have obtained."

Let us learn from David to take no steps without God. The last time you moved, or went into another business, or changed your situation in life, you asked God's help, and then did it, and you were blessed in the doing of it. You have been up to this time a successful man, you have always sought God, but do not think that the stream of providence necessarily runs in a continuous current; remember, you may tomorrow without seeking God's advice venture upon a step which you will regret but once, and that will be until you die. You have been wise hitherto, it may be because you have trusted in the Lord with all your heart, and have not leaned to your own understanding; you have said like David, "Let us enquire of the Lord," and like Jehoshaphat, who said to Ahab, "I will not go up until I have enquired of the Lord"; and you have not to ask priests of Baal, but you have said, "Is there not here one, a prophet of the Lord, that I may enquire at his hands?" Now, keep on in the same way. If Providence tarries, tarry till Providence comes; never go before it. He goes on a fool's errand who goes before God, but he walks in a blessed path who sees the footsteps of Providence, and reads the map of Scripture, and so discovers, "This is the way wherein I am to walk." This may be imputed to some one here; I thought I would begin with it, for it may be I have some young man who is about unadvisedly to take a step which may be his ruin, temporarily; I beseech him, if he loves the Lord, not to venture until he has sought counsel of God, and unless he has a firm conviction that he is doing it not merely for his own advantage but to help him in serving his God the better.

Thus I have introduced the text: but now I would refer to it in another way altogether. David was not to go to battle, until he heard a sound of a rustling in the tops of the mulberry trees. There was a calm, perhaps; and God's order to David was, "You are not to begin to fight until the wind begins rustling through the tops of the mulberry trees"; or as the Rabbis have it, and it is a very pretty conceit if it be true, the footsteps of angels walking along the tops of the mulberry trees make them rustle; that was the sign for them to fight, when God's cherubim were going with them, when they should come, who can walk through the clouds and fly through the air, led by the great

Captain himself, walking along the mulberry trees, and so make a rustle by their celestial footsteps. How true that may be, I cannot tell; my remark is only this—that there are certain signs which ought to be indications to us of certain duties. I shall use the verse in this way.

First, then, in regard to SPECIAL DUTIES. I shall confine myself, I think, to one. The office of the ministry is a special duty. I do not believe, as some do, that it is the business of everyone of us to preach; I believe it is the business of a great many people who do preach to hold their tongues. I think that if they had waited until God had sent them they would have been at home now; and there be some men who are not fit to edify a doorpost, who yet think that if they could but once enter the pulpit they would attract a multitude. They conceive preaching to be just the easiest thing in all the world, and while they have not power to speak three words correctly, and have not any instruction from on high, and never were intended for the pulpit, for the mere sake of the honour or the emolument, they rush into the ministry. They would be doing more to serve God and to serve the church if they would take a business and preach now and then as they had time to study, or else give it up altogether and let somebody come and preach to the people who had something to tell them. For alas, alas, a preacher who has nothing to say will not only do no good, but will do a great deal of harm. The people who hear him get disgusted at the very name of a place of worship; and they only look at it as a kind of stocks, where they are to sit for an hour with their feet fast, quiet and still, listening to a man who is saying nothing, because he has nothing to say. I would not advise all of you to be preachers; I do not believe God ever intended that you should. If God had intended all his people to be preachers, I wonder how even He in his wisdom could have found them all congregations; because were all preachers where were the hearers? No, I believe the office of the ministry, though not like that of the priesthood, as to any particular sanctity, or any particular power that we possess, is yet like the priesthood in this—that no man ought to take it to himself, save he that is called thereunto, as was Aaron. No man has any right to address a congregation on things spiritual, unless he believes that God has given him a special calling to the work, and unless he has also in due time received

certain seals which attest his ministry as being the ministry of
God. The rightly ordained minister is ordained not by the laying
on of bishops' or presbyter's hands, but by the Spirit of God
himself, whereby the power of God is communicated in the
preaching of the word.

There may be some who will say, "How am I to know whether
I am called to preach?" You will find it out by-and-by, I dare
say; and if you are sincerely desirous to know when you are in
the path of duty in endeavouring to preach, I must bid you do as
David did. He noted the rustling in the leaves of the mulberry
trees. And I must have you notice certain signs. Do you want
to know whether you can preach? Ask yourself this question,
"Can I pray? When I have been called upon in the prayer
meeting, have I been enabled to put my words together and has
God helped me in the matter?" So far so good. "Well then I will
go and try, I will preach in the street, for instance." Suppose
nobody listens to me, suppose I go and take a room, or go to a
chapel, and nobody comes to hear, well, there is no rustling
among the mulberry trees; I had better stop. Suppose I go to
my wife and children, and take a text, and just preach a little
wee bit to them and to the neighbours; suppose, after I have
preached to them, I should feel that they could preach a great
deal better to me, there is no rustling among the mulberry trees,
and I had better give it up. And suppose if, after having
preached for some time, I hear of none who have been brought
to Christ, there is no rustling among the mulberry trees, I
think the best thing I could do is, to let somebody else try; for
suppose I have not been called to the ministry, it would have
been a fearful thing for me to have occupied the watchman's
place, without having received the watchman's commission.

I ask you these questions. Have you tried to address a
Sabbath school? have you gained the attention of the children?
Having tried to address a few people, when they have been
gathered together, have you found they would listen to you
after you had preached? Had you any evidence and any sign
that would lead you to believe that souls were blessed under you?
Did any of the saints of God who were spiritually-minded, tell
you that their souls were fed by your sermon? Did you hear of
any sinner convinced of sin? Have you any reason to believe
that you have had a soul converted under you? If not, I believe

it is advice which God's Holy Spirit would have me give you; you had better give it up. You will make a very respectable Sunday School teacher, you will do very well in a great many other ways; but unless these things have been known by you, unless you have these evidences, you may say you have been called, and all that; I don't believe it. If you had been called to preach, there would have been some evidence and some sign of it.

I would discourage none; I would say to every young man who has a grain of ability, and believes he has been called of God, and everyone who has really been blessed, "So far as I can help you I will help you; I will do so to the very uttermost, if you need my help; and I pray God Almighty to bless you, and make you more and more abundantly useful; for the Church needs many pastors and evangelists." But if there is no soul converted under you, if you are not qualified to preach at all, you shall have my equally earnest prayers for you that God may speed you—and I shall pray for you in this way, that God will speed you by making you hold your tongue. I waited till I heard the sound among the mulberry trees, else had I been uncalled and unsent. David waited; he would not go to the battle till he had heard the signal from on high, which was the signal for the battle, and the signal of the commencement of warfare.

But now I come to something more practical to many of you; you do not profess to be called to preach; THERE ARE CERTAIN DUTIES BELONGING TO ALL CHRISTIANS WHICH ARE TO BE SPECIALLY PRACTISED AT SPECIAL SEASONS. First, concerning *the Christian Church at large.* The whole of the Christian Church should be very prayerful, always seeking the unction of the Holy One to rest upon their hearts, that the kingdom of Christ may come and that his will be done on earth even as it is in heaven; but there are times when God seems to favour Zion, when there are great movements made in the church, when revivals are commenced, and when men are raised up whom God blesses; that ought to be to you like "a sound of a going in the tops of the mulberry trees." We ought then to be doubly prayerful, doubly earnest, wrestling more at the throne, than we have been wont to do. I hear the noise amongst the mulberry trees. Everywhere I hear of the doctrine of grace being made more prominent, and the preaching of the Gospel becoming

more earnest, more energetic, and more full of the Spirit. We
have seen in our midst some called out of our church, whom God
has blessed in the preaching of the Word. There is in many
places, "the sound of a going in the tops of the mulberry trees."
Now is the time for us to bestir ourselves. Oh let us cry to God
more earnestly; let our prayer meetings be filled with men who
come full of vehement petitions, let our private altars be more
constantly kept burning, causing the smoke of prayer to ascend,
and let our closets continually be occupied by earnest intercession. Bestir thyself: there is a "sound of a going in the tops of
the mulberry trees."

That is concerning the Church at large; the same truth holds
good of *any particular congregation.* One Sabbath day the minister
preached with great unction; God clothed him with power, he
seemed like John the Baptist in the wilderness, crying, "Repent
ye, for the kingdom of heaven is at hand." He spake with all
the earnestness of a man who was about to die; he so spake that
the people trembled, a visible thrill passed through the audience.
Every eye was fixed, and the tears seemed to bedew every cheek.
Men and women rose up from the sermon, saying, "Surely, God
was in this place, and we have felt his presence." What ought a
Christian man to say, as he retires from the house of God?
He should say, "I have heard this day the sound of the leaves
of the mulberry trees." I saw the people earnest; I marked the
minister speaking mightily, God having touched his lips with a
live coal from off the altar. I saw the tear in every eye; I
saw the deep, wrapt attention, of many who were careless.
There were some young people there that looked as if they had
been impressed; their countenances seemed to show that there
was a work doing. Now, what should I do? The first thing I will
do is, I will bestir myself. But how shall I do it? Why, I will
go home this day, and I will wrestle in prayer more earnestly
than I have been wont to do that God will bless the minister,
and multiply the Church.

Well, what next? Where do I sit? Was there a young woman
in my pew that seemed impressed? When I go this evening I
will look out for her; I have heard the "sound of the leaves of
the mulberry trees," and I will bestir myself; and if I see her
there, I will speak a word to her; or, what is more, if I hear
another sermon like it, and I see any who seem to be impressed,

I will try to find them out; for I know that two words from a private person are often better than fifty from a minister. So that if I have seen a young man impressed, I will touch him on his elbow and say, "You seemed as if you enjoyed this sermon." "Yes, I liked it very well." "And do you like spiritual things?" Who can tell? I may be made the means of his conversion. At all events, I shall have this sweet consolation to go to bed with, that I heard the "sound of the leaves of the mulberry trees," and as soon as I heard it I bestirred myself that I might serve my God, and be the means of winning souls from hell.

But, alas! much of the seed we sow seems to be lost for want of watering. Many an impressive sermon seems to lose much of its force, because it is not followed up as it should be. God's purposes, I know, are answered, his Word does not return unto him void; still, I think we might sometimes ask ourselves, have we not been too dilatory, too neglectful in not availing ourselves of favourable times and seasons, when the power of the Spirit has been in our midst, and when we should have looked upon it as the signal for more strenuously exerting ourselves in the service of our Master.

Keep the same idea in view in regard to *every individual* you meet with. If you have a drunken neighbour; it is very seldom you can ever say a word to him. His wife is ill; she is sick and dying, poor fellow, he is sober this time. He seems to be a bit impressed; he is anxious about his wife, and anxious about himself. Now is your time; now for the good word; put it in well. Now is your opportunity. If you see a man a little impressed, and he is open to conviction, do what you can. If any of your acquaintance have been in the house of God, if you have induced them to go there, and *you think* there is some little good doing but you do not know, take care of that little, it may be God hath used us as a foster-mother to bring up his child, so that this little one may be brought up in the faith, and this newly converted soul may be strengthened and edified.

But I'll tell you, many of you Christians do a deal of mischief by what you say when going home. A man once said that when he was a lad he heard a certain sermon from a minister, and felt deeply impressed under it. Tears stole down his cheeks, and he thought within himself, "I will go home to pray." On the road home he fell into the company of two members of the church. One of them began saying, "Well, how did you enjoy the sermon?" The other said, "I do not think he was quite sound on such a point." "Well," said the other, "I thought he was rather off his guard," or something of that sort; and one pulled one part of the minister's sermon to pieces, and another the other, until, said the young man, before I had gone many yards with them, I had forgotten all about it; and all the good I thought I had received seemed swept away by these two men, who seemed afraid lest I should get any hope, for they were just pulling that sermon to pieces that would have brought me on my knees. How often have we done the same! People will say, "What did you think of that sermon?" I gently tell them nothing at all, and if there is any fault in it—and very likely there is, it is better not to speak of it, for some may get good from it. I do believe that many a sermon that seems nothing but perfect nonsense from beginning to end may be the means of salvation. You and I may have more knowledge of the Scriptures, we may be more instructed and enlightened: we may say, "Dear me, I do not know how people can hear that." You may think people are not able to hear it, but they are saved; that is all you have to look after.

And I think I must expressly make an appeal to you in regard to *your own children*. There are certain times in the history of my own beloved children, when they seem more impressible than at other seasons; I beseech you never lose the opportunity. Salvation is of God, from first to last; but yet it is your business to use all the means, just as if you could save them. Now there are times when your son, who is generally very gay and wild, comes home from chapel and there is a sort of solemnity about him you do not often see. When you see that, get a word with him. Sometimes your little daughter comes home; she has heard something she understands, something that seems to have struck her thoughts. Do not laugh at her, do not despise that little beginning. Who can tell? It may be the "sound in the tops of the mulberry trees." Your son, a boy of fourteen or fifteen, is often coming home apparently deeply interested, and sometimes you have thought, "Well, I do not know, the boy seems as if he listened rather more than others do. I think there must be a good work in him." Do not, by any harshness of yours, put a rough hand on that tender plant; do not say to him, for instance, if he commits a little fault, "I thought there was some good thing in you, but there is no piety in you at all, or else you would not have done it." Do not say that, that is a damper at once. Remember, if he be a child of God he has his faults as well as any other boy. Therefore do not be too harsh or severe with him, but if you find the slightest good say, There is the "sound in the tops of the mulberry trees."

There may be ever such a faint rustling, never mind, that is my opportunity; now will I be more earnest about my child's salvation, and now will I seek to teach him, if I can, more fully the way of God; I will try to get him alone and talk to him. The tender plant, if it be of God, it is sure to grow; but let me take care to be the instrument of fostering it, and let me take my boy aside, and say to him, "Well, my son, have you learnt something of the evil of sin?" And if he says yes, and I find he has a little hope and faith, though it may be rather a superficial work let me not despise it, but let me remember, I was once grace in the blade, and though grace in the ear now, I would never have been grace in the ear if I had not been grace in the blade. I must not despise the blades, because they are not ears; I must not kill the lambs, because they are not sheep; for where would my sheep come from, if I killed all the lambs? I must not despise the weakest of the saints, for where should I get the advanced saints from, if I put weak ones out of the covenant, and tell them they are not the children of God? No, I will watch for the least indication, the least sign of any good thing towards the Lord God of Israel, and I will pray God that these signs may not be delusive, not like the smoke that is driven away, nor like the early cloud and the morning dew, but the abiding signs of grace begun, which shall be afterwards grace complete.

And lastly, in regard to *yourself* there is a great truth here. There are times, you know, "when thou hearest the sound of a going in the tops of the mulberry trees." You have a peculiar power in prayer; the Spirit of God gives you joy and gladness; the Scripture is open to you: the promises are applied; you walk in the light of God's countenance, and his candle shines about your head; you have peculiar freedom and liberty in devotion; perhaps you have got less to attend to in the world and more closeness of communion with Christ than you used to have. Now is the time; now, when you hear the "sound of a going in the tops of the mulberry trees." Now is the time to bestir yourselves; now is the time to get rid of any evil habit that still remains; now is the season in which God the Spirit is with you. But spread your sail;

> *I can only spread the sail;*
> *Thou Lord must breathe the auspicious gale.*

Be sure you have the sail up. Do not miss the gale, for want of preparation for it. Seek help of God, that you may be more earnest in duty, when made more strong in faith; that you may be more constant in prayer, when you have more liberty at the throne; that you may be more holy in your conversation, whilst you live more closely with Christ.

XX

CONSOLATION FROM RESURRECTION

"I will ransom them from the power of the grave; I will redeem them from death: O death, I will be thy plagues; O grave, I will be thy destruction: repentance shall be hid from mine eyes."—Hos. 13: 14.

THIS verse stands in the midst of a long line of threatenings. Like a rock of mercy, it rises in the midst of a sea of wrath. Hence many critics have felt bound to see in it a continuation of threatening. I am quite content to accept the united authority of the Authorized and the Revised Versions, and to be'ieve that the mind of the Holy Spirit is fairly expressed in the grand old Bible of our fathers. I regard our text as a promise overflowing with delight.

Israel was coming to its very worst. The people were to be carried to Babylon, and thence to be scattered to the ends of the earth. Yet the Lord, in his great love, lets them know that this was not to be final and entire destruction. He would not utterly cast away the people whom he did foreknow, nor allow death to hold them in bondage for ever. He would open their graves, and bring them out, and make them to know Jehovah. Therefore, he drops in this word of promise when it was least expected.

I shall ask you first, to CONSIDER THE FACT WHICH IS HERE USED AS A FIGURE. The resurrection of the dead is here employed as a figure of that which the Lord was about to do for his people. At one time salvation from sin is called a creation, and creation is a fact; here it is a resurrection from the dead, and that also is sure to be accomplished in due time: we have the first-fruits of it already.

There will be a special resurrection for those who are in Christ Jesus. "There shall be a resurrection of the dead, both of the just and unjust." But for the members of the body of Christ there is a resurrection from among the dead. These are the many that sleep in the dust of the earth who shall awake to everlasting life (Dan. 12 : 2). They rise because they are one with Christ in his resurrection. His resurrection is the proof and the guarantee that they also shall rise in the day of his appearing. "If Christ be in you, the body is dead because of sin; but the spirit is life because of righteousness" (Rom. 8 : 10). Their bodies, which were redeemed as truly as their souls, though left during this life under mortgage to nature, so that they suffer pain, and weakness, and ultimate death and decay— their bodies, I say, being a part of the purchase of the precious blood, shall be raised again from the dead. That which is sown in weakness shall be raised in power; that which is covered with dishonour by the very fact of death and decay shall be raised in splendour, made like unto the glorious body of Christ. This is no poetic fiction, but a literal matter of fact, even as was the resurrection of the Lord Jesus. We hear our Redeemer say, "Thy brother shall rise again," and we accept it literally. Our dear ones whom we have laid in the grave shall come again from the land of the enemy. Concerning ourselves, also, we believe,

> *Sweet truth to me,*
> *I shall arise,*
> *And with these eyes*
> *My Saviour see.*

We accept the doctrine of the resurrection of the dead as the revelation of Christianity. The immortality of the soul was seen before the appearing of our Lord in a dim and cloudy manner; but the resurrection of the dead was not discoverable by the light of nature, and when it was at first preached, men called the preacher a "babbler"; they could not understand that such a thing could be. The philosophy of human nature rejected the resurrection, and rejects it still. Only by the revelation of Christ do we know that the dead shall rise again.

This resurrection is connected with redemption: "I will ransom them from the power of the grave." A ransom is the paying of a price for something. There was a price paid for us, to deliver us from the death which is the desert of sin. You know who paid it, and how he paid it. Remember how he opened wide his hands, and poured forth more than gold; remember how his side was digged by the spear, that the deep mines of his life-wealth might be emptied out for us. Jesus our Lord has paid the ransom price. Now are we "waiting for the adoption, to wit, the redemption of our body" (Rom. 8: 23).

Another word is used in the parallel sentence of our text— "I will redeem them from death." It refers to the redemption of an inheritance by the next-of-kin. "I know that my Redeemer liveth" is the ground of Job's confidence as to his resurrection and justification. My *goel*, my next-of-kin, to whom the right of redemption belonged in equity, has stepped in, and has fully redeemed both my soul and my body. What a blessed truth is this, that the ransom of the body is paid, so that this corruptible must put on incorruption, and this mortal must put on immortality! Though the body remains for a while subject to vanity, yet the term of this subjection will soon run out, the ransom being already paid. Regeneration has liberated the soul, and resurrection will do the like for the body before long.

The margin hath it, "I will ransom them from the hand of the grave: I will redeem them from death." O beloved, we come into the grave's hand, as it were, and firm is the grip of the sepulchre; but our God saith, "I will redeem them from the hand of the grave." Glory be to God for the sure hope of resurrection! Beloved, there remains nothing due upon the estate of our bodies for which they can be detained in the dust when the Lord Jesus comes to awaken them from their long sleep. They shall freely rise to be reunited with the disembodied but happy spirits to which they belong. We look for a resurrection from among the dead. "But the rest of the dead lived not again until the thousand years were finished. This is the first resurrection. Blessed and holy is he that hath part in the first resurrection: on such the second death hath no power" (Rev. 20: 5, 6).

This, according to our text, is *wrought entirely by divine power*. It must be so; for how could the dead contribute to their own lives? How can bodies which have been dissolved in the sepulchre reconstruct themselves? Here you have in the text the divine personality asserting itself four times— "I will ransom them," "I will redeem them"; "O death, I will be thy plagues"; "O grave, I will be thy destruction."

Who but he that made can re-make? But all things are possible
to the Creator. We have heard many objections raised to the
doctrine of the resurrection. Let them object as long as they
please. Grant us a God, and nothing is impossible or even
difficult. With a God who can work miracles nothing becomes
incredible. What a triumph will the resurrection be for the
Lord God! He hath been pleased to give the special honour
of it to his own dear Son. By the risen Christ we shall be raised
again from the dead. We shall sing hallelujahs to him that
was slain. He by death has destroyed death, and by his resurrection has torn away the gates of the grave. This is our
Lord's doings, and we adore him because of it.

Observe, next, that *by the resurrection death itself is transformed, and totally overcome.* He saith, "O death, I will be thy
plagues," as if death were personified, and then itself plagued—
its own arrows of pestilence being shot into itself. Beloved,
death no longer kills, but rather admits to a larger life; it no
more destroys, but the rather it perfects—I mean not of itself,
but through our Lord Jesus Christ. It is no longer death to
die; it is no longer punishment to the believer, but a dismissal
from banishment. Ye that are in your sins will die in your sins,
and to you death is death indeed; but to the child of God, death
is so altered that he who hath the power of death, that is, the
devil, is sore vexed. He is plagued by seeing the joy with
which the believer dies. It is a grand thing to see a man dying
full of life: the river of his mortal life comes to an end, but only
by widening into the ocean of the glory-life above. Satan
gloated over the mischief which he had wrought by death; but
lo, it is through death that Jesus has destroyed him, and
delivered his people. God makes his dying people to be like
the sun, which never seems so large as when it sets. All the
glories of mid-day are eclipsed by the marvels of sunset. Watch
the west! See how the clouds are mountains of gold, and anon
the skies are seas of fire. All the tapestries of heaven are hung
out to welcome the returning hero of the day to his rest beyond
the western sea. So does the dying saint light up his dying
chamber with heavenly splendour as he sets upon this world
to shine in another. Thus the Lord plagues death, leaving the
monster powerless to harm or even terrify the believer.

As for the sepulchre, it is destroyed. "O grave, I will be thy destruction.'' No grave shall detain one of the redeemed. The tomb is

> *No more a charnel-house, to fence*
> *The relics of lost innocence;*
> *A place of ruin and decay*
> *The imprisoning stone is rolled away.*

The grave is our bed-chamber, which our Lord himself hath furnished for us by leaving in it his own grave-clothes. It is a retiring-room whose odour is most sweet to love; for

> *There the dear flesh of Jesus lay,*
> *And left a blest perfume.*

Death, thou art not death! Grave, thou art no grave! The names remain, but the nature of the things has altered altogether.

To close this first subject—*this resurrection will abolish death and every possibility of it in the future.* I notice that certain persons, in their anxiety to suck the meaning out of the word "everlasting," so as to avoid everlasting punishment, have questioned the everlasting nature of heaven. They have even gone the length of hinting that they are not quite clear that if believers get to heaven they will always remain there. Yes, and this is what it comes to. Nothing is safe from these revolutionists. They would tear away every covenant blessing from the children of God in their zeal to make the punishment of sin a trifle. To do honour to their own intellect, they would sacrifice the eternal blessedness of the blood-washed! But it is not so. Jesus has said— "Because I live ye shall live also." As long as Christ lives we must live: as long as Christ is in heaven we must be with him where he is, to behold his glory. So long as God is God his children, partakers of the divine nature, must live for ever, and be for ever blessed. Raised from the dead, and taken up to Christ's right hand, we shall henceforth fear no second death. When sun and moon grow dim with age, and earth's blue skies are rolled up like a worn-out vesture, we shall enjoy an age like the years of God's right hand, like his own eternity. The great I AM shall be the bliss of every soul whom Christ hath redeemed from the grave, and this shall know no end.

To this the Lord sets his seal. Do you want to see the red wax
and the divine impression thereon? Look at the close of the
text, "Repentance shall be hid from mine eyes." There doth
Jehovah declare his unalterable will; it must and shall be even
so. That his saints shall rise from the dead is the immutable
decree of God. In all this let us rejoice. Our future is bright
with glory. These things are revealed to faith, but they are
not to be seen of the eye, nor even conceived in the heart, nor
pictured by the imagination.

> *I know not, oh, I know not, what joys await us there!*
> *What radiancy of glory! What bliss beyond compare!*

This much, however, we do know, that there is to be a rising
for us, even as our Lord has risen, and we shall be satisfied
when we awake in his likeness. Constantly in Scripture is this
resurrection used as the figure of God's delivering and blessing
his people; and especially as the figure of regeneration or the
giving of a new and spiritual life to those who were by nature
dead in trespasses and sins. I intend to use it so in our next
line of thought.

In the second place, IN THESE WORDS LIE AN ENCOURAGE-
MENT TO LOOK FOR DELIVERANCE OUT OF GREAT TROUBLES.
The encouragement comes in this way: God, that will surely
raise his people from the dead by his own power, can and will
as surely raise them from every kind of trouble and apparent
destruction. If there can be any comparison of ease with
omnipotence, it must be easier to raise Job from his dunghill,
than to raise Job from his grave. If God, therefore, shall restore
us from the sepulchre, he can certainly restore us from sickness,
from poverty, from slander, from depression of spirit, from
despair. That is clear; who shall doubt it?

God will delight to work the work of our deliverance. If he
takes pleasure in raising a dead body, he will assuredly take
pleasure in raising from their distresses those in whom he
delights. The Lord rejoices in our joy. He doth not afflict
willingly, but he blesses us joyfully. Therefore, we may rest
assured that he will turn again and have compassion, and raise
us up from our downcastings.

The ends and designs for which the Lord afflicts them are

very gracious and we may expect that he will end the affliction when those designs are accomplished. When the Lord puts us into the furnace it is to refine us; and as soon as the dross is consumed he will bring forth the pure gold.

And now, to come to the text, we must traverse the same ground again: *this deliverance comes through redemption*. Beloved, he that redeemed Israel from all iniquity will also redeem Israel from all his troubles. That redemption price of the Lord covers every necessity of his people, and supplies every mercy that they will need between here and heaven. Do not, therefore, doubt or despair, because your troubles seem as if they would slay you, for the Angel who has redeemed your body from death will redeem you from all evil. He that will bring your body from the grave, will love you up from the pit of trouble, even when you are ready to perish. Redemption covers all, and secures from every danger. He that died for you, lives for you, and cares for you. You shall be supplied, not only with grace and glory, but with food and raiment. "Thy bread shall be given thee; thy waters shall be sure." Oh, rest in the Lord; especially confide in the redemption of Jesus. Let the precious blood speak peace to you; for if he has bought your soul, he has bought all that goes with it, and all that is needed for this life as well as the next.

This deliverance will also be God's work. I have shown you that it was so in resurrection, concerning which the great "I will" is so prominent in the text. Now, if you are in great trouble, do not run to friends and acquaintances, nor reckon up your own strength, but make direct resort to God, who quickeneth the dead. He that brought again from the dead our Lord Jesus is he that can and will deliver you. He is the God of salvation, and unto him belong the issues from death. His name is Shaddai— God all sufficient; trust him fully. When he made the heavens, who was there to help him? What aid does he need in rescuing his servants? Oh, learn to wait only upon the Lord! Do not think that I am talking mere words. No; trust in God must be real and practical, and it must be simple and unmixed. "My soul, wait thou only upon God; for my expectation is from him." Oh, how sweet it is to rest on God's bare arm! Long have I known what it is to trust in God, and at the same time to repose on the help of many friends; but now I know what it is to rest in him unmoved when forsaken of many. I cling to that dear arm, and find it all the help I need. If you rest on God alone, as the rock of your salvation, you need never fear. Often does the Lord afflict us to this end, even as Paul saith, "But we had the sentence of death in ourselves, that we should not trust in ourselves, but in God which raiseth the dead."

When the Lord delivers his people, *his work is singularly complete, for he triumphantly turns evil into good.* We shall yet exult over that which now casts us down. That which threatened to kill us shall increase our life, and we shall hear our Lord say to it, "O death, I will be thy plagues; O grave, I will be thy destruction." He will turn mourning into dancing, loss into gain, sorrows into joys. He will enrich you by your impoverishment; he will make you strong out of weakness; he will give you health by means of sickness; and fulness by emptying you. Does the adversary threaten to destroy you? You shall be more than a conqueror. That which seemed to be the death and burial of your hope shall be the overthrow of your fears.

The Lord will do this so completely that *he will make you sing concerning it.* In the book of Hosea the Lord declared a fact in plain language; but when the work was done the Lord by his servant Paul made it into a song for his chosen in that famous chapter of the Corinthians—"O death, where is thy sting? O grave, where is thy victory?" Let us catch the spirit of this lyric, and translate it thus! "O poverty, where is thy penury? O sickness, where is thy misery? O weakness, where is thy loss? O slander, where is thy sting?" We shall before long look back upon all our afflictions with gladness, and bless the Lord for them as for our chiefest blessings. We may yet feel like that great saint who, when he recovered from sickness, cried, "Take me back to my sick bed again, for there have I enjoyed such fellowship with Christ as I never knew before." We may yet have to say, as certain saints of the Church of Scotland said, "Oh, that we were meeting among the moors and the hills once more; for never had the bride of Christ such fellowship with the Bridegroom as when she met him in secret places." The Lord knoweth how to lift us high by that which cast us low, and to make psalms for our stringed instruments out of the dirges which drowned our music. The God of the resurrection has delivered, doth deliver, and will deliver his people.

In the third place SEE HERE A DECLARATION THAT GOD WILL SAVE HIS CHOSEN FROM THEIR DEATH IN SIN. He that will raise our bodies from the grave will, according to his everlasting covenant, raise his chosen from their death in sin.

This must be so. If the Lord did not raise his people's souls from their death in sin, a resurrection of their bodies would be a curse rather than a blessing. Resurrection will be no boon to those who die unregenerate. You will all rise from the grave; but I fear that some of you will rise to shame and everlasting contempt. That is an awful passage which I quoted just now from the Book of Daniel: think much of it. Therefore since God will not have his people rise to shame and everlasting contempt he will make their souls to rise first into newness of holy life. This regeneration must come to all of you, if you are to be partakers of the glory of Christ hereafter. Ye must be quickened, though ye were dead in trespasses and sins. That fact suggests a question to each heart—Have you received the divine life?

If you are indeed made alive unto God, you will agree with me that *this resurrection comes to us entirely through redemption*. There is no quickening a dead soul, except by the process here described: "I will ransom them from the power of the grave; I will redeem them from death." Did the law of God, when you heard it, ever quicken you? Nay, it slew you. "When the commandment came, sin revived, and I died." It made your death more apparent to you, but it brought you no life. Did the eloquence of men, or human persuasion, ever raise you from spiritual death? You listened to it, and you listened, but you listened in vain. You were moved with human affections, but these human affections passed away, like the morning dew. Beloved, life only came to you when you received Christ Jesus, your Redeemer. Well do I remember when I first looked unto him, and lived! The life and the look came together. There is no receiving eternal life apart from believing in him who is the life. There is no life except by looking unto Jesus. Your uplifted eye must be fixed on the uplifted Saviour, crucified as the redemption of his people: life only comes to us through his redeeming death. God himself only maketh us live by Christ Jesus.

You will follow me in this also: *quickening is always the Lord's work*. Here he may repeat the "I will" of the text all the four times. We spoke of resurrection as solely the work of God, so must the implantation of spiritual life be the work of the Spirit of God, and of him alone. Never let us dream that we can make ourselves alive unto God, or that we can quicken our unconverted friends. You could not make the simplest insect, how could you make a new heart and a right spirit? This is the finger of God, nay, this needs the arm of God, as it is written, "to whom is the arm of the Lord revealed?" The full power of God is needed to beget faith's life within the soul of man.

Further, keep up the parallel between regeneration and resurrection as seen in the text, and notice that *whenever the Lord raises his dear ones from the dead, and makes them live, it is a great plague to death.* He that hath the power of death must often be grievously annoyed when he sees a dead sinner begin to live unto God. "I did reckon on him," saith he. "I wrapped him up in the cerements of drunkenness, I shut him up in the dark sepulchre of ignorance; and yet he is alive!" "I did reckon on the debauched man," saith he, "I saw him rotting in lasciviousness; he was so far gone in lust that he was given over by his friends; but my great enemy Jesus Christ has come here, and made even the corrupt to live!" Again and again the adversary has to feel that Christ is his plague, and that he will be his destruction. When Jesus raises men from the dead, he shows who is Master, and makes the adversary know that his dominion is soon to fall. As in his lifetime on earth the Lord overcame both the devil and death by a word, even so it is now, and his name is thereby greatly glorified.

Those who are made alive, how greatly do they plague the enemy of souls when they begin to talk aloud of free grace and dying love? When black sinners show themselves washed in the blood of the lamb, when lips that used to curse begin to sing hallelujahs, and tongues that talked infidelity begin to proclaim the testimony of the true faith, how the prince of darkness is afflicted! How the sepulchres of sin are destroyed! Right well does the poet say:

> Satan rages at his loss,
> And hates the doctrine of the cross.

This work once done is an abiding work. I point again to the seal at the bottom of the text. "Repentance shall be hid from mine eyes." God resolves that they shall live, for he has redeemed them, and his redemption price is too precious to be wasted. He has ransomed them from the grave, and they shall never return to their grim prison-house again, they shall live to plague Satan, but they shall not live to be overcome by him. What the Lord has done he will not suffer sin, death and hell to undo. Nothing shall lead him to repent of his design, or turn from the purpose of his heart. Jesus lifts his hand and says, "I give unto my sheep eternal life; and they shall never perish, neither shall any man pluck them out of my hand."

In the fourth place notice that HERE WE HAVE AN ASSURANCE THAT THE LORD CAN DELIVER FROM ANY OTHER FORM OF DEATH.

Suppose the *Church at large* should decline to a spiritual death—and I am sure it does so just now—what then? The faults which are now so apparent may only be the beginning of worse evils. Suppose error should become rampant in all our churches, as it may; suppose those who bear testimony should grow fewer, and their voices should be less and less regarded, as they may be; suppose at last the true Church of Christ should scarcely be discoverable, and that men should bury it, and dance a saraband upon its grave, and say, "We have done with these believers in atonement. We have done with these troublesome evangelical doctrines." What then? The truth will rise again. The eternal Gospel will burst her sepulchre. "Vain the watch, the stone, the seal."

Suppose I am now speaking to *some child of God*, who says, "I can believe all this; but, alas! I feel dead myself." We do sometimes faint, and are full of fears, and cry, "Will the Lord cast off for ever? and will he be favourable no more?" We trust we do really love the Lord; but we get very dull at times, and cry out:

> Dear Lord, and shall we always live
> At this poor, dying rate:
> Our love so faint, so cold to thee,
> And thine to us so great?

We feel as if we could not pray; there is no singing in us; and we feel as if we could not feel. At times we are so dull and stupid that we cannot think ourselves to be enlightened of the

Lord at all. For my own part, "I am more brutish than any man" at times, in my own esteem. Be our case as it may, let not faith waver because feeling changes. When you are down in the dumps, remember that as the Lord will raise your dead body, he can certainly revive your fainting heart. Trust in him to restore your soul. By God's grace, leave the vaults and come into the upper air of trust and thanksgiving. If you cannot do anything else, my dear friend, do cry aloud. Cry, "O God, help me! Quicken thou me, O Lord."

Do any of you say, "Well, I never get into so sad a state. I am always lively"? I am very glad to hear it, if it be true. But I have heard that the statues in St. Paul's Cathedral are never afflicted with rheumatism; and the reason is, because they have no life. I am just a little afraid that you also may have no changes and no fears, because you have no spiritual life. God knows whether it is so or not. Look to it. I would sooner have the rheumatism, and be alive, than be without pain and be a statue. The most painful life is preferable to the stillest death. Take hope NOW, for the Holy Spirit will revive you, even as Jesus saith, "He that liveth and believeth in me, though he were dead, yet shall he live."

Lastly, let us have that same hope about *our unconverted friends*. In dependence upon the Spirit of God, preach the Gospel, which is the vehicle of divine life, and you shall see them live. Have faith about those who are laid on your heart. God grant your faith a full and speedy reward, for Jesus' sake!